About the Author

This book is to be returned on or before the last date be'
You may renew the book unless it is requested by another
You can now renew your books by phone

Fiona Fullerton l'ou may renew the book unless it is requested by another actress and television presenter, Fiona is guru. For several years she wrote a popular weekly property column in the *Saturday Telegraph* which inspired tens of thousands to follow her advice. She now runs her own successful property business, buying, renovating and letting flats in London.

Fiona Fullerton has presented Carlton's *The Property Show*, Anglia TV's *Off the Beaten Track*, *Fiona Fullerton's Style Guide* on Sky TV and *Country Houses* for Meridian. Recognised for her part in the Bond movie *A View to a Kill*, Fiona has enjoyed a high-profile media presence for over 20 years.

KT-375-876

I1772029

HOW TO MAKE
MONEY
FROM YOUR
PROPERTY

FIONA FULLERTON

SANDWELL LIBRARY & INFORMATION SERVICE	
I1772029	
Cypher	05.12.02
333.3382	£12.99

PIATKUS

88   Visit the Piatkus website!   88

Piatkus publishes a wide range of exciting fiction and
non-fiction, including books on health, mind body & spirit,
sex, self-help, cookery, biography and the paranormal.
If you want to:

• read descriptions of our popular titles
• buy our books over the internet
• take advantage of our special offers
• enter our monthly competition
• learn more about your favourite Piatkus authors

visit our website at:
www.piatkus.co.uk

Copyright © 2001 Fiona Fullerton

First published in 2001 by
Judy Piatkus (Publishers) Limited
5 Windmill Street
London W1T 2JA
e-mail: info@piatkus.co.uk

This paperback edition published in 2002

The moral right of the author has been asserted
A catalogue record for this book is available from the British Library

**Judy Piatkus (Publishers) Limited and Fiona Fullerton are not responsible for any action
taken as a result of reading this book. All facts and figures are correct at time of going to press.**

ISBN 0 7499 2215 X   HBK
ISBN 0 7499 2280 X   PBK

Text design Paul Saunders
Illustrations John Egan
Illustrations on pages 26, 213, 247, 248 Rodney Paull

This book has been printed on paper manufactured with respect for the
environment using wood from managed sustainable resources

Data manipulation by Wyvern 21, Bristol

Printed and bound in Great Britain by The Bath Press, Bath

For Neil

Contents

Acknowledgements

I would like to thank the following for their help, research and patience:

Hamptons International and Scotts Kensington for information on lettings contracts
Julian Gore at Edwin Coe, Solicitors for all legal advice and information
Annabel Stokoe of Scotts Kensington for years of lettings advice
David Knight of Knight, Mason and Associates for his help on building your own home and extension
Norwich Union for their brilliant information on cowboy builders
Nick Pearce of Beaney Pearce, Estate Agents for advice and information on buying and selling
Selina Waterhouse for her research into mortgages, surveys and all those things I don't understand
Hilary Collister for getting to grips with my computer
Anne Clayton at Lloyds TSB for her financial wizardry
Mary-Anne Crafter at Hamptons International for her brilliant public relations
Mark Edmonds for giving me my column in the *Daily Telegraph*
Rachel Winning and Katie Andrews at Piatkus for their constant encouragement and advice.

There are, of course, hundreds of other people who have given me advice and help over the last 25 years when I began on the first rung of the property ladder. To all of them I am hugely indebted and say a very big thank you.

Introduction

I have always been incredibly nosy. Even as a small child I used to love exploring other people's houses and would marvel at the way they lived. I had friends who lived in tiny terraced houses and friends who lived in castles, so from very early on I was exposed to both ends of the property spectrum.

I, however, was brought up in a series of rather bland, Ministry of Defence houses as a result of having a father in the Army. The locations may have been exotic – Africa, Singapore, Germany, USA – but the houses most definitely were not.

Maybe this is where my love of interior design and decorating sprang from. It certainly is a mystery to my parents how I came to know about Georgian fan-lights and bullion fringe, when I spent a childhood surrounded by magnolia painted walls and 1960s teak furniture. I was screaming for a bit of chintz.

Having entered the movie industry at the tender age of 11, I started saving my pennies and bought my first flat at 19. Discovering a hitherto untapped flair for decorating, I managed to create a haven of Sanderson gorgeousness out of a woodchip nightmare and sold it on for a tidy profit.

This pattern was repeated a couple of times until I was eventually living in the heart of Knightsbridge, London, a mere bomb-blast away from Harrods. It was also my first foray into the lettings market, as no sooner was I ensconced in my two-bedroom apartment than I was whisked off to Hollywood.

It was then that I realised how much money could be made from letting good flats. It was 1983 and I made 15 per cent yield on my capital in the first year and 12 per cent in the second. I bought the flat for around £87,000 and sold it in 1989 for £240,000. By my calculations I made 176 per cent on my initial investment, which brought a 23 per cent return year on year for six years. Not bad. But timing is everything. I sold it just in time.

This is one of the reasons for writing this book. I discovered a knack for making money out of property and surely, if I can do it, you can do it too. It just takes a little know-how, a few tricks and a lot of stamina. They say a property doubles in value roughly every seven years, but in fact you can double your money within a year, if you have the right property, in the right location. If you regard your home as a business investment, however long you intend to live there, by enhancing its potential you are increasing its value.

I continued trading-up until 1994 when I decided to go into the lettings market properly. Having sold a really lovely place in Chelsea, South West London, I bought two flats with a view to developing and letting them. This gave vent to my creative urges even though I was still working as a busy actress.

But, oh dear, I made many ghastly mistakes as a landlord and have based this book on what I have learnt as a result. For example, I bought a studio flat (difficult to let) on Chelsea Embankment (no transport links for miles and no parking) and painted the walls terracotta (most tenants don't want red).

So now I seek advice from my lettings agents before I Buy to Let and they give me a rough idea of the projected income from the property. I'll buy a place that is fairly run down, in a good location, redesign it, do it up and let it. I also take care of the management myself. All the flats have off-white walls, neutral carpets, up-to-the-minute American-style bathrooms and are fully furnished with quality furniture. If a tenant is going to pay a hefty rent they want a home from home that is comfortable and well equipped.

After the birth of my daughter in 1995 I started writing more frequently for various newspapers and magazines, in a bid to stay at home. This led to the discovery, by the *Daily Telegraph*, that I was, shock-horror, 'A LANDLORD' and they offered me a 12-week stint as a guest columnist, writing about my experiences on the property ladder.

Two-and-a-half years later I was still writing my column and was also presenting television programmes on the subject. Much to the amusement of my family and friends I was being called a 'property expert' or 'property guru' when in fact I was just applying my knowledge and experiences that had been gathered over 24 years of dealing with estate agents, solicitors and removal men.

But property is the new big thing. The subject seems to dominate dinner party conversation and the media. There are so many television programmes devoted to house-related issues that cookery is in danger of being relegated to the second division. I now know what it must be like to be a doctor. People keep rushing up to me and saying things like 'I've got an attic, do you think I should convert it?' or 'My tenant won't pay his rent and now his Egyptian belly-dancer girlfriend, who has athlete's foot, has moved in with her four children and the neighbours are complaining. What should I do?'.

People love to talk about property. I suppose we all have to live somewhere but the idea of property as an investment is finally taking hold. The Buy to Let scheme has obviously helped the small investor like me and now landlords are popping up all over the place. Discussing your returns and your tenants over dinner is far more fun than arguing about the best place to ski this year.

I'm still making mistakes but loving it all the same. My Buy to Let portfolio is still growing and, because I do the management as well, the hassle factor is growing too. As for buying and selling, I'm still interested on a development basis but I think we've found our roots here in Gloucestershire. If all goes according to plan, I won't be leaving this house until I go to meet that great landlord in the sky.

* * *

This book is very much a 'skip and dip' book. In other words, you skip the chapters that don't apply to you and dip into the ones that do. For example, we are starting with what and how to buy a property, which is for the first-time buyer. If you already own a property but want to know how to enhance it to make the maximum profit, you will need to skip this section and look at Part III, Chapter 12.

Similarly, if you want to sell it quickly you could skip to Chapter 7. However, if you haven't got a loft there's no point reading about loft conversions, is there?

I have written this book based on extensive research and my own experiences of the property ladder and the private rental sector. However, if I have been mis-informed or have misinterpreted information I have been given, please show some forbearance. Forgive me. I have tried to be as accurate as possible but regu-lations and legislation change, and certain organisations may go out of business. This is not meant to be a guide to conveyancing or to be a substitute for the need to take professional advice in what is probably most people's largest and most important financial transaction. My opinions, as expressed, may differ widely from others, and styles and tastes change with enormous frequency. This is simply my way of sharing the highs and lows of 'trading up'.

FIONA FULLERTON – *June 2001*

How to **Make Money** from **Your Property**

part one

Buying and Selling

chapter one

Buying your home

What Do You Really Want?

OK. Assuming you're not some titled land-owner who has just inherited a castle in Scotland (if you are, I'm very flattered that you are reading my book), you need to decide what sort of property you really want to buy. More to the point, what do you need? (There is usually a huge discrepancy between what we want and what we need.)

For example, are you a first-time buyer or moving to another house for your expanding family? Are you down-sizing or getting extremely grand? Have you suddenly come into some money or just lost the lot? Are you relocating because of work?

Here is a check list to help you narrow the field. Work your way through this list as soon as you've decided to move, before you go to an estate agent. This will help to clarify your requirements. The compromising comes later!

CHECK LIST ....

- Do you want a house or a flat? (To help you make that decision, look at Chapter 2.)
- Do you want to live in the country or the town or city?
- Do you want a brand-new home or an old one?
- Do you want privacy and seclusion or do you want to live on an estate within a bustling community?

- Do you want a flat in a serviced block?
- Do you want freehold or leasehold? ('Freehold' means you own the land on which the property stands. 'Leasehold' means you have a lease on the property for a number of years, which is granted by the freeholder of the land. So you own the property but not the land. Most flats are leasehold.)
- Do you want a purpose-built flat or a conversion?
- Do you want something to restore or something perfect?
- How many people will be living in the house?
- Are you expecting to start (or expand) a family?
- Do you need self-contained separate accommodation?
- Do you want a garden?
- Do you need off-street parking or a garage?
- Do you need stables (ooh, how grand) or a paddock?
- Would you like extra acres with your property? If so, how many?
- Do you want a sea view or a riverside location?
- How many bedrooms do you need?
- How many reception rooms would you like?
- How many bathrooms would you like?
- Do you need to be close to schools?
- Do you need to be close to a mainline railway station?
- What is your maximum journey time to work?
- Do you need special disabled access?
- Do you want to be able to let out a room to help pay the mortgage?
- Are you buying to rent (see Chapter 9 for more on this)?
- Do you want to purchase a second home?

If you can answer all of the above and then put a figure at the bottom of it, which is your ceiling price, you will have a very concise brief to give your estate agent once you have decided on the location.

Mind you, we only ended up in Gloucestershire purely by fate. The house dictated the location. As both of us work from home and don't have a regular commute, we wanted to be 'in the country' but within easy reach of an airport and all major transport links. Geographically we were fairly flexible.

My own 'wish list' was very specific. With two young children we needed space; large garden; big kitchen; office; river if possible; playroom off kitchen; several bedrooms; etc., etc. We also wanted something to restore. The agents got to work. One minute we were viewing in Sussex, the next minute Northamptonshire. I have to confess to harbouring a secret longing to live in the Cotswolds, so when this house came up and it met all the basic criteria, we were thrilled. It most definitely helps the agent if you know just what you want.

> **I** hate statistics but here's a good one. In 1988 the average age of the first-time buyer was 21. In 1998 the average age of the first-time buyer was 29. So where did all those twenty-somethings live? They were renting I suppose. I bought at 19, which was a good move, with hindsight. **My tip:** buy as soon as you can afford to. *Get on the ladder.*

When to Buy and When Not to Buy

> **N**ever buy in a hurry. Rash decisions cost money and a bad investment is unforgivable. *Not the idea at all!*

Most people buy in the spring and the autumn. Blame it on the great British weather or something but most estate agents say that when March arrives the market starts to pick up again, then come July and August, when everyone is on holiday, it tends to get a bit sluggish. Then September, October and November get busy before a slow December, January and February when everyone is getting over their Christmas hangover and hiding under the duvet.

So, common sense tells me that in an off-peak season it is probably a good time to buy a property, because the agents have more time and there is less competition for the buyer. Of course, I'm not suggesting that no one else is looking for a bargain in July but let's face it, if Mr Seller put his flat on the market in December and hasn't had a nibble by July, the chances are – if he is desperate to move – that he will drop the price, or accept your ridiculous offer.

In an ideal world, you should buy when the market is depressed or coming down, never when it is at the height of a boom. However, this is easier said than done. It is difficult to assess whether prices have peaked or if they are going to keep rising. They might not come down for years. Keep an eye on the news. There is an element of chance, or gambling, in all of this, but if you read the papers they will tell you what is happening in the property market. If they start talking about it being a 'sellers' market' this means it is a great time to sell but not to buy.

A 'buyers' market' is just that: a good time to buy, especially if you are looking for an investment. The only problem with selling at the top is that, unless you are moving to Outer Mongolia, you will be buying at the top as well. The only way around this is to bank the money and rent a place, which more and more people seem to be doing, until prices 'soften'. ('Soften' is estate agents' parlance for prices levelling out or coming down.)

If you buy when the market is inflated there is a danger of getting into the negative equity trap. Negative equity is when you buy a place with a large loan, property prices drop alarmingly, as in a recession, and you are left with a place that is worth less than your loan. This is a horrible situation but, hopefully, if you buy wisely – and this book is here to help – you will never find yourself in this predicament.

CASE STUDY ....

A friend of mine was keen to buy a sweet little house in South London at the end of the 1980s, just as the recession started. He put in an offer just below the asking price but the lady seller didn't accept it. Three months later he noticed the house was still on the market at a much reduced price so he put in an offer, and once again he was turned down. The recession really took hold and prices started to tumble. Noticing the 'For Sale' board was still up outside her house he made another offer that was finally accepted. It was £60,000 *below* his initial offer.

The moral of this true story is that while it pays to wait sometimes if you are buying, it certainly does not if you are selling in a falling market.

If time is on your side:

- Try to buy when the market is falling. Even though it may fall further, if you see your ideal property, buy it. Prices will always go back up.

- Buy in the less busy seasons, so there is less competition. There should still be plenty of choice.

- Try not to buy when prices are rocketing because you will see less return on your investment. But if you read that prices are still going up, get in quick.

- Never buy in a hurry. Make considered decisions but once you find the right place, you will need to move swiftly.

If time is *not* on your side:

- In a rising market, sell up and rent. Buy later.

- In a falling market, let your home out, borrow against it and buy. Sell later. (See Chapter 9 for more on this.)

How Much Should You Spend?

As the daughter of an army accountant I come from the saving-for-a-rainy-day school of thought. Being careful with my money has enabled me to invest in property, but if I had an extravagant lifestyle I wouldn't necessarily be able to meet my loans. It is difficult for me to generalise on this subject as everyone's circumstances are different but this is something you must assess before taking on a huge mortgage. (See Chapters 4 and 5 on mortgages and doing the sums.) Never, never overstretch yourself financially as repossession is not an amusing subject. Therefore, always live within your means and settle for peace of mind. If you buy a home it will be your biggest financial asset and hopefully you can turn it into something wonderful and sell it on for a huge profit! That's the general idea behind this book. Make your home make you money and you'll be shooting up that ladder.

But getting it wrong is soul-destroying. Why put yourself in a position where you could lose the lot, including all your hard-earned income? So, assuming that you are currently renting a place, the chances are that your mortgage could be the same as, if not less than the amount, you are paying per month.

Some building societies are happy to lend up to four times your annual income but, as explained in Chapter 5, the general rule of thumb is that your mortgage repayments should not exceed one-third of your monthly net income, after tax.

If you are single, you simply multiply your gross income by three. For example, if you earn £15,000 you can afford to borrow three times that, which is £45,000. However, if you and a partner are entering into a joint mortgage, there are two possible ways of estimating the amount you can borrow:

a. 3 x major income + 1 x minor income

or

b. 2.5 x joint income

How much can I afford to pay?

Monthly Income   £

Net monthly salary (first applicant)

Net monthly salary (second applicant)

Overtime, bonuses etc.

Other income

                                            Total income

Monthly Expenses

Food and drink		Standing orders/direct debits	
Clothing		Other loan repayments	
Household items		Regular savings	
Entertainment		Life insurance	
Telephone		Household maintenance	
Car and travel expenses		Home insurance	
TV licence and/or satellite/ cable subscription		Electricity	
Mobile phone		Gas	
Subscriptions		Other fuel	
Holiday fund		Water rates	
Credit cards		Council tax	

                                            Total expenses

Available income each month   **TOTAL**

(Total monthly income less total monthly expenses)

For example,   your monthly income is   £1,000

           your monthly expenses are   £700

           the difference is   £300

How to **Make Money** from **Your Property**

This is the amount of money you can afford to spend monthly on a mortgage but remember that this figure should not be more than a third of your net monthly income to avoid over-stretching yourself.

However, you will need a **deposit** – this is your downpayment of savings, which should be as much as you can afford, to keep the mortgage lower – and legal fees, stamp duty and removals will also eat into your capital. So, therefore, only spend what you feel comfortable with and always keep some spare cash for contingencies, such as car repairs.

> **I**f I have only learnt one thing in life it is that nothing is for ever. Nothing should be taken for granted. Not your job, not your relationships, not your health and particularly not your income.

If you are buying for investment purposes your spending potential could be very different. Take advice from lettings agents, valuers, surveyors, engineers or who-ever is necessary to reassure you that this is a good buy. It may be a huge amount of money you want to spend, involving enormous loans, but if everyone agrees that the building has potential and you have a rough idea of its resale value once you have finished with it, then go for it! If you can handle the stress you won't be the first millionaire who made their money this way.

One chap I know bought a Victorian institution down in Devon for just under £1 million and converted it into apartments. He borrowed nearly the whole lot and spent a fortune converting it, but sold them on for nearly £12 million! Not a bad return. He wasn't even an experienced developer – he just had an eye for the main chance – but he took excellent advice from architects, planners and agents, and this is the key.

> **M**y first home was a tiny attic flat in Faling, West London in a Victorian house that had been converted into four flats. I bought it in 1976 for £10,250 and managed to create a cosy little home out of a fairly ordinary flat. This was the first time that my decorating skills had been put to the test and, I must say, apart from the orange bathroom (worrying I know), the rest of it looked quite good. I sold it in 1978 for something like £14,000, but in 1999 the flat was worth £195,000 according to one local estate agent. There's inflation for you!

How to **Make Money** from **Your Property**

On the other hand, a certain famous style guru bought his first house for £4,250 in 1953. It was in Regent's Park Terrace in London's Camden Town and was arranged over five floors. He only lived there for about seven years but it was worth £1 million in 1999. Which just goes to show that location is everything (for more on the importance of location, see Chapter 3).

CHECK LIST ···

Here's another check list:

- Never overstretch yourself financially.
- Your monthly mortgage payment should not exceed one-third of your monthly net income.
- Assess your lifestyle. Can you make sacrifices to pay your mortgage? (Is cutting down on your leisure expenditure an option?)
- Take advice from the experts, such as an IFA (independent financial adviser).
- Do your sums using the chart on page 11.

Spotting the Potential

The secret to making money out of property is buying what no one else wants and turning it around. Spotting the potential takes quite a keen eye because most people will walk in and go 'Yuk'. Try to look past the dilapidations or ghastly decorating to assess the potential saleability of the property. Just because the vendor likes black satin sheets, a mirror on the ceiling and purple walls, isn't a reason *not* to buy the house!

There is an element of voyeurism in buying a property because we love to nose into other people's lives and have a good laugh. I'm constantly amazed at the exquisite naffness of some of the houses I've seen, but don't be put off. Look beyond that. The more 'individual' the decorating style, the more likely it is that you will get a bargain.

Assuming that the location is ideal (see Chapter 3, Location, Location, Location) and it is within your budget:

- Does the property have interesting architectural features like fireplaces and cornicing?
- Does it have good windows?

How to **Make Money** from **Your Property**

Before: *Try to ignore the mess when viewing a property. Clutter like this should not prevent you from noticing the nicer features, such as the fireplace, window and shape of the room.*

- Is the roof sound?

- Are the floorboards in good condition?

You'd be amazed how different it will look if you take down the curtains and rip up the carpets. Try to imagine a blank canvas in the house and how it would look with you in there. After stripping and varnishing the floorboards, painting every-thing white and replacing the bathroom, what will it be worth? Ask the agent who is with you.

The trouble with most of us when viewing a house, is that we lack imagina-tion. I'm sorry, it's true! I have it on good authority. We like the property presented on a plate, in immaculate condition. Some properties are, but the rest of them suffer because they are not. Stop looking at the dodgy furniture and the funny wedding photos and take in the dimensions of the room instead.

After: Imagine the room as a blank canvas – with a lick of paint and your furniture it can become very light and charming.

Even a complete ruin can have potential. If you are not shy of architects, builders and construction engineers, and your bank has been extremely generous with its home improvement loan, you could end up with a manor house that has been neglected for two hundred years and is now worth a king's ransom.

CHECK LIST ....

- Ignore the decor and the furniture.
- Use your imagination.
- Assess the space and light.
- Ask how much it would be worth once you have done it up.
- Look for architectural features.

How to **Make Money** from **Your Property**

CASE STUDY ···

A designer I know had a development business doing up houses and selling them on. She specialised in characterless properties built mainly in the 1950s and 1960s. The only thing she insisted on was good light in all the main rooms. She then transformed each place by changing the windows to six-pane casement windows, installing fireplaces, cornicing and an interesting staircase. The exterior was rendered to get rid of pebble-dash and occasionally she would hang shutters by the windows. Hey presto! A charming home and a massive profit.

Do You Need a Granny or Nanny Annexe?

One of the most important things to do when buying a home is to think ahead. Nowhere is this more obvious than if you suddenly need some more space with self-contained accommodation. If you can anticipate this when buying, it will save another move.

For example, are you thinking of having a live-in nanny? If you are, be warned. Nannies are becoming increasingly fussy these days, and if you are moving house due to an imminent arrival and expect to house a nanny as well, you need to remember one or two things. Many nannies like a sizeable bedroom – not a box room – with their own bathroom and sitting-room with TV. Some of them require completely self-contained accommodation with a kitchen and their own entrance, which is fine if you happen to have a basement flat in your house or stables ready for conversion, but how many of us can boast two front doors?

Of course, not *all* nannies are so demanding, but a few years ago, in our old house, we had a nanny who left after a few weeks announcing that she didn't like her accommodation. I was most put out. It was the prettiest room in the house and we hadn't had any complaints before. Her agency said, 'I'm afraid Carolyn requires completely self-contained accommodation with her own front door'. I see. Carolyn obviously had a thing about hearing her very own doorbell and liked segregated post, but she was far too posh for us anyway. I was afraid to eat a chocolate biscuit in her presence.

Alternatively, if you have the space, you could build an annexe, say, over the garage. My friend Pru did this and it is now in its third incarnation. First it was the nanny annexe, then when the children got older it became the teenage den and games room, and now it is the granny annexe. (See Chapter 12, section on extensions.)

If a frail parent is coming to stay they too want to retain their independence by having self-contained accommodation. You could convert the basement or cellar, if you have one, or build an extension. Either way it will definitely add value to your property because you are creating an extra bedroom.

CHECK LIST

- Plan ahead.
- Will you need extra self-contained accommodation at some stage?
- Many nannies like their own front door!
- If you build an extension, it will add value.

> If you are going to the expense of building an extension to house a parent, put the bathroom on the ground floor. That way, if the stairs get difficult at a later date, they can live entirely on the ground floor.

chapter two

What to buy (and what not to buy)

Flats Versus Houses

Most first-time buyers will settle for a flat because it is within their budget and geographically convenient. It all comes down to available income and marital status. Not many singletons want to live alone in a house in the country, but if they were married with children they might. Not all retired people want to live in houses because a lot of very active older people actually love urban flat-dwelling.

It really depends on your preference. Do you like stairs and gardens? Do you hate stairs and gardens?

> **Of** course there are wonderful flats on the market but, if you can afford it, buy a house.

I've only ever lived in three flats, or apartments as the Americans call them – or it could be a duplex, maisonette, walkup, condominium, tenement or penthouse – but when it comes to flats versus houses, I'm afraid the house wins every time. Call me detached, but the idea of sharing a roof with a bunch of strangers holds no appeal. I do own a few flats, but they're for other people to live in, not me. Besides, I like the fact that I can re-hang pictures or do the washing at midnight without anyone complaining. I like the fact that I can wander into the garden on a hot summer's day. I like the fact that I can paint the outside of the house when it needs it and not when somebody tells me to. I like not having service charges.

Living in a house, however, means you have the extra responsibility of maintenance and paying your own buildings insurance:

- the roof may leak;

- the walls need pointing;

- the gutters need clearing;

- the aerial needs fixing;

- the lawn needs mowing;

- the weeds need killing;

- the chimneys need sweeping;

- the windows need painting, and so on, and so on.

Before you buy a house try to work out in advance what your quarterly bills will come to (the vendor should tell you about heating bills and water rates etc.) and then add on what you think maintenance will come to. It could be an alarming amount of money spent annually but forewarned is forearmed.

CASE STUDY ••

Inheriting a mature garden can sometimes prove a very expensive undertaking. I heard about one lady who bought a house with a magnificent cedar of Lebanon in the garden. It was hundreds of years old and absolutely massive. Everyone would comment on its beauty, size and rarity, but what they didn't realise was that it was costing her about £2,000 a year in maintenance, for tree surgery, disposal of debris and hiring equipment such as shredders. A rotten branch fell on a car once on a windy day and left a nasty dent, so she has to be extra vigilant about preventive care.

Sex

Bear in mind that when it is time to sell your property, if a couple are viewing, it is usually the female who will decide whether to buy or not. This is well documented and researched! A chap might say, 'Oh, it's OK. Let's have it', but the lady will intervene, 'Good grief, I'm not buying this. The bathroom is far too small.'

Therefore, have you considered the gender of *your* flat?

Most flats are either male or female, with the occasional hermaphrodite thrown in, and it could be extremely important when you come to sell. (Houses have a less definite gender but it pays to be wary.)

I bought an amazingly masculine flat a few years ago and proceeded to make it even more masculine. I knew it was male because it had a huge studio area with a spiral staircase leading up to the galleried sleeping area (no door) and a kitchen the size of a filing cabinet. So I redesigned it to make it feel like a gentleman's club. Lots of black granite and mahogany, and eventually it became a very horny bachelor pad. It all sounds groovy I know, but it was a huge mistake. It looked divine, but it wasn't easy to sell because it was too butch. The conclusion one draws is that female properties will always sell because, let's face it, most guys don't really mind where they live, so both genders will buy. On the other hand, the stylish bachelor pad has a minuscule male market, that the female will never buy.

Also, beware of studio flats. There is such a tiny proportion of the market looking for, or prepared to buy, a studio flat that you could find yourself saddled with a property that is hard to shift. Most people like a separate bedroom with a door on it.

Remember that most flats will have a **service charge**, which is controlled by the managing agents. The bigger the block of flats the higher your service charge will be. It covers:

- the cleaning of the common parts;
- the maintenance of any lifts;
- the entry-phone;
- the porters' (if any) salaries;
- pest control;
- buildings insurance;
- the lighting of communal parts;
- general maintenance;
- sinking fund in case of major works.

Dos and Don'ts of buying flats

If you want a flat that is easy to sell later:

- **don't** buy a basement flat – most people worry about security and lack of light;

- **don't** buy a studio flat – the majority of buyers want a separate bedroom;

- **don't** buy a flat above fourth floor if there is no lift;

- **don't** buy a very masculine flat;

- **don't** buy a very short lease flat (see overleaf);

- **do** buy a flat in a mansion block (but remember those service charges);

- **do** buy a garden flat with good security;

- **do** buy a 'female' flat;

- **do** buy a flat with a terrace or balcony;

- **do** buy a flat with a nice view;

- **do** buy a flat in a modern riverside development.

Before you buy a flat, make sure there isn't a herd of baby elephants living upstairs. The poor insulation between the floors of most Victorian flat conversions means that the noise levels can be dreadful. The fashion for wood flooring – instead of carpet – is making it worse. Go and see it in the evening when everyone is home from work or school.

Houses Versus Flats

With houses you can't really go wrong – assuming the location is good (and we will cover that one in Chapter 3, Location, Location, Location). Whether it be a terraced house, semi-detached, detached or in the middle of a huge estate, it is your own space and if you maintain it well it should be a sound investment.

When buying a house:

- **do** buy a house with a garden;

- **do** buy a house with separate access (as opposed to shared access);

- **do** buy a house that is freehold. Leasehold houses are rare but try to avoid them.

Freehold or Leasehold

A **freehold** property is one where you own the land on which it actually sits. Most houses therefore are freehold, with a few exceptions, and there will be no ground rent to pay.

A **leasehold** property is one where the land is owned by somebody else (the freeholder), but you own the property for the duration of the lease. This most often occurs with flats in large blocks or houses that have been converted into flats. There will also be ground rent to pay.

> **Pets** The one drawback of some leasehold flats is that the managing agents have a 'no pets' policy. If you plan to take your spaniel with you, it will be worth asking first before you start doing surveys, etc. If the lease states 'no pets' and you choose to ignore this clause, the freeholder is within his rights to take action. Also, you may be miles from the nearest park, so walking your pet could become a problem. Are you familiar with the 'Pooper Scooper'?

The secret with leasehold property is only to consider buying something with a lengthy lease. If it only has 21 years left to run you will be handing it back to the freeholder on the expiry of the lease, so where is the investment in that? You might as well rent.

If it is a 99-year lease or even a 999-year lease, which you quite often get with new builds, it's a pretty safe bet that it will see you out! Even if you don't want to live there for ever, you may be making an investment for your children or grandchildren, so the length of the lease is important.

When buying a leasehold home, bear in mind how long you anticipate living there. This is because the value of a property will be affected by the lease when you come to sell, and if it is getting short your capital growth will not be as great.

The general rule of thumb is that anything under 50 years is getting risky. A girlfriend of mine wanted to buy a flat in a *very* posh part of London but the lease was only 47 years. The price was fairly reasonable because of it, but when we asked around and she did her sums, we discovered that if she lived there for five years, she would make a loss when she came to sell it. This seemed daft to me so I advised her against it. Short leases are only for the very rich.

Mortgage companies don't like short leases either. They will be unlikely to lend you the money if it is too short.

However, if it still has 87 years left to run, which one of my properties did, when I sold it six years later the lease still seemed a reasonable length so the price wasn't affected.

Buying the Freehold

Occasionally on a leasehold property the freehold is offered for sale to be shared equally among the various leaseholders. This happened to me a few years ago on a flat in a Victorian house in Kensington, West London. There were only four leaseholders in the house and we all thought it a very good idea indeed. The main benefit is that you can take control of the running of the house, will no longer have to pay ground rent and can appoint your own managing agents to take care of it. Also, owning a shared freehold property can be a lot more desirable when it is time to sell, since there is no limited timescale as with a lease.

Leasehold Reform, Housing and Urban Development Act 1993

The above has enabled leaseholders to buy their freeholds collectively, and individuals to extend their leases by 90 years. However there are strict rules as to residence and the procedures can be lengthy and the cost uncertain. It is essential to take advice from a solicitor or agent who specialises in this field.

In order to proceed you need collectively to appoint a solicitor to act on your behalf. The freehold must be purchased by 'one body' and in order to do that you will need to form a company that can act as the 'nominee purchaser'. It can be called Acacia Avenue Ltd or whatever the address is!

Even though the freehold can be acquired for a fairly reasonable amount each, being shared proportionally, this is exclusive of costs including solicitor's and landlord's fees, which may run into thousands, but once you have the freehold it will make your property more attractive.

The only recurring problem with sharing the freehold is that some owners like to manage the block between themselves instead of employing a managing agent, which can seem an unnecessary expense. This can lead to a breakdown between the freeholders if one or two of them decide not to pay their share of important repairs or buildings insurance.

CASE STUDY

One owner discovered there was no reserve fund due to a couple of non-payers and on Christmas Eve she received a letter from the insurance company cancelling the buildings fire cover because some electrical repairs had not been carried out.

This is a ghastly situation to find yourself in, so it is always wise to have a managing agent to run the building if you buy the freehold.

- Good managing agents act as a mediator between flat owners and can insist on repairs and payments.

- Make sure your managing agent is a member of the Association of Residential Managing Agents.

- If the Leasehold Reform and Commonhold Reform Bill becomes law, it will make owning a leasehold flat much more like being a freeholder, with the right to collective management.

In 1987 the Landlord and Tenant Act stated that if a non-resident freeholder wished to dispose of his property he must first give the leaseholders the opportunity to club together to buy the freehold. This is called the Right of First Refusal – but they weren't prosecuted if they ignored it. However, on 1 October 1996 when the Housing Act came into effect, they could be fined up to £2,500 for not explaining tenants' rights and another £5,000 if they sell the property despite those rights. So don't let anyone sell your freehold without consulting you first. It could be worth buying.

New Build Versus Old Timer

Old

The Victorians certainly knew how to build a house. They make ideal family homes and, because the Victorians had such huge families, they are usually fairly spacious too. Victorian vicarages and rectories are always worth a look because the Church was so wealthy in those days and vicars certainly knew how to live in style and comfort. They are awash with ornate architectural features, such as plaster cornicing, fireplaces, beautiful staircases, tiled floors and stained glass doors. Unfortunately for the vicars, the Church sold off a lot of property in the 1970s due to lack of funding. Their loss was most definitely the house purchaser's gain.

Victorian properties are also much easier to adapt to modern family life than Georgian houses. Putting in *en-suite* bathrooms can present a problem as Georgian rooms are so perfectly proportioned and there are also far more listed buildings of the Georgian period, so extending upwards is often restricted.

Victorian houses will always be a sound investment because, no matter what you do to them – within reason – they hold their value brilliantly. A minimalist decor works just as well as the traditional style, and you can even take out floors to create areas of double height. This is possible because planning consents are rarely required. They are very flexible and spacious. Flats in Victorian mansion blocks are usually a good investment too.

> The Victorian Society treats any building up to 1914 as Victorian, even though the old dear packed her hair-net in 1901. They aim to protect anything built during that time, whether it be a stable or a stately home. They get 10,000 applications for demolition every year and fiercely protect what they consider to be of architectural importance.

Mind you, I happen to love old property, living as we do in a 17th-century house. Whether it be a Queen Anne, Jacobean, Georgian, Edwardian or even Tudor property, it is the history and curiosity about a place that is so fascinating. There was a tendency during the late 20th century to cover everything up, so look carefully behind all that plasterboard. Timbered houses and barns usually sell very well. Buyers love old houses with timbered ceilings and huge inglenook fireplaces. Beams should be exposed wherever possible.

How to **Make Money** from **Your Property**

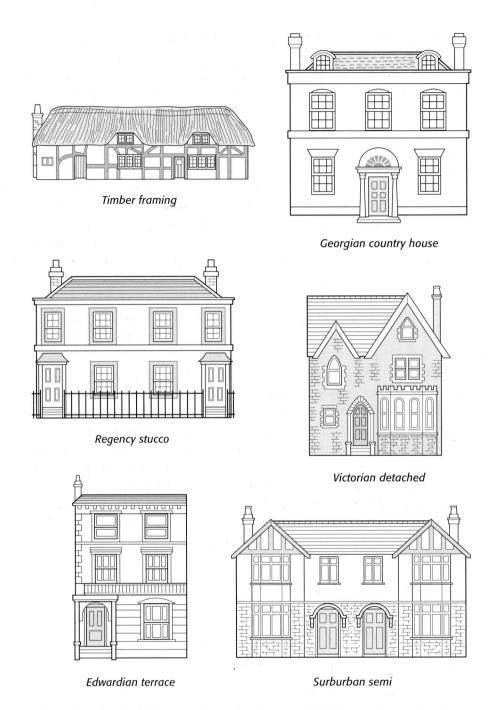

Timber framing

Georgian country house

Regency stucco

Victorian detached

Edwardian terrace

Surburban semi

I have always loved old houses and now developers are building new houses in various period styles. Victorian houses make excellent family homes.

An old property with historic connections will definitely have an added selling point. Estate agents are quick to add historical detail to their brochures in the hope that this might persuade you to buy. If Nell Gwyn lived there once it is a great conversation piece. If a king actually slept there it is of even greater significance. I know of one house where Queen Anne stayed – allegedly – on her way to take the waters in Bath and of another that belonged to Catherine of Aragon's Lady of the Bedchamber. How quaint. But no matter how tenuous the connection, if a property has a historical story attached to it, this will immediately set it apart and therefore will not only be interesting to buy but easier to sell. The price is not necessarily affected by its history, but it will be another quirky selling feature.

However, most historic or old houses are 'listed buildings' and this can be very restrictive. A 'listed building' is one that is deemed by English Heritage and/or the local council to be of great historic or architectural importance. (See Chapter 12 for more on listed buildings.) Before you buy a famous or listed building it would be wise to ascertain exactly what you can or cannot do to it. There may be restrictive covenants preventing you from selling off the barn in the garden or whatever. (A covenant is a legal promise imposed on the purchaser by a previous owner that certain things would not be done on the land.) If it is Grade I or Grade II* listed, it usually means that you cannot change anything externally or internally without permission. The local planning department have officers who will come to the property offering advice and they have excellent literature telling you all about how to preserve your home in the most sympathetic way.

English Heritage also have booklets on restoring listed properties, with the various dos and don'ts explained. Remember, before you do *anything* you must seek permission. (See Chapter 12, Making the Most of Your Property.)

Buying an old house brings with it all sorts of other problems, even if it isn't listed. Plumbing and wiring, for example, were very different in the old days. The maintenance costs will be higher on an old house if you think of all the various things that can go wrong like:

- rising damp;
- subsidence;
- dry rot;
- rotting window frames;
- wood infestation;
- frost-damaged stone;
- roof leakages;
- high heating bills;
- rusting gutters;
- electrical failure –

and that's on a good day!

However, the upside of all this is that you will have a home that is totally unique, has a rich history (if it hasn't, make it up!) and is much in demand. After all, they're not building them like that any more.

> **Y**ou can never truly own a property. We are only caretakers, merely passing through. Our role, our responsibility, is to protect, maintain and cherish a property for the next generation.

New

The attractions of a brand-new house are obvious:

- efficient central heating;
- fabulous bathrooms;
- state-of-the-art kitchen;
- all mod cons;
- low maintenance;
- no work to do;
- you can move straight in.

The National House Building Council (NHBC) is the independent regulator and standard setter for the new homes industry in the UK. They have 18,000 house builders registered with them who are put through a technical and financial vetting system. Builders must comply with NHBC Rules and Standards or risk investigation.

The NHBC provides a ten-year Buildmark Cover Warranty on the structure of a new house, and a range of warranty and insurance services for conversions, community housing and self-build projects. For the first two years after your home is completed it is up to the builder to put things right and for the remaining eight years you are covered by the NHBC in respect of major structural defects.

A new house might not be to everyone's liking (I hate straight lines in a house as I happen to like wonky walls and sloping floors), but at least you can move straight in and everything *works*! What bliss. I have looked around several new builds, both flats and houses, and have been hugely impressed by the finish and attention to detail. Depending on which areas of the market you are looking at, a new house will usually provide good value for money.

Most people haven't got time to deal with builders and take on a 'project', so moving into a new home is quick and easy. It will be freshly painted, warm and, most of all, the plumbing works. The purchaser usually has to carpet a new property, but that will be the only major expense. Try to find out all you can about the reputation of the developers. If someone's already moved into an estate, ask them if everything is OK.

Security is good these days in new builds, with video entry-phones, exterior lighting, video cameras and on some developments there is a gated community with security guards.

Storage is also taken into consideration, which is a problem in most homes. There will be good wardrobes in most bedrooms, linen cupboards with the hot-water tank, under-stair storage and special utility areas for the washing machine. The problem is that room sizes can only be measured up to the face of the wardrobe, not the recess, so it is important to look at the floor plans to get a clearer picture.

> This reminded me of my time living in Los Angeles in the 1980s when everyone was completely loopy, had fabulous teeth and plenty of storage. My apartment was fairly spacious and had wardrobes the full length of one wall in my bedroom, but the real plus factor, and most American apartment blocks provide this, was my own storage space in the basement. It was like a little lock-up garage. Brilliant or what?

When you move into a new build you will be given two years by the builder to list all the 'snaggings'. This is everything that doesn't work or isn't quite right. For example, a cupboard doesn't shut properly, the toilet flush is too long, a crack appears under a window or the window doesn't open – that sort of thing. For two years they will fix these things free of charge. Well, they *should* do. Obviously, if you have broken something they might dispute this. More serious structural defects will be covered by your NHBC warranty.

So here are the ups and downs of old versus new.

Old

Ups	*Downs*

Ups
- interesting architectural features;
- a history;
- mature garden;
- good capital growth;
- will sell well;
- unique.

Downs
- may be listed;
- may have restrictive covenants;
- high maintenance;
- more things to go wrong.

New

Ups
- all modern facilities;
- latest kitchen design;
- good storage;
- good security;
- read to move into;
- good value for money.

Downs
- no history;
- less character;
- garden minus planting;
- slower capital growth;
- may have restrictive covenants;
- teething troubles;
- rest of estate unfinished – may take a while to mature;
- less individualistic.

Buying a Repossessed Property

Buying a repossessed home can sometimes be a very sad experience but it can also provide a bargain. Repossessed properties are normally disposed of in the usual way through estate agents or by public auction, but there is a commercial list of repossessions that you can buy, which is advertised in the property sections of some national newspapers.

There are usually around 40,000 repossessed homes on the market in the UK and the majority of these used to belong to people who simply over-stretched themselves financially. (This is why doing the sums is so important (see Chapter 1). Heaven forbid you should ever find yourself in this situation.) The lending companies and banks will do everything to stop having to take control of a property and insist that communication is vital to prevent it happening. However, more often than not the home-owner ignores all letters and warnings, and that is when they have to take legal action.

When you are viewing a property through an estate agent you won't necessarily be told that it has been repossessed. However, it becomes painfully obvious when you see the anger and frustration that has been taken out on the poor house. A friend of mine bought a house in such a state that every fixture and fitting had been removed in a fit of pique. She said bathroom tiles, fireplaces and even the ceiling rose had been removed and the whole place had been trashed. This sort of damage can cost a great deal to rectify.

This is when you really need to be able to spot the potential of a property and look past the sadness. Properties from every section of the market are represented, from a humble little terraced house to a detached mansion in Mayfair, and the price will obviously reflect the state that it is in. It is a myth that they go for well below market value and that mortgage companies just want to cover their loan, because everything has a value to somebody and it just depends who is viewing or who is bidding on the day.

> **R**emember, when you buy a property it is essential to change all the locks, as you don't know how many sets of keys are floating around.

chapter three

Location, location, location

Where to Buy

That tired old cliché about the three most important things to remember when buying property – location, location, location – has an incredible ring of truth to it. Unless you get the location absolutely right and, even better, can predict trends (see check list for how to identify an up-and-coming area), you will never make any serious money on the property ladder. I know this to my cost, having bought a property that I could neither sell nor let, due to the fact that it was

a. on a busy road, so had to be double-glazed;

b. at least 12 minutes' walk from the underground;

c. had no parking.

And that was in a prime Chelsea address overlooking the river. I got my fingers burnt on that one and learnt that no matter how lovely the flat, location is everything.

You want to buy something that will be really easy to sell, so if you are looking at living in a city, try to spot the hot new areas. In Leeds and Manchester, for example, there is such demand in the city centre that hot new flats have been shooting up over the last few years and these will always be a good investment. In Oxford, the place to buy is right by the canal, where you can walk to the city centre.

Sometimes, just outside a city or town can be a good location if there are good rail and road links. People are governed by where they work so transport links are important. In fact, if you buy within 60 minutes' commuting distance of any major city it will be a good investment. Take London for example. Houses that are near (not too near) a mainline station into Waterloo, Paddington, Euston or Liverpool Street will usually be easy to sell (particularly Waterloo, because of the direct access into the City of London). This will apply to all cities.

Buying in the country on the edge of a village is still very desirable but it shouldn't be too remote and must have easy access to the major road networks. Property with a lovely view is ideal. Property with a sea view will always fetch a good price and is a guaranteed location. Anything near a golf course is quite popular (particularly if you are looking to buy a holiday home to let).

CHECK LIST ·

Your where to buy check list:

- easy distance to a train station or major road network;
- on the edge of a village;
- just outside a town is good;
- city centre is even better;
- something with a view or sea view;
- close to a golf course;
- not too far from the shops.

Where Not to Buy

It may be a bit rash to generalise on where not to buy because every property has its unique qualities and if you want to buy a flat overlooking a cement factory then that is your decision. The flat is probably wonderful. This book, however, is all about making money out of your property and the re-sale factor of that flat will be quite marginalised.

So here, in my humble opinion, are a few to avoid.

CHECK LIST ·

Your where not to buy check list:

- anything too remote – a house in the middle of nowhere, down the end of a track, will have a very small market;
- next to a sports ground or stadium – your life will be hell when it is in use;

- next to a very busy road or dual carriageway;
- close to a major railway line;
- anything with a nasty or obstructed view;
- a flat higher than the fourth floor if there is no lift;
- a flat where the common parts are really shabby;
- next to a sewage works;
- next to a milk depot (unless you like waking up at 3 a.m.) or bus depot;
- close to a river that has high risk of flooding;
- anything on a flood plain;
- next to the edge of a cliff, with a history of erosion! (They do come on to the market and are usually cheap);
- under a busy flight path;
- anything with a shared access (i.e. your driveway is used by others);
- next to a pub.

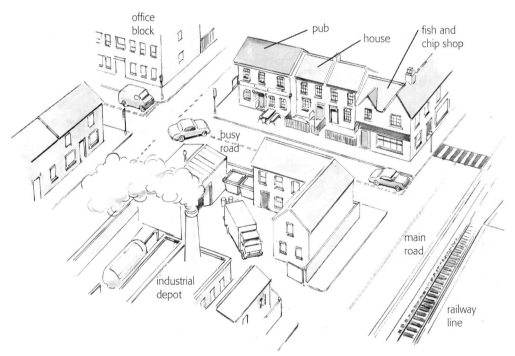

Bad location: *This poor house is in the worst possible location. It is surrounded by chaos and noise on all sides (next to a pub, near a fish and chip shop, on a busy road, opposite an industrial depot and close to the railway). There is nowhere to park, no green spaces and it is miles to the shops.*

Living next to a pub might be *your* idea of heaven but it will definitely be difficult to sell. You can never find anywhere to park if you live next to a pub. This is only one minor irritation in a list that includes:

- late-night disturbance;
- drunk and disorderly behaviour on your doorstep;
- brewery deliveries blocking you in when you are trying to leave in a hurry;
- pint glasses and crisp packets littering the pavement in summer;
- ghastly hanging baskets;
- the occasional fight resulting in GBH;
- the Live Band – horror of horrors.

If there are two very nice flats on the market in the same street, but one of them is slightly cheaper because it is next to a pub, buy the other one!

Good location: This is a similar style of house in a quiet residential street. You can park outside the house which overlooks a pretty park. The school, shops and the station are not far away.

Question: What do Michael Caine's films and the Duke of Westminster's houses have in common? **Answer:** They're all in the best locations. Ha ha. Location, location, location. The old cliché about buying property also applies to making films. Apparently, Caine has only three basic criteria when choosing a film script. Does it have 'loads of dosh, nice nosh, and a lovely location'? This is hugely important if you're going to have a good time. Hence, we see Caine in Rome (Italian Job), Rio (Blame it on Rio) and Cape Town (Zulu). Me? I get Bracknell.

In 1990 I was cast alongside Anthony Hopkins, Lindsay Wagner, Christopher Casenove et al. in one of those glossy American mini-series in which my entire part took place in either New York or the deep South. I was deeply excited. My agent promised ten days in New York and a buy-out. This is joyous, I thought. Half-way through costume fittings I got a call to say 'Lindsay Wagner's coming here. Forget New York. It's gonna be Bracknell.' Apparently Bracknell is a dead ringer for New York.

So there I am, all lip-gloss and bad attitude, driving a '67 Chevy the wrong way down a street on the outskirts of Bracknell. I'm surrounded by policemen and maniacal production assistants on walkie-talkies, all screaming at each other because they want to open the road and the yellow cab hasn't arrived yet. But – that's showbiz folks.

Identifying an Up-and-Coming Area

Transport links are the key to this trick. If accessibility to a certain area has increased due to improved railway or road links then this is usually an area to target. Also, an area adjacent to an already popular location can suddenly have potential. If you see little coffee bars popping up this could mean that a developer has already identified the area as becoming the next big thing. This has been happening in London, of course, with places like Islington suddenly becoming trendy. When people can't afford Islington any more they look at King's Cross.

The move from Kensington to Notting Hill Gate would have been decidedly downmarket 20 years ago but who'd have thought that it would be so chic now.

Hackney in East London has become the new Chelsea, with the largest concentration of creative people anywhere in Europe. Actors, designers, architects, writers, artists, musicians and ceramicists all live there. So sniff around. Ask questions at local estate agents because the same thing is happening up and down the UK.

Sometimes the indications that an area is changing are fairly obvious. Liverpool, for example, is undergoing a massive regeneration scheme that will enhance trade, travel, retail and housing, so property prices are bound to be affected. Town centres such as Walton-on-Thames are being updated, rebuilt and improved, which will make them once again a desirable place to live. The trick is to buy early before house prices rise too much.

A friend of my husband's has lived in Leeds for 30 years. He bought a modest terraced house not far from the city centre. 'Since Leeds went all posh with the arrival of the Harvey Nichols store, my house has quadrupled in value,' he said. He wasn't clever, he was just lucky.

CHECK LIST ···

Checklist for identifying up-and-coming areas:

- improved transport links are vital;
- is it close to an already popular area?
- try to spot a trend;
- good parking is essential;
- ask around.

Doing Your Research

As far as location is concerned not everyone wants to live in an urban environment. It is perfect for the first-time buyer and the young, free and single, but there comes a time, let's face it, when you yearn for some peace and quiet. Quite simply, your circumstances change. In my case it was getting married, having children and finally growing up! I longed to live in the country, have a battered Land Rover and lots of dogs.

Serious research and homework is absolutely necessary before any major change of lifestyle. This is fundamental to save you a fortune if it all goes horribly wrong. Here are some questions to ask:

- Is the house near a noisy railway line or main road?

- How far is the station?

- Are there farm smells when the wind changes direction?

- Does the farm have a cockerel or noisy dogs?

- Does your lane get flooded?

- How far is the nearest supermarket?

- Where are the schools?

- How long does the school run take?

- Does your village attract tourists?

- Are roads congested with tourists in the summer?

- Is the house under a flight path?

- Does its proximity to the coast or a river mean it's at risk of flooding?

- Is there a lot of heavy traffic on the roads?

There is no point discovering the answers to all these questions after you have moved in. Some of the loveliest houses in the country fail to reach their asking price because of one of the above. If you buy a house in that category (i.e. near a main road), you must be aware that it may be difficult to sell and its capital growth may not be as rapid as you would hope.

There are no department stores for miles around and excellent restaurants are not two a penny in the country (unless you live in Ludlow, Shropshire, which has four Michelin-starred restaurants!). The nearest cinema is miles away and if you have children you will be a constant chauffeur. Having said that we all *love* living here in Gloucestershire and wouldn't swap it for anywhere else, but it doesn't suit everyone. I have one girlfriend who starts to hyperventilate if she can't go shopping every day.

With children, the first part of our research started with the schools. In your case you may want to be near family or friends or be moving to a new job. Either way, research is *vital*.

A good tip to researching an area could simply be to rent a furnished house there for a few weeks. Take the children and see how much there is to do in the area and how convenient the location is. If you don't like it after all, you won't even have any boxes to unpack!

The reason research is so vital is that it will cost you dearly to rectify your mistake, if you make one. The cost of moving these days is astronomical if you take into account stamp duty, land registry fees, agent's commission, your solicitor's fees, removal company and those hidden extras. A friend of mine moved from London to Kent and back to London within two years. She missed the restaurants, the shopping and the bright lights. It was 1999 and it cost her poor husband £60,000.

Neighbours

Here's a favourite joke of mine: a man runs off with his neighbour's wife. The neighbour complains, 'They've only been gone a week but I miss him already'.

Part of researching an area and a property is to check out the neighbours, especially if you will be living in close proximity. My solicitor said that sometimes he is asked to do searches on the neighbours as well as the area, which I think is a very good idea. Check out the situation in advance before buying next door to the drummer in a rock band. Unfortunately, much as he would love to, the vendor is unlikely to impart this information readily because it's probably the reason he's trying to sell in the first place.

CHECK LIST ···

Research check list:

- The local amenities?
- The location?
- The neighbours?
- The transport links?
- The nearest shops?
- The schools?

Country Idyll Versus Urban Dwelling

Country idyll

I've had a nomadic life until now, living in such diverse places as Singapore, Nigeria, Dusseldorf, Los Angeles, London, Atlanta and Watford. But the only place where I feel I belong and where I can be truly happy is the English countryside.

After three years in Wiltshire as a teenager and three years in Dorset, I have now come to settle in Gloucestershire and wild horses couldn't drag me from this idyllic place.

Investing in property in the countryside, whether it be England, Wales, Scotland or Ireland will always do well, particularly if it is a detached house with a bit of land. Good family houses are in short supply, so if you stumble across one that looks like a neglected wreck, snap it up quickly. Prices for houses like that tend to exceed expectations.

Houses with a **sea view** are always a fairly safe bet, as are houses **in a village** or on the **edge of a market town**. Try not to buy anything **too remote** as this will limit the market. **Cottages with charm** and character will always sell well and make an excellent rental investment too. (See Chapter 11 for more on buying a holiday home.) Anything called **The Rectory** or **The Vicarage** will immediately attract a buyer.

Thatch Don't be put off by **thatched cottages** because of the various negatives associated with them:

- fire risk;
- high insurance premiums;
- poor insulation;
- the expense of re-thatching.

Thatch is, in fact, the best material for keeping homes warm in winter and cool in summer, while insurance rates have dropped dramatically in the past ten years. The annual incidence of fire in thatched properties is less than half that of ordinary homes and the cost of re-thatching is fairly reasonable if you consider that most of them last around 50 to 60 years.

Good investment in the country:

- in a village;

- cottage with charm;

- sea-view;

- stone farmhouse;

- a bit of land (more than half an acre);

- good-size family house;

- detached;

- thatched cottage;

- outside a market town;

- a rectory or vicarage.

Bad investment in the country:

- anything too remote;

- a grand house near an industrial area;

- a farmhouse too close to the dairy;

- a historic house soon to be surrounded by a new development;

- anything with shared access, such as farm tracks;

- anything with the slightest risk of flooding.

Urban dwelling

Of course, country life doesn't appeal to everybody. One girlfriend came to our house wearing beige trousers and cream sling-backs and said things like 'Ooh, it's so muddy round here. How can you stand those church bells? Frankly, I'd die if we didn't have a Marks and Spencer five minutes away. How do you manage darling?'.

My parents are committed city-dwellers too, who love the fact that they live right in the centre of the action. The shops, food-halls, theatres, restaurants and concert halls are all within easy walking distance. The noise, smell and hassles with parking are minor irritations.

How to **Make Money** from **Your Property**

You won't get as much space for your money, but whether you buy a flat in the Albert Docks in Liverpool or next to the Albert Hall in London it will be a major investment with rapid capital growth (depending on the location). For single-tons, first-time buyers and the youthful active retired who like the buzz, where better than the city?

Good investment in the city:

- riverside warehouse conversions;
- flat with a terrace or balcony;
- flat with parking;
- close to all amenities;
- close to a park;
- freehold house, if you can find one;
- long-lease flat;
- trendy new development.

Bad investment in the city:

- history of flooding;
- basement flat;
- nowhere to park;
- can't walk to shops;
- no view;
- very short lease;
- next to a pub;
- on a main road.

> **I**f your circumstances change and you need to move away from the city, think about renting out your property instead of selling. (See Part II.) Your urban dwelling will keep a steady capital growth and the rent will cover your mortgage.

Getting Value for Money

Buying in the so-called 'new towns' can provide excellent value for money as long as you don't mind living on a new development – or an estate – that hasn't matured yet and in fairly close proximity to your neighbours.

A few years ago people would snigger at the mention of new towns like Milton Keynes, Harlow or Crawley, but if you'd invested in property there 15 years ago, it would have been a very smart move. When so many companies relocated to Milton Keynes in the 1980s, house prices rose dramatically and the rental market there, even now, is surprisingly buoyant.

The same is happening in Telford, Shropshire, where brand-new developments are springing up on green-field sites. (That is land that has never been built on before and that used to be part of our countryside.) These days a great deal of care is taken over the landscaping of these developments and the architectural styles tend to echo periods of the past.

Buying off-plan

When it comes to buying new houses, buying off-plan (i.e. it hasn't been built yet!) is becoming increasingly popular. Committing yourself at this early stage means you get to buy the property at the initial offer price. During the first phase of development prices are lower and they increase once the developer has completed a few sales. Once the property is complete you can sell on at a profit or move in knowing it has already made you money.

If you are the first-owner of a brand-new house – or flat – on a development, you can also choose the best plot and customise your property according to the choices provided by the developer. You may have a choice of kitchen finish, or tiles or door handles etc. You can even choose how many plug sockets you need. These will all be extras but should still be value for money. They will have a show-home for you to look at so that you can envisage the end result. But don't be fooled by the clever styling. If the house you are looking at is quite small, the designers will have employed all the tricks in the book to create the illusion of space. These include:

- lots of mirrors;
- clever lighting to brighten the space;
- under-scale furniture;

- small beds in bedrooms;

- pale colours;

- beautiful accessories;

- some missing doors.

To get a clearer impression, ask to see a house that is completed but undecorated. This will usually be possible.

The only risk of buying off-plan is if the bottom falls out of the property market, and you find yourself committed to purchasing a house that is now worth less than you paid for it. But this can be true for any property. The other downsides are that the completion dates are usually on the optimistic side. You may find your moving date slips back and you encounter some delays. You will need to scrutinise the plans and find out exactly what will be included to avoid any disappointments when you move in. Also, if you do encounter any problems, make sure you write down your complaints as soon as possible (see pages 28–29).

> **M**ost new estates provide value for money – not just in 'new towns' – but the various developers and familiar building companies do vary a lot in their quality of finish. Have a good look around at what is on offer. Most estates have three or four different companies building on them, to varying standards, so ask any owners who have already moved in what they feel about the quality.

CHECK LIST

Before you buy check list:

- Study the property specification carefully.
- Ask to see the architect's plans and other working drawings.
- Check the square footage and what it includes.
- Consider the position.
- Check out local property values.
- Visit other sites by the same developer and question owners.
- Check the development is covered by NHBC Buildmark Warranty or an equivalent scheme.

How to **Make Money** from **Your Property**

- If you're buying a flat, ask about service charges and how they are assessed.
- Check whether a parking space is included in the price.
- Make sure your finances are in order.
- Remember you will have to pay a reservation fee which is non-refundable, but often deducted from the deposit at exchange of contracts.
- A 10 per cent deposit is payable on exchange which you will lose if you fail to complete the deal.
- Check with a solicitor before signing any contracts and make sure any special deals you have agreed with the developer are included.
- Request a clause which will give you your deposit back if your home is not ready by a certain time.

Face the fact that you get what you pay for, but that a small, beautifully finished family home with a tiny garden *and* garage, on an estate, will be fairly competitively priced compared to anything else around.

> **B**uying brand new, on an estate, usually means that your capital growth will be slower than buying elsewhere. Why? Because of supply and demand. But it will still be providing excellent value for money because you will be getting a three-bedroom house that could cost a great deal more elsewhere.

CHECK LIST ···

Value for money check list:
- buy in new towns;
- buy on an estate;
- buy off-plan.

How to **Make Money** from **Your Property**

Is a Bargain Really a Bargain?

The chances of finding a real cracker of a bargain on the property market is as likely as finding Lord Lucan working in a Balti restaurant in Wolverhampton. The fact is, they are usually snapped up by eagle-eyed developers before the rest of us can say 'Ooh potential, I like it.'

However, there are one or two ways of finding a property below its market value, but you have to be prepared to rummage. (For more details, see Chapter 4, How to Buy It.) You are not going to find a four-bedroom townhouse in Oxford in immaculate condition for £210,000.

Most bargains – if you can call them that – are in a pretty ruinous state. They are only bargains because you need to spend squillions putting them straight. This is fine if the location is great but if it is a grotty little flat next to a pub, beware. A bargain is only a bargain if you are going to make a whacking great profit when you sell it on. Location, therefore, is everything.

Buy privately

One way to strike a mean deal is to buy privately, by-passing the agents. Most newspapers and magazines carry advertisements placed by people anxious to sell but wanting to save their 2 per cent agent's commission. What they fail to realise is that most agents will push the price up in negotiation and help the owner achieve a better price.

Most vendors are tempted by speed and cash. They will accept a lower price if you say 'Look, X is my final offer but it's a cash deal (i.e. no loans to arrange) and we can exchange on Tuesday'.

The internet

The internet now has several sites dedicated to putting buyers into direct contact with vendors. Again, you will only get the bargain if you are in a position financially to move swiftly. If you are waiting to sell your home first, the bargains will be gone. Speed is of the essence.

Auction

Another good way to snap up a bargain is buying at auction. Housing associations, local councils, trustees, banks and building societies are all selling off property this way, as well as established estate agents. Repossessions sometimes present a bargain but you must know what you are doing otherwise the price could end up higher than an estate agent could achieve.

Build it

Alternatively, you could always build your own bargain. If you want a conventional family home, £80.00 per sq ft would give you 1,400sq ft for £112,000. That's assuming you can find a plot of land. You could register with the local land agent or buy a plot at auction and then have the hassle of dealing with the builders. You might get a bargain, but rather you than me.

TIPS ....

Property bargain tips

1. Be in a position financially to exchange contracts swiftly. Speed and cash will often secure a bargain.

2. Spot the potential of a property that no one else wants. It may look ghastly but is the location good?

3. Be prepared to deal with builders as most bargains are in need of modernisation.

4. Check the internet and small ads for people selling privately.

5. Try to identify an up-and-coming area.

6. Use auctions to buy repossessions or housing association sell-offs.

7. Make all your arrangements prior to auction.

8. Stick to your ceiling price at auction.

9. Buy a plot of land and build it yourself.

10. Have a lie down.

chapter four

How to buy it

The Basic Nuts and Bolts of Buying a House

This is the basic procedure for buying a house if you are a first-time buyer. Obviously, if you are selling one home in order to buy another then the procedure is slightly different and can be a great deal more complicated. This is covered in Chapter 5, Mortgages, Surveys, Contracts and Other Nasties.

So let us assume that you don't have to worry about your buyer dropping out at the last minute or gazumping. (Gazumping is when a seller has accepted your offer but then takes a higher offer from a third party.) You haven't had to tidy up before every viewing and you're not in a chain. Lucky you! You've got all that to look forward to.

You have found a place that you would like to buy and after doing the sums to make sure that it is financially feasible, you ring the estate agent and formally **make an offer**. This should be 'subject to contract and survey'. If your offer is below the asking price, the agent will put it to the seller and there will be a bit of negotiation until everyone is agreed on the price. This means your **offer has been accepted**. 'Subject to contract' means that they will sell it and you will buy it *only* if both parties are happy with the various contractual negotiations. After your survey you may decide not to buy after all or to re-negotiate the price.

The agent should then agree this in writing and will ask for your solicitor's details. If you do not already have a solicitor there are plenty of High Street solicitors who specialise in conveyancing and who will do it for a fixed fee plus disbursements. That's the extra costs for searches etc. (See Chapter 5 for more on contracts and dealing with solicitors.) I think it's better to use a solicitor who is recommended by a friend though.

Solicitors and licensed conveyancers can both carry out the basic legal work for you. There are few licensed conveyancers around, and they offer a highly specialised service limited to house buying transactions.

The best solicitors will offer a full service including conveyancing, guidance and acting on your behalf if things go wrong. They are obliged to ensure you fully understand the obligations you are undertaking when buying (or selling) your home. They should also explain any legal jargon in plain English – and if there is anything you do not understand keep on asking until your solicitor explains it properly.

The legal procedure is different in **Scotland**. Once you have made an offer on a property it is legally binding. This prevents people making several offers on different properties and also prevents gazumping.

Now, the money. Ten per cent of the sale price will be required on exchange of contracts and this will be held by the seller's solicitor. If you have already been offered a loan, that's terrific. If not, you will need to **arrange a mortgage**, but ideally you should do this before you even start to view properties. The lender can offer you a 'mortgage in principle' or 'decision in principle' (see Chapter 5 on mortgages). The lender will probably want to do a **valuation of the property** to make sure that their percentage is secure. If you are borrowing 90 per cent of the total and the property is undervalued by the lender you may have a problem making up the shortfall.

Assuming all is well, your mortgage company will make an official offer in writing. You should **arrange a survey** of the property before proceeding, for your own peace of mind. You do not want to invest in a home with chronic subsidence and rising damp. Most estate agents can provide a surveyor. Use one from a different company to the sellers (see Chapter 5 for more on surveys).

The **surveyor's report** will tell you all sorts of things about the property (such as 'Garden wall unstable'), which hopefully are not too scary. If, however, it does highlight a serious problem, such as subsidence, you may be able to negotiate the price down even further. If everything is then OK, you will receive a long and boring list from the seller's solicitor listing all the **fixtures and fittings** that are going to stay and those that are not. Go through this carefully as you may be under the impression that certain things are being left, such as garden benches and pots or light fittings and curtains.

When everything is agreed and your solicitor has done the searches (this is to make sure there isn't a bypass planned past your front door), has all the answers to his enquiries and has seen the title deeds (these outline the details of your property such as whether it is freehold or leasehold and any rights you will have over restrictions imposed on the property), he will then draw up a contract and you will need to **arrange a date for completion**. This is traditionally 28 days after **exchange of contract**. However, it can be brought forward or delayed to accommodate both parties. Exchange of contract is when you will need to get 10 per cent of the sale price to your solicitor so that he can pass it on to the seller's solicitor.

Then you can *exchange contracts*… Hurrah! You are now in a situation where you are legally bound to complete the sale of the property. If you decide to back out at this stage you will forfeit your deposit and could be sued by the owner for his losses for your breach of contract.

The good news is that the property is now as good as yours and no one can sneak in and take it from you. The bad news is you now have to find the money to pay all that horrible stamp duty and legal fees etc.

As the **date of completion** approaches you can start making plans for the move (see Chapter 8, Moving House Painlessly). If you want to take measurements at the property or show your decorator around for a quote, gaining access should not be a problem. You have committed to buy the property after all but some sellers can be quite emotional about this and don't want to let you in again until completion. Try sweet-talking them, or take round a bunch of flowers.

On the **day of completion** the property will be legally yours when the seller's solicitor has received the balance of the money. This is usually wired (sent by bank transfer) direct from your solicitor.

Congratulations. Have a glass of champagne and take a deep breath. Now the real work begins.

Be warned that on a Friday the banks and building societies sometimes go into overload and the BACS system they use to wire money around can be subject to delays. More people move house on a Friday than any other day of the week, so many is the time that removal men have been sitting in their van outside a property waiting to be let in. The seller is staunchly protecting his land until the phone rings to say that the money has arrived!

Of course, your removal company will be more expensive on a Friday because of the Busy Friday Factor. So why not move house on a Thursday?

To sum up, here is a rough schedule of events:

1. Arrange a mortgage.

2. Make an offer – if accepted.

3. Give your solicitor's details to agent.

4. Get a property valuation.

5. Organise a survey.

6. Exchange contracts.

7. Set date for completion.

8. Day of completion – move in!

The costs

This is a rough estimate based on the costs of buying a house for £93,000. If you have previously sold a home you will have to take into account your estate agent's commission of approximately 2 per cent of the sale price plus VAT.

Asking price	£100,000
Your offer	£90,000
Accepted offer	£93,000
10% of sale price on exchange	£9,300
Your deposit/downpayment	£5,000
Your mortgage	£88,000
Stamp duty at 1%	£930
Legal fees (land registry and search fees)	£600
Survey	£350

How to **Make Money** from **Your Property**

This is just an example. Stamp duty is now being abolished in some inner city areas to encourage regeneration. Legal fees vary from town to town and are often based on a percentage of the price of the property. The cost of the survey will vary, too, depending on the type you choose. If you want to get an idea of how much these charges might be in your area ring round a few solicitors and surveyors to get some average figures to help you when working out your finances.

Council tax, buildings insurance, life assurance cover and removal costs are other variables you will need to consider.

Various Ways of Finding Your Property

Internet, magazines, estate agents

So, you've decided what you want, or need, as a home and how much you can afford. Now all you have to do is find it and arrange the finances. No one said buying a home was easy, but finding it first can be even trickier. There are various ways to search for a property and I've tried them all, trawling through magazines, scrolling through internet sites, calling estates agents and even searching the private ads.

It took us nearly two years before we found our house in Gloucestershire and being tenacious certainly pays off if you are searching for your dream home. However, not everyone has that much time and we all have different reasons for moving house, so let's assume that you need to find somewhere fairly quickly.

Geography can present huge problems when buying because if you live in Kent and need to buy somewhere in Leeds then obviously you're not going to be able to drop everything every time an estate agent says he's 'got a good one for you'.

Internet

This is where the internet can be invaluable. Most estate agents have their own sites and there are numerous other sites where people can advertise their properties privately. Be very specific with your requirements – the price range, location, number of bedrooms, whether you need a garage or garden, number of bathrooms etc. – and the relevant properties will pop up for you to choose from. Some sites are very slow and the pictures take ages to appear, but the internet is

How to **Make Money** from **Your Property**

changing rapidly and things will improve. Some sites even have a video walk-through so that you can see right round the house.

> **O**ne word of caution if you are a single female. If a property appeals that is being sold privately – i.e. without an agent – make sure you take a friend along for the viewing. You may think I'm daft, but it's just common sense isn't it? Would you walk freely into a strange man's house and let him close the door behind you? I don't think so.

Magazines and newspapers

Magazines and newspapers are a good source of inspiration through their advertising and editorial pages. Get a friend – or the company you are going to work for – to send you as much local information on property as possible. Most local estate agents have their own gazette or freesheet and local newspapers carry lots of advertising. Most ads that are placed by agents are fairly truthful these days, due to the Misdescriptions Act. It's what they don't say that is the problem. For example, they won't tell you that the three-bedroom semi is on a main road. Always ask questions before seeing a property that interests you. (See Chapter 6, Selling Your Home.)

Glossy magazines, such as *Country Life*, or local glossies like *Cotswold Life*, *Cheshire Life* and *Shropshire Life*, show plenty of lovely houses for sale from the upper end of the market.

The national newspapers all have property sections, which are worth scouring every weekend and you will quickly discover whether the area you are considering in Leeds is within your budget. The newspapers tend to list their ads county by county, which makes things a bit easier.

Estate agents

Let your fingers do the walking! Telephone several estate agents in the targeted area and get them to send you details of available properties. Explain that you cannot afford the time to see unsuitable properties – they will always try to get you to see something way over your budget. Be very charming on the phone – a little schmoozing goes a long way!

With all this information winging its way to you, all you have to do is wade through it all and choose half-a-dozen that you would like to see on one day. Be persistent if your agent is not returning your calls and remind him that you are coming all the way from Kent to Leeds (to continue our previous example) and would like to see one property every hour. Make the agent work for his money! He wants to sell you something after all. As time is of the essence, don't bother with anything that is already under offer. It could be a complete waste of time. This will let him know that you are a serious buyer. However, if you are under no pressure to move, then seeing a property that is under offer could be beneficial. You may lose it but then again the other offer could drop out and you will get the house you want. It will also give you an idea of the real value of properties in the area.

If geography is not a problem and you are living or working in the area where you want to buy, you could drive around, making a note of agents' numbers on the For Sale boards.

Buying privately

If dealing with estate agents is anathema to you (you are not alone), then you could always buy privately, bypassing the agent entirely. This is hard work for the seller (see Chapter 6 for more on selling privately), but good news for the buyer. I found a flat that was advertised in the small ads of a Sunday newspaper, when I was looking for another rental investment. It was in a frightful state, having been a student squat for four years. It had a turquoise carpet and ghastly 1970s bathrooms but the location was perfect, being in the middle of Kensington, close to transport links (see Chapter 3, Location, Location, Location) and I could see its potential. As I tend to drive a hard bargain, I got the flat for a really good price. This can sometimes be a great way to buy if the seller is in a hurry. Otherwise the advantages of negotiating without an agent are loaded in favour of the seller. *He* is the one saving on commission.

But I'm all in favour of dealing direct with the seller. It's so much simpler. When you need to ask them a crucial question, you don't need to first ask your solicitor, who asks their solicitor, who asks the seller, who tells the solicitor the answer, who tells your solicitor, who tells you. You can just pick up the phone and say, "Ere Brian, where d'you keep the blinking stopcock?".

TIPS ···

Tips for Buying Privately

- Ask the seller lots of questions on the phone before you bother to see it, e.g. How long is the lease?, Where is the flat exactly? etc.

- Take someone with you for the viewing, for security.

- Get the seller's solicitor's details.

- Make sure the seller tells you about service charges, ground rent, etc.

- Be prepared to negotiate.

Swapping

Finally, there is buying and selling property on the direct swap basis, which can work marvellously to your advantage. The small ads on the property pages have hidden treasures that cut out the agents or you could take out an ad in the local paper of the area in which you wish to buy. For example, 'Do you own a barn near Chippenham? Need a flat in Putney? Why not swap?'.

A girlfriend of mine swapped houses with her mother-in-law recently because she needed a bigger house and her mother-in-law wanted a smaller home. They both lived in the same town in Hampshire and after a brief discussion decided it was the most sensible thing to do. They had both houses valued, their solicitors drew up the contracts and deposits were paid on exchange of contract. On completion, my friend only had to pay the difference in the value of the two houses plus her stamp duty. Here's how it could work:

> A has a house worth £140,000
> B has a house worth £165,000
> They swap properties.
> A has to pay £25,000 to B plus £1,650 stamp duty.

Apparently this is happening quite a lot in post-divorce cases with the necessary down-sizing. The real financial advantages are that you save on estate agent's commission and the stamp duty only has to be paid on one property (the higher value property) since a change in legislation. If you are really clever you can even do your own conveyancing and save on solicitor's fees but this is a bit ambitious. Searches still have to be carried out and proper contracts drawn up so that the swap is a fully legal transaction, but you could end up saving yourself thousands of pounds.

CHECK LIST ··

- Check the local newspapers.
- Jot down numbers on For Sale boards.
- Use the internet.
- Read the ads in national newspapers.
- Telephone local agents with your brief.
- Look in estate agents' windows.
- Check the glossy magazines.
- Check the private ads.
- Make friends with your chosen agent and be persistent.
- Let your fingers do the walking.
- Be selective.
- Never view without an agent or friend (if you are female).

Reading Details, Floor Plans and Photos

Once you have received all your information and property details from all those various sources, you will need to sort the wheat from the chaff. Oh boy. Poor you! I remember being totally overwhelmed by the stuff arriving through the letter-box each morning, but it's easy to play property sleuth when you know how.

Details

First, stick to your original brief. You have arrived at a property specification that meets your minimum requirements and a budget that takes into account all the extra costs, so don't be swayed by anything else. This will waste time. Bin all the details that look tempting but cost too much. Going to visit houses that you can't afford is fine if you are aspirational or voyeuristic, but it just wastes everyone's time and leaves you feeling inadequate. If you need three bedrooms don't look at anything with fewer than three. Read the details carefully. These days estate agents' details are a lot more honest than they used to be, thanks to the Misdescriptions Act, but there are still words to be wary of:

- **Individual** is one. 'Decorated in a very individual style' means that no one likes it! However, if you're not averse to rectifying someone else's bad taste with a load of white paint, then you might be on to a good investment. If it has been sticking on the market for six months, offer a price and see what happens. You could make a tidy profit when it's time to sell.

- **'In need of modernisation'** is another beauty. At least it's honest but are you really up to a massive overhaul? If you need a fairly standard family home, for example, sometimes reading the details is not enough.

- **'Store room/Bedroom 3'** probably means the bedroom is the size of a shoe-box.

- **Georgian style** means a brand-new house with Georgian features.

Floor plans

Floor plans are becoming increasingly important and some people would rather see a good floor plan than pictures. I am a huge fan of the floor plan because it can tell you far more than words can about the layout of the property. For example, if it says 'from hallway through into a large open sitting room', which way did I turn? Left or right? With a floor plan you can see exactly the location of the sitting room off the hallway, and you can also see where the windows and fireplaces are, and the geography of the bedrooms and bathrooms. Especially if you have children, things like this are very important.

When we first saw the details of our house, it was the floor plan that sold it to us, not the photographs or the words or the history. It met all the basic criteria I had for moving to a house in the country. This is why you must be absolutely clear on what it is you need to buy.

Photographs

Photographs should only be viewed as a guideline and are often misleading. If you are buying a Victorian terraced property then the house is, presumably, the

This is a floor plan of a bungalow, which shows clearly the layout of the rooms and their relation to each other. You can see where the windows and cupboards are and which way the doors open. Remember that a floor plan is only a guide and is not usually drawn to scale.

same as the one next door. They are used as the emotional key to pull you through the door. 'If there's only one photograph on the details, it's got to be a good one, otherwise the purchaser isn't grabbed', said one estate agent. He admitted that sometimes they have to go back to rephotograph a property if the original shot isn't doing the trick.

On a rather grander scale, one agent said, 'The photographs are the cornerstone of our marketing and publicity. After all, if the purchaser is sitting in Hong Kong, the pictures have to be beguiling if he is to make that journey'. Of course the internet is making life much easier for the foreign investor but with photographs they've got it down to a fine art. They only take exterior pictures in certain months of the year, when the garden looks perfect and the sky is the clearest blue. Like the wording, photographs can be economical with the truth. They say the camera never lies? Oh yes it does! So don't be taken in.

We'll come to this later if you are selling. That's a different story! But if you're buying, be careful. Don't be tempted to go miles out of your way to see a property that looks wonderful, fits your criteria and seems much cheaper than everything else in the area. There has to be a catch.

Ask questions: so why is it cheaper?

Once again, let your fingers do the walking. Call the agent and put him on the spot. 'Before I view, can I ask you a few questions? 47 Burfield Road seems a very good price. Why is that?' 'Well actually it's next to the main railway line.' 'Oh, what about 30 Binmouth Avenue, that looks so chic.' 'It's a gorgeous flat but it's next to the busiest pub in the area.' 'What about Holborn House? That seems perfect for us, but why is it so cheap?' 'Well, it is lovely but people seem put off by the fact that aircraft seem to skim their chimneys.'

Believe me, if you ask enough questions you will save yourself an awful lot of viewings. The agent has to be honest if you ask him direct questions. When we were looking for our house, I was very taken with one house in Northamptonshire. It seemed perfect for us, so we went to have a look, without me grilling the agent first. Big mistake.

The house was lovely. Except it had a public footpath 10ft from the front door going right along the edge of the garden!

Use a map

Getting out the map to see the exact location of a property can save a great deal of time too. It's a great way of discovering all the things they don't tell you in the details. Some time ago I fell in love with a house that I had read about in South West London. I got out the A–Z to check the location of the street and discovered it was next to Chelsea Football Club! Now, you might not think that such a bad thing, but when it's time to sell it will either stick on the market for too long or its capital growth will not be comparable with other houses in Chelsea. This should be taken into account.

When buying a house in the country, the details usually only give you the name of the village. Look it up on the map and you'll discover exactly *why* it is the price it is. Eight acres doesn't normally go for a snip unless there is something seriously wrong with the location. (Unless you *want* to live next to a quarry.)

If you become proficient at reading details, floor plans and photographs it will save you a great deal of time when it comes to viewings.

CHECK LIST ··

- Don't be taken in by the photos.
- Study the floor plans carefully, as they will tell you more.
- Stick to your original specification.
- Grill the agent to extract more information before viewing.
- Use a map for exact locations.

Viewing the Property

It always amazes me that some people spend longer choosing a fridge/freezer than they do a home. When I buy a property I view it not once or twice, but six or seven times, sometimes more. This is because the property will take on a different character at different times of the day. Depending which way it is facing, some rooms may be really gloomy when you want them to be brightest. After the first viewing, and assuming you are really interested in the property, make arrangements with the agent or the seller to see it again after work. They want to sell it, so they won't mind. This will show you things like how difficult it is to park your car after work and how noisy it is with the children back from school. If the seller is there, don't be afraid to ask lots of questions. How are the neighbours? How long have you lived here and why are you moving?

This last question can sometimes be very revealing. If they stammer and start waffling about it being 'time to move on' it probably means that they've had a row with the neighbours or the flight path is getting too much. Remember, most people move home for a reason, so you must do your research. (See Chapter 3, Location, Location, Location.)

Look out for any tell-tale patches of damp or dark staining on the ceiling, which could mean there is a leak above. If all the lights are on turn them off and see how dark it is. Ask when the central heating boiler was last serviced. If you really like showers, turn the shower on to test the pressure. If it is a pathetic dribble you may need to install a pressure pump. Here are some more things to check for:

Interior

- Any cracks in the walls?
- Is it double glazed?

- Peeling wallpaper (due to damp)?

- Condensation on windows?

- Fresh paint – is that a cover-up?

- Springy floors – are the joists rotting?

- Woodworm or dry rot?

- Does it have a damp-proof course?

Exterior

- Damaged or blocked guttering?

- The state of brickwork and rendering?

- Bulging or cracked walls?

- Damaged chimneys?

- Missing roof tiles?

- Is the drive in good condition?

- Is there a garage?

- Is there off-road parking?

- Are sheds and greenhouses included in the price?

- Is it on a steep slope?

- Is the garden south facing and is it big enough?

- Are the drains OK?

Check each room fits your requirements: Is it large enough? Are there enough windows? How many plug sockets? Is there storage space? Are the stairs well lit? Will a double bed fit in the bedroom? Is there an airing cupboard? Is there a loft?

Don't be put off by flaking paintwork or other people's ornaments and knick-knacks. Just because the owner has a ghastly collection of porcelain rabbits everywhere, it isn't a reason not to buy the house. Look beyond that. (See Chapter 2 on spotting the potential.) This book is all about making a profit when it is time to sell, so the more time you spend on the viewing, the more informed your decision will be.

Dos and Don'ts

- **Do** view the property as many times as you feel necessary.

- **Do** ask lots of questions.

- **Do** check the plumbing.

- **Do** take measurements if a beloved piece of furniture is coming with you.

- **Do** research the location and local facilities.

- **Do** get a survey (see Chapter 5 for more on surveys).

- **Do** trust your instincts.

- **Do** check that the price is competitive.

- **Do** take your time.

- **Don't** view anything that doesn't fit your basic brief.

- **Don't** believe everything the agent says.

- **Don't** be put off by a pushy seller.

- **Don't** be put off by the seller's ghastly choice of wallpaper!

- **Don't** be put off by a posh estate agent.

- **Don't** forget the costs of stamp duty, council tax, ground rent, service charges, etc.

> **D**on't waste time viewing a property if you know within the first five minutes that you don't like it. The agent won't mind as it will save his time and his voice. I once went to see a house and hated it on sight. Instead of viewing for the next hour I said, 'I'm very sorry. I think I've made a terrible mistake. This isn't what I'm after at all.' He said, 'Thank God for that. I've got a mountain of paperwork at the office.'

Is the Price Right?

Whether you are buying a one-bedroom flat in Birmingham or a vast town house in Bristol, every property is only worth what someone is prepared to pay for it. There is no such thing as a market price because the market fluctuates so enormously, but there will be a **guide price**.

The price at the bottom of the agent's details is known as the 'asking price', but there is no guarantee that they will get it! It may be much lower or indeed much higher. If you have seen something you like and are considering making an offer, compare the property with other similar properties. For example, if it is a two-bedroom flat in a large block of flats, did the agent sell another one recently? Check prices in other agents' windows. Ask around.

If it is a Victorian terraced house and you discover that the one next door – which has exactly the same dimensions – sold three months ago for £50,000 less, I would want to know why. Perhaps next door is unmodernised but it could be that the one you like is overpriced because the owners have just put in a new kitchen. With an inflated price you will be losing out when it is time to sell. Discuss this with the agent and make an offer accordingly.

In most instances, if you ask what the agent thinks the seller will accept, he will guide you. Obviously, the more expensive the property, the bigger the margins, so if the seller is asking £700,000 you could start at £630,000. At £85,000 you could start at £79,000.

However, the bottom line is how badly you want the property and what it is worth to you after you have done all the sums. (See Doing the Sums in Chapter 5.) If you really love it **do not procrastinate**. Put in an offer and keep going up until it is accepted. Alternatively, if you feel it is fairly priced and want it badly, offer the asking price. Sometimes speed is essential if other parties are interested. Of course, this can lead to horrid situations like gazumping and sealed bids (Chapter 5 on both), but hopefully neither of these things will happen to you.

Service charges

Remember, if you buy a leasehold flat, there are usually service charges involved. This can make a huge difference to your annual outlay, as service charges can be very hefty. So remember to include them in your sums!

One of my rental flats in West London has a service charge that is an eye-watering amount. This is paid by me, not the tenant. It covers:

- the cleaning of all the common parts, such as corridors and the reception area;

- the maintenance of two lifts;

- the entry-phone;

- the salaries of several porters;

- pest control;

- buildings insurance;

- the lighting in the common parts;

- general maintenance.

It also provides a sinking fund in case of major works such as redecoration or roof repairs, but these will usually be accompanied by an extra bill. Yikes!

Fancy Buying this One?

When the very rich want to sell their houses they might not want the world to know, so even if they are not officially on the market, they are being quietly shown. These are known in the US as 'pocket listings'. In Bel Air, Los Angeles, a very wealthy arts patron has been allowing a select few billionaires to view her Louis XVI chateau, La Belle Vie. The asking price for the 34,000sq ft mansion was a breathtaking $50–$60 million.

CHECK LIST ···

- Get your finance arranged first.
- Compare prices in estate agents' windows. Know your market.
- Ask other agents' opinions.
- If the price is inflated ask why.
- Be businesslike – not too keen and not too cool.
- Don't be afraid to make a lower offer of around 10 per cent less than the asking price.
- If the price is right *do not procrastinate*.
- Speed is of the essence.
- If you can offer a fast exchange, you will sometimes get a better price.
- Don't forget the extras: service charges, rates, council tax, legal fees, etc.
- Ask which fixtures and fittings are included in the price.
- Remember stamp duty. (See Chapter 5 for more on this, but, briefly, if a property is priced at £260,000, negotiating a £10,000 reduction will save you another £5,300 because you only pay 1 per cent stamp duty up to the £250,000 threshold.)

Buying at Auction

Buying property at auction can be a fabulous way to secure a bargain, but you must know what you are doing and it is most definitely not for the faint-hearted. Every time I've been to an auction I feel as if my heart is going to pound its way out of my chest! It is a real adrenalin rush but it helps if you can have a couple of dry runs so that you know what to expect.

Most property auctions are announced or advertised in the local newspapers or at the local auction house. They are arranged through the estate agent's office and once details have been released you are able to view the property and arrange surveys etc.

The main advantage to buying this way is that you avoid protracted negotiations, as once that gavel has gone down, there is no turning back. The property is sold that day to you, assuming you are the highest bidder, and the accepted bid is the completed contract with completion 28 days thereafter. You can also take comfort in the fact that you have paid a price only one bid higher than the under-bidder.

There is a down-side I'm afraid. The buyer must make all his arrangements prior to the auction – mortgage agreement, valuation, survey, solicitor's fees etc. – and these will inevitably involve expense. As there can only be one successful bidder, all the other bidders will have met these expenses in vain. It's a risk you must be prepared to take.

This is how it works. Once you have found the property you want, make sure with your solicitor that the property is free of any legal problems. Often properties with title problems are those that end up being auctioned. Then you should arrange a survey if you are getting a mortgage. A number of houses with structural problems which make it difficult to get a mortgage, are put up for auction. The lender will probably want a valuation anyway. The most important, and scary, thing is that you must be in a position to sign the contract in the auction room and to pay the 10 per cent deposit of the purchase price there and then (the guide price is usually the seller's reserve price, so it will only go higher!).

You must then be in a position to complete the purchase on the date agreed in the contract. This is usually 28 days from the auction date, so make sure your solicitor has all the legal documents in place.

The auction itself will either be held in the local auction rooms, in a hotel or pub (I've been to one in a pub!), at the agent's offices or at the site. It is usually very fast-paced and will all be over in minutes. It is essential that you keep a cool head and stick to your ceiling price. Don't get carried away with the emotion of it all, as you could end up paying far too much for the property. If you can't cope – quit.

CHECK LIST ···

- Get a loan agreed.
- Decide on the property you want.
- Get the survey done quickly.
- Have a solicitor to check documentation.
- Have 10 per cent of the guide price ready, either a personal cheque or bankers draft. The balance will be required in 14–28 days.
- Know your financial limit and stick to it.
- Get there early so you don't miss your lot.
- Bring someone to support you.

CASE STUDY ···

A local auctioneer in Wiltshire told me that you shouldn't expect to acquire an absolute gem for a knock-down price at auction. The fabulous houses normally go for above market price because the demand is so high and everyone wants them. 'It's the difficult houses that do well at auction. The quirky ones that no one wants to buy through the normal channels. I've sold water towers, windmills, house-boats, bunkers, you name it. The very neglected, derelict houses usually end up at auction. If you're prepared to spend time doing them up, *they* can present a bargain.'

One lady bid successfully for a disused farmhouse and seemed delighted with her damp pile of bricks. It transpired that her grandmother had been born in that house and she has now turned it into a delightful home.

Feng Shui, Bad Vibes and Ley Lines

Buying a home is such an emotive thing and often our initial instincts are absolutely right. If it doesn't feel right, don't buy it. I remember going to view a small house some years ago and meeting the owner who was a thin, nervy woman. The house had been on the market for over a year and had lots of crystals and wind-chimes all over the place. 'Because of the ley lines' she explained, 'the energy force-field in this house is rather peculiar. I had to move the sitting room from the front to the back of the house because I simply couldn't concentrate in there and I like to read.' Er, exactly. Not one I thought I should buy, so I beat a hasty retreat.

One hears stories of priests having to exorcise demons from houses and of properties lying empty for years simply because everyone who enters is severely spooked. Houses definitely give off an aura. They have good vibes and bad vibes, and some have a history that is very sad. If a house has a series of short-term ownerships it is always worth investigating why. It may be simply a coincidence but it could be something a lot more sinister. One house I went to see felt distinctly odd. It transpired that the three previous owners had all died in the house in tragic circumstances. This is not information readily passed on to a purchaser.

Of course, if the previous owners have been in a house for 21 years then it's a pretty good bet that it's a happy house. My advice is always try to meet the owners before purchasing a property. They can speak volumes without uttering a single word.

You could always call in a feng shui expert to tell you whether the house is a good buy or not. Feng shui is the Chinese art of placement of furniture and objects to create harmony and to bring you luck, wealth and good health. Well, that's what it says here.

I always thought feng shui a bit faddish, but it is big business now and deadly serious. The experts are much in demand and wielding immense power. A few years ago I was selling a flat in London and the chap who was keen to buy it insisted on delaying exchange of contracts until his feng shui expert had flown back from Brussels. The expert finally arrived and there was a lot of whispering and sucking of teeth.

He suggested that my spiral staircase was going to drain his energy. This was a bit like telling me Mrs Thatcher was a Martian. I didn't understand. My buyer nearly backed out because of the spiral staircase and the lift-shaft outside the front door. Apparently this causes negative *chi* (energy), but can be rectified by hanging an eight-sided bagua mirror between the door and the lift. Plus seven red ribbons. To solve the spiral staircase problem, he was advised to create a screen around it and as a divorcee he should have 'many empty pots to represent new beginnings'. Excuse me? I would have thought a beautiful plant in a pot was a lot more life enhancing.

But there you are. We all make choices and deciding on a new home is one of the biggest, most expensive decisions we will ever make, so try not to let other people sway you. Trust *your* instincts and intuition and you won't go far wrong.

If the owner of the property has recently died – peacefully one hopes – the property will be a 'probate sale'. This means that the property is part of the deceased's will and therefore you will be dealing with the executors of that will. Once they have agreed to sell it, you will be dealing with their solicitor in the normal way. The good things about a probate sale are that the sellers might not be dependent on a purchase so avoiding a lengthy chain. They are also likely to be reasonably flexible about the completion date. However, you are unlikely to meet the sellers and the information you can gather from them may be rather sparse.

CHECK LIST

- If the house gives off bad vibes, don't buy it.
- If it has had several owners over a short period, find out why.
- You could always ask a feng shui expert to check it out.
- Trust your instincts.

Building It Yourself

If you can't find anything to buy that suits your particular specification then you must be a real fusspot! You could always build your own home but this is a rather radical, stressful way of solving the problem. It could, however, provide all the answers.

A friend of mine bought one of those green-oak timber-framed barns that come in kit form and had it built for her. They come in varying sizes and there are now several companies that manufacture them. I must say they look really wonderful – particularly after a few years when they have weathered down.

Building your own home can prove to be quite economical. For example, a typical family home for two adults and two children is usually approximately 1,400sq ft. At an industry standard rate of £80.00 per sq ft this would provide a home for £112,000. Depending on the level of quality and finish your require you pay accordingly.

Finding a suitable plot in the first place can be a major problem. You could register with the local land agent and buy the local newspaper, and there are details of plots available through specialist publications. The local planning authority will tell you what their development guidelines are.

You will need planning permission, of course, and the land most likely to get it lies within an imaginary line drawn around a village. This is known as the 'village envelope'. If you can't find any land you could knock down an existing property and start again but this is pricey as you will be paying over the odds for the plot. However, there are lots of beautiful villages with seriously dodgy 1950s built bungalows sitting on prime sites that are crying out for some sympathetic architecture.

I hope you like living in a caravan, because that's what most people tend to do during construction of their home. Think of it as an adventure. We were camping here for three months and it's amazing how quickly the memory fades once the builders have gone and you are happily ensconced in your beautiful home.

> **R**emember that, even though your building costs look reasonable, the general rule is that the house's market value will be about 15 per cent less than the costs involved.

Before you start constructing your own house you will need:

- full planning permission;

- one full set of construction drawings, including
  a. architectural drawings
  b. plumbing layouts
  c. electrical layouts
  d. heating and ventilation layouts (mechanical)
  e. roofing
  f. Building Regulation Approval;

- architect's contract with phased payment and performance schedule;

- contractor's contract with phased payment and performance schedule;

How to **Make Money** from **Your Property**

- insurance for both architects and contractors, naming you, your project manager and your site as additional insured;

- bond (both architects and insured), naming you and your site as additional insured. Get a copy for your files.

You will be unable to sell your newly built property if an NHBC Buildmark Warranty (or equivalent) is not available when it is completed or a structural engineers report is not obtained confirming the property has been built to a good and workman-like standard and in accordance with planning permission and building regulations.

You *must* use industry standard contracts for all your consultants, as this will protect you, and ensure high standards and quality control during the entire building process. Dealing with builders can be extremely complicated and difficult (see Chapter 12, section on dealing with builders), and most of us do not have the time or the expertise to deal with the construction of our home. This is where a project manager is invaluable. He is your liaison between the builders and you. He has your best interests at heart and will take orders from you and manage the day-to-day activity on the site.

On a much larger scale your project team will usually consist of the following:

- project manage/owner's representative;

- architect;

- engineer;

- quantity surveyor;

- contractor;

- landscape designer and contractor;

- decorator/interior designer.

CASE STUDY ··

The Barstons bought a plot of land in rural Shropshire from a farmer in need of extra finance. Mrs Barston needed to be near her ailing mother and Mr Barston had just been made redundant. 'It worked really well,' said Mrs Barston, 'because my husband was able to be on site every day co-ordinating the job (as in project managing). We saved a lot of money that way. The builders took nine weeks longer than estimated but the results are worth it. We have the house we wanted for a price we could afford. If I did it again though, I would rather build through the summer months. Building in the winter was a bit daft.'

Just pray that you don't unearth a Roman mosaic while digging foundations. Watching archaeologists for two days will be very exciting but after 18 months it won't be so amusing. Your caravan will seem smaller by the day as they won't let you continue with your building until everyone is fully satisfied that they have unearthed absolutely everything.

CASE STUDY ··

A couple from Gloucestershire were granted permission to build an extension on their house providing an archaeologist was on site to record any findings. They budgeted for the archaeologist being there for two days. Under Planning Policy Guide 16 (PPG16) developers and owners have to bear the costs of any discoveries. However, the archaeologists found some pottery and thought it might be the kitchen of a Roman villa, so they were there for eight days. This cost the couple an extra £2,000 for the archaeologists, the report and the delay to their builders.

Once the evidence was recorded they were free to build on top of the findings, but not destroy them. (If human remains are found the delays can be quite protracted.) The local authority also allowed the couple to keep some of the pieces, which they put on display in their home.

chapter five

Mortgages, surveys, contracts and other nasties

Mortgages

Now we get to the nitty-gritty. This is all about borrowing money but making it grow for you. Most of us are bemused by mortgages and insurance policies but try thinking of it as a means to an end. You borrow, you buy, you improve, you sell. The difference between what you borrowed and the sale price is now 'X'. You invest 'X' in the next property, plus a mortgage, and repeat procedure. Hey presto! You're working your way up the property ladder.

Before you even step through the door of the estate agents, you should sit down and work out how much you can realistically afford to borrow from a mortgage lender. There are some very simple calculations that you can do to work this out. Most reputable lenders use these calculations as they are felt to indicate affordable monthly mortgage repayments.

Doing the sums

To recap on Chapter 1, if you are single, then you simply multiply your gross income by three: for example, if you earn £15,000 you can afford to borrow three times that, which is £45,000. However, if you and a partner are entering into a joint mortgage there are two possible ways of estimating the amount you can borrow:

> a. 3 x major income + 1 x minor income
>
>   or
>
> b. 2.5 x joint income

If you are self-employed, the amount you can borrow is usually based on your average earnings over the last three years. You will need to show the lender your annual accounts and/or tax assessments.

It is important to bear in mind that the mortgage lender will take into account any outstanding loans or higher purchase repayments that you may have. They will deduct the amount of those commitments away from your gross income before calculating your borrowing potential.

Also remember that even though a lender may be willing to give you £100,000, it doesn't mean you can buy a house for £100,000 if you have no savings. If the property needs renovating you will need to budget those costs. If you need £15,000 for building work then the property should cost no more than £85,000.

A warning

There are lenders out there who are willing to consider four times your gross income, but beware. Remember, these standard calculations are in place to make the life of the purchaser easier. What is the point of owning the perfect house, if every month you are just scraping by, with no money left over to pay for the decorating? It may be worth calculating what your living expenses are, so you know how much you need (look at the income and expenditure chart in Chapter 1).

Everyone is entitled to a mortgage from the age of 18 to 80, whether you are a pensioner, a student or self-employed. If you approach a bank they will ask you to open an account with them and will run the usual credit checks to check your financial history.

Deposits

When you have worked out how much you can borrow, you need to decide how much money you can afford to put down as a deposit on the house. The deposit is your hard-earned cash, your savings, your capital. If you have been saving like mad then you are very wise because you won't need to borrow quite so much, but don't forget your savings will also need to cover legal fees, surveyors fees and stamp duty. For example, if you have saved £5,000 and want to buy a house for £60,000, you can use that as your deposit/down payment, so you will only need to borrow £55,000. The average amount for a deposit is somewhere between 5 and 10 per cent of the asking price, although it is possible these days to get 100 per cent mortgages. These are very handy for first-time buyers who may not have savings set aside for a deposit. However, I don't recommend a 100 per cent loan because if there was another recession and property prices took a dive, you would immediately find yourself with negative equity, i.e. a loan larger than the value of the property. The amount of deposit affects how much you need to borrow, which in turn will affect your monthly repayments.

Mortgage indemnity fee

The size of the deposit will also affect the mortgage indemnity fee (or mortgage indemnity guarantee – MIG). The indemnity fee is a kind of insurance policy that most mortgage lenders have to protect themselves against you defaulting on your loan.

The MIG is a one-off payment that is made to the lender before you start repaying the mortgage. The size of this fee depends on how much of a deposit you can raise. If it is more than 25 per cent of the asking price you will be exempt from this charge. The fee is calculated in a typically complicated way.

You must find 8 per cent of the difference between 75 per cent of the asking price and the amount actually borrowed. Confused? For example, if you wanted to buy a house for £100,000 and you put down a deposit of £5,000 you would need to borrow £95,000 from the lender. Therefore:

75% of asking price	= £75,000
Amount borrowed	= £95,000
Difference	= £20,000
8% of £20,000	= £1,600 MIG

So, the fee can seem quite hefty, what with all the other expenses involved in house buying. Some lenders soften the blow by allowing the cost of this fee to be added on to your loan, which pushes up the charges on your interest. (If you have a 100 per cent mortgage and you add the MIG fee on to your mortgage it would immediately put you into negative equity.)

Remember the MIG protects the lender, not you, from their lending you more than 75 per cent of the value of the property. The insurance company issuing the MIG can still come after you in the case of your defaulting on the mortgage loan.

Choosing the right mortgage

Repayment mortgage

When tip-toeing through the mortgage minefield, the first thing you have to decide is whether you want a repayment mortgage or an interest only mortgage. A **repayment mortgage** lets the borrower pay the interest plus some of the capital off the loan per month. In the early years the purchaser will be mainly paying off the interest and only a small amount off the capital, but as the capital gradually decreases over the years, so does the interest and the payments will gradually chip away at the capital. This means that the borrower will usually pay off the loan within the agreed repayment term.

The repayment term in the UK is usually 25 years. This standard period of time means that the repayments are a lot more manageable than, say, a mortgage paid off over 15 years. However, you can choose the length of repayment term.

Interest only mortgage

The other type of mortgage available is an **interest only mortgage**. You simply pay off the interest each month but do not touch the capital, which means that by the end of your repayment period you still owe exactly the same amount you borrowed from the lender in the first place. However, as you are not paying off the capital each month, the surplus money that you have is invested in a separate repayment vehicle. There are two kinds of repayment vehicle, an **individual savings account** or **ISA** and an **endowment policy**. Both of these work in a similar way in that the money that you pay in each month is invested into, and trades on, the stock market. The ISA or endowment provider will advise you as to which sector of the market to invest in and can estimate the return you will get from your ISA or endowment policy. They should be able to calculate whether your savings plan will earn you enough money to pay off the mortgage and how long it will take. In some cases this type of investment can result in your mortgage being paid off early.

Endowment

'Low cost' endowment policies have received a bad press because they haven't been performing as well as they were expected to and left some borrowers with a deficit in their mortgage. Low cost endowment policies are policies where the sum insured is less than the amount borrowed but the projected bonuses are supposed to make up the difference. During the economic boom of the 1980s, financial advisers were projecting that long-term interest rates would remain high and that consequently growth would continue to increase, so the return on your investments would adequately cover the cost of your mortgage. Unfortunately, they got it wrong and their vision did not materialise.

What actually happened was that the economy slowed down so that long-term interest rates were running at an all-time low. The assumptions made by the advisers in the 1980s were basically too high. The higher the assumed rate of growth, the lower the monthly premium, therefore the borrowers were simply not paying enough into their savings plans. This situation has now been reassessed and the assumptions being made are a lot more conservative. This, too, has a knock-on effect, because the adjusted projections mean that the borrower must pay more into their savings plan, making endowment mortgages prohibitively expensive.

Loan amount:	How much do you want to borrow?	£50,000	£50,000
Loan term:	Length of time for repayment	25 years	15 years
Interest:	The current rate for the mortgage you are interested in	7%	7%
Your monthly payments:			
	Interest only	£291.67	£291.67
	Repayment	£353.39	£449.41

Remember you will also have to take into account the costs of the repayment aspect (ISA, pension) on an interest only loan. Mortgage calculators are available on most building society web sites. Your bank or building society will be able to show you the figures when you apply for your mortgage.

The Difference between ISAs and Endowments

ISAs work in a similar way to Endowments but there are three major differences:

1. ISAs cost the borrower less, as the savings plan provider for an ISA does not charge as much commission as an endowment provider.

2. ISAs are also cheaper because they don't automatically have life cover built in. If you want life cover to ensure that your mortgage will be paid in the event of your death you have to make specific arrangements for this. This lack of compulsory life cover only really benefits the single person with no dependants, because, if they die, the property would simply be sold and the mortgage lender would recoup their money that way.

3. Finally, ISAs are tax free. Endowments are taxed at a basic rate within the fund. An ISA is a pure savings plan whereas an endowment is two things joined together; a savings plan and a life insurance policy.

Flexible mortgage

A flexible mortgage is rather like a bank loan where you can pay off as much or as little as you can afford without being penalised. In other words, if you are feeling flush or have just had a cash windfall you could pay off a lump sum, or if things are a bit tight you could take a 'payment holiday' where you don't pay anything for a while. Flexible mortgages are very popular and the rate is usually just above Base Rate. The interest is calculated on a daily basis.

With *some* flexible mortgages you can even amalgamate all of your financial commitments, so your savings and your current account are all in the same fund with your mortgage. By doing this, the interest calculated on your mortgage can be reduced, saving you a small sum.

Rates of interest

Whether interest rates are interesting or not, it's time to look at the different rates of interest that are available – these rates are mostly calculated by reference to the Bank of England's Base Rate, whatever that is at the relevant moment. There are more choices to be made here, as there are lots of different deals and options concerning the rate at which interest is charged. On the following page are some rates you may come across.

- **The variable rate** your monthly repayments will reflect the fluctuations in the Bank of England base rate. This means that repayments will increase and decrease in line with Base Rate, making it much harder for the borrower to budget how much comes out of their accounts each month. This option is usually the least popular but lenders often sweeten the pill by offering attractive cashback deals. **Cashback** payments are used as an incentive by lenders to gain loyalty. They can be a good idea as long as you are prepared to stay with the lender for a minimum period – sometimes 3 years or more – otherwise there may be hefty penalties if you decide to cash in early, i.e. if you have to move house or decide to move to another lender.

- **Discounted rate** means that your mortgage will still go up and down shadowing Base Rate, but the amount to have to pay will always be a little less than the actual Base Rate itself. The discount is approximately 2 per cent lower than base rate.

- **Capped rate** your mortgage will again go up and down with Base Rate but it cannot rise above a pre-set fixed percentage. For example, if Base Rate is running at 6.9 per cent and your cap is 7 per cent, if Base Rate were to rise to 7.5 per cent your repayments would not be calculated above the 7 per cent cap.

- **Cap and collar rate** similar to the capped rate but the percentage cannot go above a certain rate or drop below a fixed rate either. This deal obviously benefits the lender as well, as it means that should interest rates drop below the collar, they will not be losing too much money.

- **Fixed rate** this means that you will pay exactly the same amount of money each month as your rate will remain constant for however long your fixed period will be. No matter what happens with Base Rate your rate will stay the same. These are quite popular with first-time buyers because the fixed monthly repayments mean that they can budget more easily.

Paying the penalty

The lender will usually operate all the rates listed above (except for the Variable Rate) over a fixed term and once you have settled with one particular offer, you will be tied into this agreement for that stated period. Any breaking of that tie-in period will result in what is known as a **redemption penalty**. So, if you move

How to **Make Money** from **Your Property**

your mortgage to another lender or you pay off the mortgage before the set period has expired, you will be fined for breaking the agreement.

This is very important. No one can see into the future and your circumstances might change considerably within that period, so it is always wise to see how long the tie-in lasts for and how much you would be charged if you had to terminate the contract early. Shop around, because some lenders will have lower redemption penalties than others and shorter tie-in periods.

Will I get a mortgage?

There are basically three things that could affect whether you will get a mortgage or not:

1. **Income** – Whether employed or self-employed, do you earn enough to pay for the prospective property? How many other outstanding loans and finance deals do you have? How much do these loans impact on your monthly outgoings? Can you afford to pay all the fees involved in house buying?

2. **Credit history** – Do you have a bad credit history because you have defaulted on any payments? Have you ever been bankrupt? Do you have a County Court Judgement (CCJ) against you?

3. **The property itself** – Is it in such a state of disrepair that it is structurally unsound and will cost a lot of money to rectify?

Lenders don't like ruins because they have to be sure they can get their money back. However, if you are refused a mortgage you will usually be informed as to what the problems are and a good lender should be able to give you some advice as to what to do next. If you think that you have not had a fair judgement or there has been an incorrect assessment, you could always contact the Council of Mortgage Lenders (see Useful Addresses) who should be able to advise you on such matters. However, even if you have a problem such as those listed above, there will always be *someone* prepared to lend you money. But beware. This comes at a price.

Applying for a mortgage

There are several documents you will need to take to your mortgage lender so that they can look into your financial and employment history, to ensure that all the details you have supplied are correct. You will need some or all of the following:

- evidence of identity – driver's licence, passport, etc.;

- proof of address;

- 6 to 12 months' bank statements;

- 3 years' proof of earnings;

- landlord's reference or previous mortgage statements.

Once you have all these the lender will be able to give you a **decision in principle** – a tentative agreement saying that should you want to borrow X amount, they would lend you the money. This is not set in stone. They are entitled to change their minds at a later date but usually this won't happen. The good thing about a decision in principle is that it can prove to a seller or an agent that you are serious about their property and have the potential funds available to buy it! This would give you preferential treatment over someone else who hasn't got a mortgage already lined up.

Where to get a mortgage:
- building societies;
- banks;
- direct lenders;
- finance houses and credit companies;
- some developers arrange a loan for you on a new build allowing you to move in for a downpayment of only £99.00;
- local authorities – if you are buying a council house;
- internet comparison sites (see Useful Addresses).

The costs

These are the costs involved in applying for a mortgage:

- **The arrangement fee.** This is a fee charged by the lender to cover their time and administration costs involved in setting up your mortgage. Some lenders **waive** this charge and some will let you add it to your loan.

- **Lender's valuation** or a **valuation survey**. Before the lender will agree to loan the buyer the funds to purchase the house, they want to satisfy themselves that the house is worth the asking price and that their money is secure in the investment. Some waive this fee too.

- **The deposit** – your downpayment.

- **The mortgage indemnity guarantee** (MIG). If you are borrowing more than 75 per cent of the value of the property.

- **Mortgage protection**. This is an additional payment that protects you against unemployment and inability to work due to prolonged illness. With this arrangement, your mortgage will continue to be paid until such time as you are able to work again.

- **The monthly repayments.**

The other costs

This is the ouch factor. The cost of moving home is huge and most of this money you will never see again. This is why choosing the right house is so important. If you think 'Oh, it'll do for now' you are making a huge compromise, both financial and emotional, which will cost you dearly when you move again. Here are some of the extra costs you will have to meet:

- **Stamp duty**. This is a tax that you have to pay to the government when you buy a house. Any property less than £60,000 is exempt and some more expensive properties in targeted inner city areas are also exempt. The payments are:

  £60,001 to £250,000   = 1% on the whole of the purchase price

  £250,001 to £500,000 = 3% on the whole of the purchase price

  £500,001+   = 4% on the whole of the purchase price

  Therefore, on a £70,000 house the stamp duty will be £700.
  On a £260,000 house the stamp duty will be £7,800.
  On a £600,000 house the stamp duty will be £24,000.

- **Legal fees (including Land Registry)**. These will vary depending on the value of the property and any resulting complications.

- **Surveys.** (See overleaf for more details.) Costs vary depending on which type of survey you have.

- **Life assurance cover**. The lender will need some sort of insurance in case of death of the borrower.

- **Buildings and contents insurance**. A lender will insist that the building is insured against fire etc., but whether you insure the contents is up to you.

- **Estate agents commission**. (See Chapter 4, section on choosing an estate agent.) Commission varies from 1.75 to 3 per cent plus VAT up and down the country, and only the seller pays this.

- **Removals**. (See Chapter 8, Moving House Painlessly.) This cost depends on the quantity of belongings being moved, the distance the van has to travel, the number of men required and the number of days packing.

- **Maintenance fees**. Does the roof need fixing?

- **Council tax**. The local authority offices will tell you what the current annual charge is for the type of building you are buying.

- **Service charge**. If you are buying a flat. (See Chapter 2 to help you decide whether you want a flat.)

- **Household bills**. Most estate agents and financial advisers have budget planners who can help you work out your monthly expenditure.

- **Water rates**. Or metered charges for water and sewage disposal.

Surveys

Why surveys are so important

Although the lender will have already organised a valuation survey to be carried out, it is advisable to hire the expertise of a chartered surveyor to report on the condition of the property. A valuation survey simply takes into account the estimated value of the property, but does not take a specific look at the condition of the various aspects of the building. (Ask your lender what their valuation fee will be – some will waive it completely.) A proper survey will highlight areas of the building that need attention. This is crucial information as it not only makes you aware of what you are committing yourself to, it can also give you some leverage in reducing the asking price as well. Although it is yet another expense, it is one you ignore at your peril.

There are three different types of surveys available:

Home buyer's report

The most basic survey is known as the Home Buyer's Report. Every element of the building is considered. However, it is important to note that this appraisal is made by simply looking and assessing, and no extensive tests are carried out. Most people opt for this type of survey because it is the least expensive, but it is only really recommended for relatively new houses, i.e. those built from the middle of the 20th century onwards. Allow about 0.3 per cent of the asking price, e.g. a cost of £180 for a £60,000 house and £600 for a £200,000 house. The report will normally include a valuation and an insurance valuation.

Building condition survey

This is a more detailed survey that should be recommended for any house that predates the Second World War. This is generally the most favoured type of survey as the surveyor will give a fuller explanation. The building is examined carefully and the surveyor will then produce a written report on his findings. As with the Home Buyer's Report there will be a list of caveats – areas that have not been examined, such as drains and foundations. This is perfectly normal, but it is important to look through these omissions and make sure that you are happy to exclude them. Costs vary enormously. No valuation figure will normally be given unless specifically asked for.

If the vendor has had any work done on the house in the past to improve its condition such as a damp-proof course, wood worm or dry rot treatment, there should be a guarantee with the improvements and your solicitor should ask for verification. Any special treatments will have a guarantee lasting approximately 20 years.

Full structural survey

This is the most expensive survey available, but it is essential if the house you are buying is clearly in very poor condition, is extremely old or has had a lot of alterations. This report is similar to the Building Condition Survey but there are no caveats, everything is checked and areas of the house will be opened up for extensive inspection and testing. This survey may be the most expensive (costs vary, depending on the state of your property) but it will definitely give you peace of mind. Again, it will not include a valuation unless asked for.

I heard about a house that was built on a flood plain. It sank about a foot every month! Not a good investment. Don't risk buying anything too close to the cliff edge either.

These surveys can take anything from 7 to 20 days to be completed. Before you seek the help of a surveyor here are some important things to think about:

- Always ask beforehand how much the survey will cost.

- Ask the surveyor to recommend which kind of report is suitable to the prospective property.

- Ask the surveyor to estimate the cost of repairs in the report.

- Check that your surveyor is part of the Royal Institute for Chartered Surveyors (RICS). They are assessed yearly on their performance, have regular training updates and are insured.

- Ask your surveyor to organise an electrical, plumbing and heating survey from suitably qualified firms if he thinks it is advisable. Asbestos cladding and insulation can be a very expensive problem with pre-1970 houses. Do not forget that once you have exchanged contracts, it is too late to renegotiate the price.

CASE STUDY

Surveys can be heartbreaking things. Just when you've set your heart on the home of your dreams, it throws up all these negatives. But forewarned is forearmed. The last thing you want is a bill for £50,000 for rising damp.

When our house was surveyed we discovered the main staircase was riddled with woodworm and therefore unsafe (it had been propped up 10 years previously), drainage was a problem, the roof was leaky and there were damp patches. This did allow for a bit of renegotiation, but we decided we wanted to go ahead.

However, it was enough to put off several other buyers who withdrew their offers. Luckily for us.

Contracts

Conveyancing – dealing with your solicitor

Solicitors are not to be feared, they are there to help you. If you don't understand anything, just ask! The term conveyancing literally means that the property will be conveyed or transferred from one party to another.

If you don't already have a solicitor to do your conveyancing they are fairly easy to find. Either ask a friend for a recommendation or go to any High Street solicitors. Most conveyancing is done on a fixed minimum fee plus disbursements and VAT and any extras, such as Land Registry fees. The conveyancing fee is usually based on the value of your property, as is The Land Registry fee:

Land Registry fees in England and Wales		Land Registry fees in Northern Ireland	
Up to £40,000	£40	Up to £10,000	£100
£40,001–£60,000	£70	£10,001–£20,000	£150
£70,001–£100,000	£100	£20,001–£40,000	£200
£100,001–£200,000	£200	£40,001–£200,000	£300
£200,001–£500,000	£300	£200,001–£300,000	£400
£500,001–£1,000,000	£500	Over £300,001	£500
Over £1,000,001	£800		

Land Registry fees in Scotland
These are also based on house cost, but it is divided into much smaller bands. For example, for a house worth £20,000–£25,000, the fee would be £55 and for a house worth £35,000–40,000, the fee would be £88.

Not all land is registered in the UK. Some parts of the countryside have never been registered because the land hasn't changed hands for hundreds of years, having stayed in the same family. For instance, most inherited land, such as great estates, will not be registered but as soon as the land is sold on, it will be. Most of London and the large cities are registered.

Once you have put your offer in and arranged for a survey, your solicitor will leap into action to get you to the next stage, which is exchange of contracts. (See Chapter 4 on the basic nuts and bolts of buying a house.) This is what he should be doing on your behalf and if you are selling and buying simultaneously it is obviously wiser to have the same solicitor to do both.

How to **Make Money** from **Your Property**

Understanding the contract

The seller's solicitor will prepare a pre-contract package, which will consist of copies of the draft contract, proof of seller's ownership and a seller's property information form (SPIF). This will also include a Fixtures, Fittings and Contents form showing what is included and what is excluded from the purchase price. This pre-contract package isn't law yet but most solicitors use it to speed things along. It may also include some land searches that have already been investigated, which give additional information regarding the property.

The buyer's solicitor must follow a number of procedures. First, they must make sure that the terms of the draft contract are in accordance with the buyer's wishes. The contract is a standard document including all the information essential for the purchase of the property, i.e. details of the property, address, purchase price, deposit, date for completion, name and address of both seller and buyer, plus any rights that third parties have over the property.

These third party rights could be:

- **A covenant**, which is a promise made by previous owners that certain things would not be done on the land, like to build on it, or prohibit the use for business purposes (change of use);

- **An easement**, which is a right for someone to do something on your land, such as walk across it in order to gain access to their property or the right to have light coming into their property.

No two conveyancing transactions are alike and complications can arise to do with boundaries or the lease, which is why you are paying a professional to deal with the process.

Your solicitor will also make some local authority searches to find out if there are proposed plans for the area. For example, are there extensive building or regeneration schemes, or maybe you are buying in a conservation area so future building may be restricted. He will also complete searches at the Land Registry that will provide further information about the property.

If, however, he slips up and misses something in his searches – you discover 4 months later that there are plans afoot to build a motorway through your back garden – you can sue for negligence. This is very rare.

All search and registration fees are costs to be paid by the purchaser. These costs are known as disbursements and can't be avoided I'm afraid. They will be added on to the fee charged by your solicitor.

When everyone is happy you will be asked to sign the contract and then hand over the agreed deposit. Both parties sign separate copies of the same contract, which are then exchanged and a date agreed for completion. Up until the point of actually exchanging contracts you can pull out of the proceedings without incurring any penalty. Once you have exchanged, there is no going back.

The final part of the solicitor's job is to arrange the completion of the sale – the finalising of the deal. One important point for the solicitor to check before completion is that the buyer's mortgage arrangement is satisfactory, the money is standing by and the client is happy with the conditions.

You have **completed** on the property when:

- the terms agreed in the contract have been included in the final transfer deed;

- the buyer's funds have been transferred from the lender to the seller's account;

- the buyer can now have the keys to the property; hurrah!

- after completion the solicitor registers the transfer deed with the Land Registry. Until this is done, the buyer will not have legal ownership of the property. The deeds are then sent to the lender, or, if you have bought without borrowing any money, can be sent to you or left for safekeeping with your solicitor. He should provide you with a copy of the Land Certificate showing you as the 'registered proprietor'.

Other Nasties

Gazumping

This is a horrible experience. It is when a seller accepts another, higher offer from a third party, even though a sale has been agreed. This can only happen before a contract has been exchanged and is immensely frustrating for the buyer. It depends how much you want the property as to whether you up your offer or not. If the seller is being greedy, just walk away. In Scotland the law is different. Once you have made an offer, it is legally binding, which saves a lot of wasted time.

How to **Make Money** from **Your Property**

Gazundering

This is when the buyer, just before exchange of contracts, informs the seller that he will only proceed if the price is reduced.

Sealed bids

These occur when there are a number of offers for the same property. Each potential buyer will put a separate bid into an envelope. On the day of the sale the envelopes are opened and the property, rather like at auction, will go to the highest bidder. There are two kinds of sealed bid:

- **Formal tender** – once the envelopes are opened and the bid is accepted, the sale is complete. There is no going back.

- **Informal tender** – the sealed bid is subject to survey and contract. In other words until you exchange contracts either party can pull out.

However, there is no way to guarantee success when buying property this way, unless you have very deep pockets and are prepared to put in a very high bid.

Guarantor

A guarantor is someone who promises to pay for your mortgage repayments if you default on them. Some lenders require this when arranging a mortgage – usually only when the borrower is considered a bit risky.

Equity

This is the difference between the value of your property and the outstanding amount of your loan. If you buy a house for £65,000 with a 100 per cent mortgage, and it is valued at £72,000, you would have £7,000 in equity in it. *Negative equity* is where the reverse is true, i.e. the value of your house is less than the amount you originally borrowed on it.

chapter six

Selling your home

Maximise Your Property

It is essential that you achieve the best possible price for your property, whatever your reasons may be for selling. Even if you're in a hurry (see Chapter 7, How to Sell Your House in One Week), you should think about maximising the potential of your home.

This could be something as simple as rearranging the furniture or painting the hall, but before you put it on the market take a good look around. The Americans call it 'house styling' and sometimes employ a professional (a house doctor) to take a look at their house and offer advice on how best to present the property. This isn't as daft as it sounds and you can do it yourself for nothing. (See Chapter 12, Making the Most of Your Property.)

When to Sell

Traditionally, spring is the most active time of year for selling a property. The days are getting longer, and the light is improving. I suppose once we see those spring flowers appearing we feel better about making new plans. In fact more people put their homes on the market between January and April than at any other time of the year. Whether this has anything to do with the fact that more relationships break up around Christmas than at any other time, I'm not entirely sure!

Autumn is also a good time to sell. After the summer holidays, when things are very quiet and people start to think about the new year and new schools etc., is when the market starts to move again.

Of course, your circumstances may dictate that you move in mid-winter, in which case an agent will be only too delighted to take your instruction but don't be put off if he says the market is quiet. Discuss placing it with several agents instead of sole agents. It may well affect your fees but will cast a wider net. But do not despair. If you follow the tips in this book on presentation and making the most of your property, you should be able to shift it at any time of the year.

However, don't forget how much is involved between issuing instructions and actually getting your home on the market.

The agent has to measure up (some will draw a floor plan), take all the details, prepare any historical information (this is always helpful), and then prepare the sale particulars, organise the photography and prepare the advertising campaign. If the property requires it, he will also arrange the printing of glossy brochures. Discussing the style of brochure and selecting photos can take for ever. 'Landscape or portrait? Four sides or six?' You then have to agree the descriptions in the sale particulars and which papers to advertise in.

Then your solicitor has to be briefed, as the title deeds – if you can't find them, check with your mortgage company – will be needed so that the description and boundaries of the property can be accurately checked. While all this is going on you are painting, polishing, cleaning and tidying up both inside and out in the hope that the first person through those portals is your buyer.

I remember thinking, after three weeks of preparations to sell our house, that if the brochures didn't arrive from the printers I was going to burst. 'It is very important at the preparatory stage of the sale, let alone during the sale itself, for the owner and agent to work closely together', said an agent I spoke to.

Time spent on the preparatory work can reap considerable benefits when the actual marketing commences. If anybody is thinking of selling their property in the spring, they should contact their agent as early as possible.

One good tip which might help rush the process along a bit is to have some fabulous photographs taken of your home, on a sunny day with the blossom out against a clear blue sky, whether you are thinking of selling or not. You never know when you might need them. For some obscure reason I had our old house photographed over a year before it went on the market, which proved pretty handy in the circumstances.

CASE STUDY ·

Mr and Mrs Wallop planned to sell their house next spring. So the previous summer they had some fabulous photos taken of the house and the garden in full bloom (so much better than a winter garden). After Christmas they started freshening up the paintwork and emptying all the rubbish out of the house because Mr Wallop had a penchant for collecting spare parts for his valve radios. In February they instructed the local agent to sell their house. He prepared everything and on 4 April they put it on the market. The house sold quickly thanks to all the preparation. Mrs Wallop was convinced the daffodils helped.

If you are trying to sell your house at Christmas, beware of going overboard with the decorations. 'Christmas is not an easy time to sell a property', said one agent, 'and the decorations can sometimes prove to be a real distraction. Hiding a beautiful staircase under swags of holly is definitely not a good idea.'

I remember once viewing a house that looked like a bomb had gone off in the tinsel department of Woolworth's. I was so agog at the sheer quantity of tinsel and the ingenious placing of it all – it was round all the light switches – that I hardly remember the house at all.

The basic rules of selling still apply at Christmas. Keep it tidy, uncluttered and simple.

CHECK LIST ·

Check list if you are selling:

Right way

- Plan ahead;

- Get the paint out;

- Instruct agents early;

- Have all the work done before marketing commences (i.e. viewings).

Wrong way

- Instruct agent to sell half-way through spring and viewings take place *while* you are painting;

- You see a house you want to buy before attempting to sell your own house.

How to Choose the Right Estate Agent

I know they get a bad press a lot of the time, but let me reassure you that there *are* some good estate agents out there. It is up to you to do your homework when it comes to selling your property.

You will need to shop around to find the agent who is most appropriate for your type of property. One of the grand 'country house' type agencies isn't likely to be interested in a one-bedder in Skegness, so you could start by trying the following tips:

TIPS ···

- Look at the For Sale boards in your area to see who is selling similar homes to yours.

- You could check in the local newspapers and magazines as well, to see which agencies are advertising homes like yours.

- You should pop into a few local agencies to test the water. Do you get a friendly reception?

- Some local independent agents have now joined forces with the larger city-based agencies. This could be useful if you're looking for a country cottage.

- Do their details look attractive? Is the window display eye-catching? If you get one of those spivvy types or they keep you waiting, walk away.

- Ask a friend in the area which agent they bought their house from. If their experience was pleasant, that agent might be the one to help you sell.

- Make sure they are qualified professionals, as most of the problems occur with people who have set themselves up as estate agents without any qualifications at all. It is surprisingly easy to do. They should be ARICS (Associate of the Royal Institute of Chartered Surveyors) or ANAEA (Associate of the National Association of Estate Agents) or ASVA (Associate of the Society of Valuers and Auctioneers). Or sometimes all three!

- If your home is unusual or exceptional or historic you may want one of the larger, up market agencies who have contacts, or offices, overseas. The national newspapers and glossies will alert you as to who they are.

Once you have decided who you like the look of, choose three agencies to come to your home to give you a valuation. They should have a good look around both inside and out; take their time and not seem hurried and have good local knowledge of the area.

> **M**ake an effort with the presentation of your home, as if the agent was a potential purchaser. He may value your home according to the way it looks and its decorative order. If you are about to paint the bathroom or the exterior of the house, tell him, because this may well make a difference to his valuation.

What it really comes down to is whether you like them or not. Do you trust them enough to sell your home? Can you develop a rapport with them? Trust your instincts. If you don't feel comfortable with the person doing the valuation, male or female, then you probably won't want them to sell your home. Not only that, why would you give all that commission to someone you don't even like? If you *do* like them, here are a few questions that you should ask.

Questions to ask the estate agent

- What are their fees? These can range from 2 or 3 per cent in the South East to 1.25 per cent in the North and West. These fees are always open to negotiation and VAT is charged on top. If you have a desirable property in a fabulous location you should be able to do a good deal.

- What are the agent's qualifications? Make sure he is a professional.

- Will you be showing the property or will he be? Ideally they should do the viewings because you may not be available, don't need the hassle and an agent can sell it for you in a more impartial way.

- Is the agency open at weekends? Sometimes Saturday staff are students brought in especially, with very little knowledge.

- Do they charge for advertising in the local paper? How many ads will be appearing?

- How much will the photographs cost and how many do they use on the details?

- Will they do a floor plan? If so, how much does it cost?

- Do they have other offices where your property will be marketed?

- Do they do mail-outs? If so, how often?

- Will your details be in the window?

- Do they insist on sole agency? You may want to go elsewhere as well.

- Will they put up a For Sale board? You might not want one.

- Do they have an agency magazine or paper? If so, will your home appear in it?

- What other marketing do they use?

- Do they have a web site and will your home be on it? Is there an extra charge for this?

- Ask to see an agreement form and several sets of details, so that you can compare them with other agencies. First impressions are very important and you will find that some details are presented in a much more attractive way.

After you have received your three valuations, sit down and take a deep breath. Chances are that you will be pleasantly surprised at how much your home is worth. However, don't be tempted to go for the highest valuation as this may just be flattery to get your business.

Weigh up the answers to all the questions you have asked and choose the agent who *you* think will do the best job of selling your home.

Issuing instruction

Call up your chosen agent – always insist on speaking to the same person because this will help to develop the relationship – and tell him that you would like him to sell your home, 'because he was the most professional/the most knowledgeable about the area/the most likely to succeed'. A little flattery goes a long way! I know I'm a creep but it works. Anyway, once you have done this – **issued instruction to sell** – the agent should confirm his fees in writing.

You should check carefully how much notice you need to give in case you decide to change agents or how long your agreement with the agent lasts before you can instruct someone else. You don't want to be tied in to an agent for 12 weeks if after a month you realise they are useless and you have made a mistake.

Upmarket Agencies

If you own a substantial home and are thinking of approaching one of the upmarket agents, you will have a choice of size and style of the glossy brochure. Be warned that the printing of these is very expensive and some of them use dozens of photographs. In my experience, it is the floor plan that is the most crucial part of any brochure. People are becoming more used to reading floor plans and the photographs are really just the icing on the cake.

Advertising your smart home in the glossy magazines, especially the ones associated with Scottish castles and baronial halls, is jaw-droppingly expensive. It can run into several thousand pounds for a full-page advertisement and your agent will try to persuade you that it is a necessary part of the marketing. Again, in my experience, the agent is using your money to advertise the estate agency; it all looks very lovely but is it really necessary?

By the time the picture appears in the magazine, most of those homes are already sold. If yours hasn't sold yet it may generate a dozen phone calls, maybe more, but it won't guarantee to sell it. However, you can negotiate all these costs against your commission, which will presumably be a whopping amount.

On a £600,000 house, a 3 per cent commission will come to £18,000 and your extras for advertising and brochures etc. *could* come to as much as £4,500. So don't be shy! Negotiate on:

- photographs;
- brochures;
- floor plans;
- web site;
- newspaper advertising;
- glossy advertising;
- all marketing;
- commission fees.

A lot of these posh agencies have a press office with a PR department who have access to all the national publications. Sometimes publicity helps to sell a home, particularly if it is featured in editorial because of its unique/quirky/historic/unusual qualities. Ask them to push the publicity because more people read editorial than adverts. Strange but true.

Those naughty estate agent's tricks

As I've said before, not all estate agents are the unscrupulous, slimy types that one hears about. My dealings with agents have always been honest and fair but maybe that's because I can tell a liar at 20 paces and will not deal with them. It's up to you to sort the wheat from the chaff.

However, it pays to be wary and here are a few of the tricks that the less likeable ones may try to pull:

- **Misleading For Sale boards**. Boards will appear on houses that are not for sale but as a means of pulling in the customer. Similarly they will put sold on houses that they have not sold.

- **Unrealistic valuations**. They will give you a high valuation in order to get your business but when they can't sell your house you find you are locked into their contract and they try to persuade you to reduce the price.

- **Priority customers**. They promise to put you on their 'Priority' list only if you take out a mortgage with them or agree to sell your house through them.

- **Selling on**. They undervalue your property, then get a friend to buy it who sells it on for a vast profit and they split the proceeds. Very naughty.

- **Ring-fencing**. They accept a bribe from a buyer not to pass on any further offers.

- **Misleading publicity**. They tell you that the house once belonged to a famous person when in fact it belonged to the famous person's granny.

My name once appeared on a press release issued by a very smart agency stating that the house they were selling for several million pounds had once been visited by me! Big deal. Apparently I went to a party there in the dim and distant past.

Secretly, I was quite flattered but thought that this was taking a tenuous celebrity connection to a property a bit far. I rang the agents and was told 'Oh, it's just a lighthearted gossipy bit. The publicity helps draw attention to the house.' Another agent said, 'There is no purpose to name-dropping. People don't buy because of a famous connection. It's slightly salacious in fact.' Exactly.

In the US all estate agents are fully trained and licensed so this sort of sharp practice doesn't exist. They have to renew their licence every five years because Americans are so litigious! There is no gazumping and no lawyers are involved. Once an offer is made, a minimum of 3 per cent of the sale price has to be paid and the buyer is locked in. The seller cannot accept any other offer. Agents get 6 per cent, which is held in escrow, as a neutral intermediary deals with the surveys, deeds and transfers.

If you feel the need to complain about your estate agent, you should approach the National Association of Estate Agents (NAEA). Their address is at the back of this book.

Do women make better agents?

I'm afraid the general consensus of opinion is, Yes! So, who better to sell your home?

'Men don't measure kitchens' said a female agent, quick as a flash. 'Size matters, after all. We're much better at the detail and tend to take a softer approach. I've found that a lot of female buyers and sellers prefer dealing with a woman for that reason. Men aren't as patient when it comes to closing the deal. Women are far more tenacious and better all round. Men are slicker, I suppose, when it comes to sales.'

I spoke to one of those slick operators who told me, 'Of course we're better. We're stronger and tougher at negotiating, get less emotionally involved with a property or a person, don't say things like "Ooh gorgeous curtains" and don't have off days every month.' Charming. I'm glad I didn't have to deal with him.

Apparently, there are more males in sales and females in lettings. Certainly, as a landlord I have only ever dealt with women agents regarding my flats and finding tenants, and they certainly do know the rental market inside out. Also, I have only ever been given wonderful advice by a female agent. That's not to suggest I'm biased either because in sales I've dealt mainly with men and have no complaints at all. One of my all-time favourite male agents told me, 'There's room for both, of course, but one of the best estate agents I ever came across was a woman. In fact, the very best agents at the top of the profession are all women. Even in the commercial world, the top agents are women.' How did they get there? What makes them such good agents? 'Tenacity. Men are inclined to give up more easily.

However, because we get less emotionally involved, we find it easier to sell a property that we *don't* like. It's just a deal.'

So there you have it. In the country, as it happens, there are very few women selling houses, so this argument is mainly city-based, but I'd say it's pretty even-stevens. Don't be deceived by that pretty young thing in the local agents. She'll be running the company one day.

Hidden Costs

Even though you are selling your home for a nice tidy profit, the costs of selling up and moving on can be astronomical. Firstly there is the **commission** to the agent. If your home sold for, say, £100,000, at 2 per cent commission that is £2,000 (plus VAT) you are giving away. As we have already established, you can negotiate this fee, but don't be taken by surprise by all the **extra costs**. You may be charged for:

- the photographs;

- the details;

- the floor plans;

- the advertising;

- the marketing;

- the web site.

Some agencies don't charge for any, or most, of these services but it is best to ask first because they can be expensive, depending on the size of your property.

Then there are your **solicitor's costs**. These can vary enormously, depending on whether there are complications with the title deeds or not. Conveyancing should be a fairly straightforward practice, which some High Street solicitors will do for a fixed fee. (See Chapter 5 for more on conveyancing.)

Assuming you are buying as well as selling, your **survey** can be a fairly reason-able cost, but sometimes it is a good idea to be there with them to make sure that they are really thorough. (See Chapter 5 for more on surveys.)

Finally, there are the **removal costs**. (See Chapter 8, Moving House Painlessly.) If you're a minimalist sort of person whose only possessions are a lava lamp, futon and a handful of crystals then obviously this category isn't going to stretch your wallet. For the rest of us though – especially if you have children – it is quite a major expense.

These hidden costs can add up to quite an alarming amount of money, so bear in mind when you sell your home that several thousand pounds will disappear into the ether.

To sum up, your costs when selling will include:

- agent's commission – from 1.75 to 3 per cent of sale price;

- advertising or marketing extras – from nil to thousands;

- surveys – if buying, could cost £250 upwards;

- solicitor's conveyancing fee – approximately £450 upwards;

- disbursements and Land Registry – approximately £200;

- stamp duty – only if buying, see scale on page 81;

- removal company – costs dependent on distance and cubic capacity;

- Valium!

What You Should Expect from Your Estate Agent

Once you have chosen your estate agent, communication is vital. Don't just leave them to get on with it because they have dozens of other properties to sell, with all those sellers giving them grief. So **regular contact**, with **humour** and **charm** will go a long way. Don't hassle them unnecessarily but if you haven't seen the details yet or haven't had a viewing for a few days, give them a call and a gentle nudge. I have found that rather than going on the attack, humour helps.

You must let them know of any timescale involved. For example, you may not want to sell it next week but have put it on the market with a view to selling in a few months' time. Of course this is very tricky to achieve but sometimes a purchaser will agree to exchange contracts with a **delayed completion**. This means they put down their 10 per cent deposit on exchange and will complete when you are ready. However, this is quite unusual, especially if everyone is in a chain.

Your agent should be knowledgeable about the area, enthusiastic, positive, polite and presentable. I would expect him to report back to me after a viewing because getting some feedback does help.

Press him for information about the reaction because it could be that he is holding back on telling your something. Most estate agents are not 'house doctors' and will not advise you on presentation (see Chapter 7, How to Sell Your House in One Week), but if he says there was a 'terrible smell in the kitchen or the hallway was dark', he might be trying to say 'Please empty the bin and replace the light bulbs'. If, however, he is very forthcoming on the state of your home, take his advice, because he knows what sells and what doesn't.

Your agent should be utterly professional. If he starts using bad language, go elsewhere. If he starts getting negative, go elsewhere.

One agent confessed to me that once a property has officially gone on the market, if nothing happens within two weeks, i.e. no offers – they start to get bored with it and move on to the next one. There is a two-week window when the agent will have all guns blazing and give it his full energy but after that they will go off the boil. It is up to you, therefore, to keep him focused and working for you. Threaten to go elsewhere.

CHECK LIST

- Every time there is to be a viewing, your agent should ring to inform you, even if they are holding keys, because you may be at home that day.

- The agent should get to the property before the client – especially if you are *not* there – to open up and turn on the lights or whatever is necessary.

- If you are at home make yourself scarce because some would-be purchasers are intimidated by the owner being present. The agent can be impartial. If they return for a second viewing, however, this is usually good news and it can be helpful if you are around then to answer questions.

- The agent should be talking all through the viewing, about the efficient central heating and the wonderful parks etc.! If he stands silently by the front door, fire him.

- You must like your agent and develop a rapport with him. It is important that you feel he is honest and trustworthy.

Floor Plans and Photos

I've already mentioned how important floor plans can be when you are buying a property, therefore it goes without saying that if you are selling something, *insist* on a floor plan. It doesn't matter whether it is a two-bedroom flat or a vast Georgian mansion, the floor plan will be invaluable.

The buyer will see your details, or brochure, and immediately be able to make sense of the layout of the home. This helps enormously. The words may say 'Tiled hallway with steps down to open living-room area', but which way is the living-room? What is the geography in relation to the kitchen? This is why floor plans are so wonderful. (See Chapter 4 for more on details and floor plans.)

The photos are another story. The camera can deceive and tell downright lies with its magic lens. It can obscure and obliterate the bad bits (you don't see the main road in the photograph) and enhance the good bits (it can make the garden look huge), so that your humble abode looks like Buckingham Palace. (That's assuming you've got a whizz photographer.)

Discuss beforehand which aspect is most likely to sell your home (it doesn't have to be the outside, if you have a wonderful kitchen or amazing back garden) and insist on seeing the results before they run off 250 copies for their details. They may decide to use more than one photo, in which case make sure you are there on the day and that everything looks perfect.

The photographs are the marketing tool that pulls the punters through the door so here are some tips to remember.

TIPS

Tips on presenting the exterior:

- The exterior should only be photographed on a bright sunny day.
- The front door must be immaculate. Repaint it if necessary.
- Put some flowers or shrubs on either side of the front door.
- The garden should look fabulous with newly mown grass.
- Take down net curtains and clean the windows.

Tips on presenting the interior:

- Tidy up the room that is being photographed.
- If there is a fireplace, light the fire. (It doesn't matter what time of year it is.)

- Adjust the furniture slightly to create the most pleasing angles. (The photographer should do this but some are lazy and you don't want a photo of the back of your sofa.)

- Switch on table lamps and use flowers to lighten, or fill, a corner.

If you are selling through one of the upmarket agents who are putting together a brochure for you, then their photographers are usually pretty good at styling the shots and rearranging the furniture. Some of the laminated brochures require eight or ten photos, and this will set you back a bit. Photos, brochures and floor plans all cost money. Quite a lot of money, so make sure you negotiate first.

'If there is only one photo on the details, it's got to be a good one, otherwise the purchaser isn't grabbed.'

CASE STUDY ·

A friend of mine was selling his terraced house recently and fired his agents when he saw the ghastly photograph they had taken of the outside. So he decided to take it himself. He painted the door Royal blue (did you know that blue doors sell more homes than any other colour?) and stuck some plastic daffodils in a borrowed window-box. He waited for a really sunny day and parked his mate's Jaguar outside the house. He then asked a friend to swing on a branch of next door's beautiful magnolia tree so that it just peeped into the shot. The results were fabulous! Who says the camera never lies?

If the property is empty the photographer should concentrate on the exterior only. However, if there are some beautiful features such as fireplaces, cornicing or balustrading, use arty close-ups on the details. Developers often go to the expense of hiring furniture to make the photo look good. There's nothing worse than an expanse of beige carpet.

Sole Agency or Multi Agency?

If you only issue instruction to one agency to sell your house this is called **sole agency** and your commission fee will be negotiated accordingly. If you decide to place it with several agents in order to spread the marketing and hopefully ensnare a buyer more quickly, the fee will usually be half a percent higher. They are working in competition with each other but the fee will only go to whoever introduces the buyer. This is called **multi agency**.

If you decide to put your home on the market with two agents who will work together on the marketing, and split the commission, this is called **joint sole agency** (JSA). The fee for JSA is also half a per cent higher than sole agency.

> For example, a London agent would charge:
> Sole agency   – 2.5% + VAT (elsewhere it can be 1.75%)
> Multi agency   – 3% + VAT
> JSA   – 3% + VAT

Most properties only need to be with one agent, unless you don't mind spending the extra money. There is a certain amount of cross-fertilisation among agencies anyway.

> **T**ry to avoid something called **'sole selling rights'** with your agent, because if you happen to sell the house yourself to a friend or relative, some agencies will insist on their commission. They should only take commission if the buyer was introduced by them.

When to change agencies

It is such an emotionally charged and stressful time, when you are selling your home, that it is hardly surprising that most agents get it in the neck if nothing happens for a while.

Once you have agreed terms and signed the conditions make absolutely sure you are not locked into an exclusive arrangement for months on end. Read the small print because you may find that if you are unhappy with your agent, you are unable to move for a specified time.

How to **Make Money** from **Your Property**

Most agents insist on six weeks after it has officially gone on the market and I think that's fair. Give them a chance, for heaven's sake! Advertising lead-times (the time between placing the ad and publication) mean that sometimes your home won't appear in the ads for three weeks.

If, after that time, you get very few viewings or feel that you are not getting the right attention, it is time to move on. Shop around again and choose another suitable agent. You may already have a second choice but ask the first agent why he feels your home is 'sticking'. It could be something you could so easily rectify or it could be over-priced.

Drive-bys

Drive-bys are the bane of the agent's life – and the seller's – because it means that a would-be buyer is literally driving past your home for a quick look at the outside, to see if it is what they are after. Now, everyone knows you shouldn't judge a book by its cover and that some homes have a frontage that totally contradicts the interior style and – more importantly – size of the property. So if you discover this is happening to you, you need to do two things. One is to smarten up the outside (see the section on kerb appeal in Chapter 7) and the other is to ask your agent how proactive he is being. He should be ringing up customers and persuading them to come for a viewing. If he is not, then it is time to move on.

Saturation point

If they have done everything within their powers to sell your home – mailed out hundreds of details, advertised, marketed, had dozens of viewings – and you still haven't received any offers, your agents will have reached saturation point and will start to lose interest. This is human nature, unfortunately, unless you have a little terrier of an agent who has got it between her teeth and refuses to let go.

Remember the 'two-week window' confession? I believe this to be true, so it will help to put your home with a new agent, with a fresh approach.

> **I**f your home is not selling, there must be something wrong with it! Sorry to be so blunt but it's true. Either the price is way too high or the naffness is overwhelming. Take a long hard look (see Chapter 7, How to Sell your House in One Week) or ask a friend for their honest opinion. It may not be only the agent you need to change!

How to **Make Money** from **Your Property**

A girlfriend of mine was trying to sell her flat, and out of loyalty to a friend, placed it with his agency, which was miles away across town. He managed to arrange a few viewings but it sat on the market for too long. Eventually, feeling very embarrassed, she withdrew her flat and placed it with an agent based in her area. She sold it two weeks later. The second agent told me 'Firstly, I was able to be more honest about the property and the price than her friend and secondly, to be quite frank, geography is very important. If you're selling a place in York, why put it with an agent in Hull? Buyers for York will go to York, not Hull.'

Small and Friendly Versus Large and Formal

I remember back in 1976 when I was looking to buy my first flat, I made the mistake of going into one of those frightfully smart agencies in Central London and inquiring as to what was available. The gentleman asked me what sort of price range I was looking at and I said, 'Oh, about 10 to 12 thousand pounds.' He gave me one of those patronising, poor-you sort of looks and said, 'I'm afraid we don't have anything of *that* price. We handle rather more exclusive homes.' That put me in my place.

I suppose I have always been of the opinion that small is beautiful. Small is certainly more personal when it comes to estate agents. You don't get swallowed up in the machinery of a large company. I have dealt with both large and small agencies over the years, and they both have benefits and drawbacks, but it really comes down to what sort of property you are selling, the price you would like to achieve and whether you want to be a small fish in a big pond or vice versa.

For example, a small local agent will know the area well, whereas one of the larger chains will have staff from all over the place.

Don't be impressed by the familiar High Street names as the smaller operations, who may only have one office, have a higher incentive to sell your home. One agent with a small agency told me, 'We are not governed by a large corporation and do not offer financial services but we do provide a very personal service with expert local knowledge. Our business is purely to sell houses for which we charge 2 per cent and we work on personal commission.'

You will find with the smaller agencies that they specialise in one specific area of the market and it's not necessarily the lower end. One top agent I dealt with many years ago was specialising in houses at the upper end of the bracket, but he only had one office. He was competing with the big companies but his service and style was unique and his brochures were fabulous. He now has two offices!

Some small agencies share the commission among the whole company rather than have their negotiators competing with each other. This makes for a less pushy, aggressive style. Also, you tend to only deal with one person in the office, which I happen to like because you can get to know them and use emotional pressure, if necessary. In the large agencies there are so many people all running around like headless chickens that you never deal with the same person twice. When you want to speak to them they are 'out of the office' because they spend the whole time on viewings.

Of course, the advantages of putting your home with a large company, whether it is formal or not, are that they have a built-in network of offices and offer a marketing service that is often global. Most of them now have offices overseas, so if you are selling the sort of property that might interest a Japanese businessman, this sort of international company is the one for you.

You are less likely to get the naughty tricks from the older, established agencies but they still employ young men, who sound as if they have swallowed a plum, with a strong competitive edge. This is where the aggressive sales talk comes in. Sometimes it is so over the top, I find it corny and clichéd. Don't be taken in by it and put yourself in the shoes of the buyer. If you think he might find the patter nauseating too, don't use the agent.

It all comes down to your personality and instincts. A small, smart agency is going to do just as good a job as the bigger High Street ones. Remember, the smaller ones are hungrier!

CHECK LIST

Small agency

For	*Against*
• personal service;	• may not get the plum properties;
• specialises in local area;	• no network of offices;
• higher incentive to sell;	• may not have a web site;
• you deal with one person.	• no international marketing.

How to **Make Money** from **Your Property**

Large agency

For	Against
For	*Against*
• network of offices;	• may lack personal service;
• international marketing;	• will be more expensive;
• upmarket image;	• may put off some buyers;
• has a web site;	• the rapid turnover of properties;
• plenty of staff.	mean they get bored with yours more quickly;
	• it can take ages to get your property on the market.

Selling Privately – Doing It Yourself

This is not for the faint-hearted. If you really do begrudge an estate agent his commission fee then you can set about selling your home yourself. It will make the whole process even *more* stressful and, of course, there is expense involved in the marketing of your home. Have you thought about:

• preparing and producing the details;

• fixing a price;

• printing the details;

• taking photographs;

• measuring the rooms;

• placing advertisements in newspapers, magazines and on the internet;

• answering the phone;

• arranging viewings.

One lady who tried this said that about half the people who arranged to view her house didn't turn up and as a busy young executive, she knew that time is money.

The internet has made selling privately much easier, and there are several sites dedicated to putting buyers and sellers in direct contact with each other, but it is all very time consuming.

How to **Make Money** from **Your Property**

> **Y**our personal security is of paramount importance, so if you are a single female selling your home this way, you *must* have a friend with you when you are showing viewers around. Preferably male.

If you want to sell your home privately, all the newspapers and magazines have a property section where you can place an advertisement. The weekend national newspapers are probably the best for this. The glossies do it too but they have a very long lead-time and are *very* expensive.

Make your ad as eye-catching as possible (it might be worth putting it in a box so that it stands out a bit), because usually there are no photographs, only words. Remember to include:

- the location;

- the period of the building;

- the size or number of bedrooms;

- number of reception rooms if it is huge;

- any special or quirky features;

- whether it is freehold or leasehold;

- the price;

- your phone number.

> **I**t could read something like:
>
> 'Unique barn conversion dating back to 1710 in the middle of Shropshire countryside 10 miles from Ludlow. 4 bedrooms, 2 bathrooms, 3 receptions all with stone fireplaces. Freehold. £250,000. Phone Gerald on blah blah blah for details.'
>
> Alternatively it could read:
>
> 'High-tech, minimalist 90s built pad. 3,000sq ft. Shoreditch. Must see. 300K o.n.o. Call Oliver on…'

Get the picture? Short and snappy is good but you must hook them with one or two words. **Unique** and **high-tech** in these examples. When people start calling they will want you to send details with a picture so have these ready to mail out. The down-side to all this is that you will inevitably get some time-wasters who just want to look around. You have no way of knowing whether they are serious buyers or if they have the means to buy.

If someone makes an offer it is up to you to negotiate and it depends how brave or tough you are. You have no intermediary to act for you to ascertain how high the buyer will go. Sometimes an agent has information that he can pass on to the vendor such as 'I know he'll go to 460K but that's his absolute final offer.' If you don't know this you may accept his offer of 440K thinking he won't go any higher.

Anyway, good luck. All I know is that it is quite a delicate matter getting the price you want but not losing the buyer in the process. You could always ask your solicitor to do the negotiating, I suppose. As soon as the sale price is agreed get the purchaser's solicitor in touch with your solicitor, so that the contracts can be drawn up.

However, it may be wise to keep on showing your home until exchange of contracts as there is many a slip between the ship and the wharf, and I have heard of people pulling out of a deal, even after surveys etc., on the day they were due to exchange.

When I was living in Los Angeles I discovered 'Open House' on Sundays. This is for people selling their homes – usually through an agent – who are prepared to open their doors between 1 and 4 p.m. every Sunday to complete strangers. The property section of the *Los Angeles Times* has several pages of houses that are on the market, with pictures, accompanied by a brief description and the address. The price range is spectacular.

I loved it because you can just turn up and have a good gawp. They take your name and address on arrival, offer you coffee and cookies, and then the estate agent (or realtor) shows you around. The owners are not usually present.

It struck me as a wonderful way of showing a house. The agent stays put and the punters just wander in. However, there must be dozens of time-wasters just there for the cookies. In one house I went to, it was getting pretty busy so she just let me wander around on my own. I suppose my English accent helped a bit, but how many times do they have people casing the joint?

CHECK LIST •••

Check list for selling it yourself:

- Prepare some details with photographs.

- Write an eye-catching advertisement.

- Place ad in newspapers or on the internet.

- Arrange viewings every half-hour to suit you.

- Send out details.

- Have a friend with you during viewings.

- Be tough but not greedy when you negotiate.

- Accept a good offer.

- Instruct a solicitor. The conveyancing fees will be the same, even though you've sold it yourself.

- Keep showing until you exchange contracts.

Being In a Chain

Eek! This is so horrible and stressful I'm having palpitations just writing about it. I'm sure you all know about being in 'a chain', because even if you haven't been there yourself, we all know someone who has.

Being in a chain is when you are selling your house to someone who is buying your house only when he has sold his house to someone else who has to sell their house first and so on and so on. You may be trying to buy a house as well – have set your heart on it – but the sale is dependent on you selling first. Or even, you are buying but the seller won't move until he has found somewhere to buy.

Confused? Being in the middle of the chain is horrific and awful, and often the whole thing collapses because one buyer drops out, so you all have to wait until another buyer is found.

I have only been involved in a chain once and then I vowed never again. The problem is that most people want to sell and buy on the same day. Completion is synchronised so that you move out of one property and into another on the same day. This is madness. It is totally dependent on your buyer coming up with the money in time for your solicitor to pass it on so that you can have the keys to your new home. This is why we hear stories of removal men sitting outside a house for hours on end, waiting to be let in, because the money has got stuck somewhere along the chain.

Mr A bought Mr B   Mr C   Mr D   Mr E   Mr F   Mr G

Mr B selling to Mr A is buying Mr C

Mr C selling to Mr B is buying Mr D

Mr D selling to Mr C is buying Mr E

Mr E selling to Mr D is buying Mr F and so on.

Unfortunately Mr C has received a low valuation on Mr D's house so his mortgage isn't going to be big enough. He can't afford to buy the house now, so is dropping out. The chain collapses.

Mr D, however, is so desperate to buy Mr E's house that he takes out a bridging loan in order to meet the deadline and puts his house back on the market. His wife is having a nervous breakdown. This is very risky as the bridging loan (a very high interest loan for just such an occasion) is hugely expensive and he might not get another buyer for months. He will soon own two houses.

There are endless permutations and combinations of being in a chain, but there are also ways of avoiding it:

- Be a cash buyer. This means you are not dependent on selling a home and you don't need a loan (either you are very rich, have won the lottery or your granny just died).

- Sell your home first before you start looking to buy. Rent for the interim period and then when you see something you like you can move swiftly. Speed always strikes a mean deal. Estate agents always favour the buyer who doesn't have somewhere to sell or who is a cash buyer.

- A first-time buyer will be at the end of the chain.

- Buy a brand-new home with no previous owner.

- Buy at auction.

- Sell at auction.

- Buy a property with 'vacant possession'. (The owner has already gone.)

- Sell your home to a cash buyer.

chapter seven

How to sell your home in one week

First Impressions – Kerb Appeal

Everyone knows that first impressions are hugely important and with the advent of 'drive-bys' the outside of your home is crucial. (This is when the buyer receives details of your property, then drives by to take a look.) If it looks like something out of the Munsters with a jungle in the front he will hardly be impressed.

Stumbling over a broken baby buggy, past the dustbins and being dripped on in the porch, while staring at a chipped door is hardly the best of omens. The approach to the front door should be clear and welcoming, so here are a few tips on presenting the outside of your home to achieve maximum **Kerb Appeal**.

- If there is a garden gate it should be clean and freshly painted and left open to welcome people towards the house. A closed gate seems negative.

- The name or number of the house should be clearly visible. There is nothing more annoying than not being able to find the property.

- The front garden should be neat and tidy. Clip the hedges, mow the lawn, weed flower beds and trim roses or brambles. Even the tiniest space can look shambolic, so tidy it all up.

- Hide dustbins. If your house is divided into flats and all your bins are at the front you can hide them away with a length of fencing or bamboo sheeting

Before: Smelly dustbins and a broken bike sitting in an unkempt garden are hardly likely to create a good impression.

attached to a timber frame. If it is an improvement, the other residents could hardly object.

- Re-paint the front door to make it look glossy and fresh. (I mentioned before that blue seems to be the most successful door colour for selling houses!) Polish up the brass letter-box and knocker.

- If the windows need re-painting I'm afraid you should re-paint them. If it is shabby and peeling outside, the viewer will assume it is shabby and peeling inside and may not come in.

- Re-paint the whole frontage if necessary.

- Remove bicycles, prams, toys, buggies, roller-blades etc. from the path and porch. The approach should be entirely free of obstacles.

How to **Make Money** from **Your Property**

After: *The panelled door is a vast improvement, the grass has been cut and the gate replaced. The tubs either side of the door are a lovely touch which you can take with you when you move!*

- Remove hoses and tools.

- Introduce colour to the front with seasonal flowers in some tubs or window-boxes. This can make all the difference and, when you've sold, you can take the whole lot with you!

- The windows must be sparkling clean.

- Replace the light bulb in the porch with a higher wattage for those winter evenings.

- If all this doesn't bring them through the door, I don't know what will. But, remember you must do all these things *before* viewings commence. You don't want people tripping over paint pots and ladders.

TIP ●

Most viewings happen on a Saturday, so Friday afternoon is a good time to spruce up the garden.

> **W**e had a problem with drive-bys when we were selling our old house. I prepared the outside as much as I could. We even painted the whole thing but the problem was the fact that from the road it looked like a rather small white cottage, attached on both sides. What the viewer didn't realise was that it opened up like Dr Who's Tardis into a classic Georgian house with a galleried hallway and a massive garden. There's not much you can do in those circumstances except bamboozle your agents into being more proactive about dragging people through the door.

First Impressions – Presenting the Property

Having given your property a facelift on the outside, it now needs a thorough internal examination. (It is *exactly* like going to the doctor!)

The biggest no-no when presenting your home is **clutter**. We all have it, collect it and keep it. Heaven knows why. We need to get rid of all the clutter in order to present a tidy, spacious, calm environment that someone would really like to buy. So chuck out and tidy up – be ruthless.

Your prospective buyer doesn't really want to see your family photos, videos and old newspapers, so put everything away. Let the house speak for itself.

The first hurdle is the **hallway** and a buyer will often make a judgment about a property within the first 30 seconds, so here are the rules:

• Put away all coats, hats, dog leads, etc.

• Replace light bulbs (with higher wattage, if necessary).

• Clean hall mats or rugs.

• Wash down walls and doors that may be splattered with rain and mud.

• Remove racks of boots and shoes.

It may be necessary to overhaul the entire front of the house to improve your kerb appeal. Fixing the gutters, painting all the windows and then re-painting the render will make a huge difference. The curtains have been removed to create symmetry.

- If it is any colour other than neutral, I'm afraid it will have to be painted. Sorry. Orange won't sell! One-coat paint is available in soft creams and neutrals, which will make the hallway much lighter and more appealing.

- Use a mirror to increase light.

- Flowers are always a lovely bonus but not essential, as this can get expensive.

These basic rules also apply for the **rest of the house**:

- Tidy, tidy and tidy again.

- Keep all the rooms well aired, as there is nothing worse than a house that smells musty or damp.

- The route around the property should be free of obstruction, i.e. don't walk into the sitting room into the back of a chair. Move it and open up the space.

- Don't hide things behind a door. All doors must open fully.

- De-clutter the kitchen completely and clean it like mad. It must sparkle. Chuck out anything that doesn't have a useful role.

- Don't over-furnish any of the rooms. Space is what people want.

- Take down any old curtains that may look a bit past it.

- Ensure routes to windows are clear of clutter. Estate agents say that most viewers walk into a room and make a bee-line for the window.

> **O**bviously the whole place should be really clean, so if you don't have a cleaner and don't have much free time, invest in a phone-call to a spring cleaning company. They can work miracles and see things that we ignore. For some reason we can tolerate our own dirt and chaos, but not other people's and this could make the difference between selling or not.

Some more basic rules:

- Complete any little unfinished DIY jobs. If the bathroom is half-tiled and you can't be bothered to finish it, get someone in to do it. It will be money well spent.

- Leave the loo seat down.

- The bathroom must be clutter-free and really, *really* clean. Throw away empty shampoo bottles, and if you have a shower curtain that has seen better days, buy a new one.

- The sitting room must have a focal point. Ideally it would be a fireplace but if you don't have one, a piece of furniture will do.

- Pile CDs into shoe boxes and use a throw to cover an old sofa.

- Make sure all the windows are clean.

- Make all the beds. Nicely.

> **G**ive yourself an extra 10 minutes every morning to tidy up before leaving for work, in case there is a viewing in your absence.

Smells

Market research has shown that **smells** play an important part in selling in retail outlets and this could just as easily be applied to your home.

Everyone knows about the coffee trick because of the subliminal effect and psychological power of the feel-good factor. 'Coffee smells nice so this is a nice place.' The same goes for something baking in the oven. The viewer will feel it is a very 'homey' sort of home.

- Nowadays, aromatherapy oils are used in the home, such as lavender oil, which promotes tranquility.

- Scented candles are good too, particularly if you are a smoker, as a non-smoking purchaser may be put off by nicotine odours.

- Flowers are wonderful of course, both visually and for their scent, but can get a trifle expensive if you haven't sold your home after six weeks.

- Pot-pourri in little bowls smells nice.

- If you can bake bread or cookies, clever you. Time it to coincide with a viewing!

The way you present your home will definitely affect the sale price, so if you invest a small amount of money to get it just right, the rewards should be tremendous. Ideally, you should implement all these changes *before* the estate agent has seen it. A tidy, cared-for and well-maintained home will get more attention than one that isn't.

Space and light

The trick to selling your home quickly is to maximise the **space** and **light** in the property. These are the two words that estate agents use the most often.

Obviously, if you are selling a penthouse loft conversion of 3,000sq ft with acres of glass walls, then space and light are not going to be a problem. Lucky you.

The majority of people live in homes where light is in short supply and space is something we dream about. However, there are several things you can do to give the illusion of space and light:

- Take down curtains to let in the light. If you have a lovely bay window, why hide it? (I always maintain that no curtains is better than bad curtains.)

- Take down roller blinds if they are not necessary. The kitchen doesn't need blinds (unless you like cooking in the buff!).

- Install little spotlights in the kitchen to light every corner.

- Use uplighters in the sitting room to bounce light off the ceiling.

- Replace any blown light bulbs.

- Remove some pieces of furniture if they are getting in the way of viewing. Less is more.

- Keep all thoroughfares unobstructed. A laundry basket behind the bathroom door is not a good idea.

- Tidy up and de-clutter as I mentioned before. Then tidy up again. **Space** is the key word here. If necessary you can box everything up in readiness for your move.

- If you are fond of strong colours on the walls this will not be creating light. A burgundy sitting room or Royal blue bedroom is fine while *you* are living there, but not for selling. Neutral colours sell a house much quicker, so invest in some paint – white or cream – and get painting.

- Clean all the windows and keep remaining curtains drawn well back.

> **I**f you are present for the viewings then you will know which lights to put on, but if the agent is doing the viewing, make sure you tell him the routine.

The Quick Fix – Redecorating on a Very Tight Budget

The two most important rooms that influence the sale of your home are the kitchen and bathroom. Most women are swayed by those rooms more than any other so it would be wise to fix them up first if you want a quick sale.

If you have already followed the tips above about space, light and presentation, but feel there is still something lacking, it could be that some drastic measures are required. **Paint** is the most wonderful product for affecting a rapid, inexpensive transformation, so get those brushes out.

Anyone can paint, but if you feel (a) unsure or (b) lazy, get some help. A friend might help or the local handyman or decorator. Remember, I'm only trying to help you get top dollar for your home, so if you want to leave it the way it is, then fine. That's your decision. However, with a little motivation, it could give your home the edge.

Obviously, if you are just about to leave a place, you might not feel inclined to start spending money on it but believe me, even on a VTB (very tight budget) you can achieve amazing results.

> **I** redecorated the kitchen in a friend's house in April 2000 for £235, giving it a completely different look. It increased the value of her property by £2,500.
>
> If I'm doing the painting myself, I use **paint pads** to apply emulsion to the walls. Decorators sniff at these but I think they are quick and easy to use and you only need apply one coat. I can do a whole room in half a day! They are available at all DIY stores.

Kitchen

Fixing a kitchen can be relatively easy. A little effort could bring rich rewards. You may need to do some or all of the following:

- Give it a good scrub first to remove all the grease. Most of the paintwork will immediately look better.

- Take down curtains/blinds/pelmets.

- Paint all the walls in white emulsion and the doors and windows in white eggshell.

- If the cupboard fronts are very old-fashioned you can replace them with new doors (keep them plain and neutral) or paint the existing doors white.

- If the vinyl flooring is dark or old-fashioned, replace it with a light-coloured vinyl. Most carpet warehouses do off-cuts.

- If you're feeling brave you could lay wood laminate flooring instead. It instantly makes a room look more glamorous.

- If there is a tiled splash-back that is dark or old-fashioned (anything patterned or coloured) you could tile over it with cheap white tiles from the DIY store, or even paint them.

The results will be amazing. Do not replace any of the clutter! Just some white china, olive oil bottles and a fruit bowl will do. Remember you are selling a lifestyle as well. You will have to live in a very purist, tidy way until you have sold. If you have a pine kitchen table that is *not* an antique you could cover it with a bright, fresh tablecloth.

These are just suggestions and ideas. Obviously if you have a wonderful country-style kitchen with an AGA and timber beams then a fresh lick of paint will do. But still keep it tidy.

Bathroom

There is only one colour that a bathroom suite should be – white. If yours is not white, oh dear. Never mind! I'm not going to suggest that you change it. (This is a quick fix after all. For bigger transformations see Part III Maximising the Potential.)

Before: *The kitchen is dark, old-fashioned and cluttered. The flooring has worn through in areas and the wall tiles are overpowering.*

After: *All the walls and units have been painted white and the flooring has been made lighter using large white vinyl floor tiles. The old wall tiles have been replaced by white ones and the pelmet and curtains have come down. What a difference!*

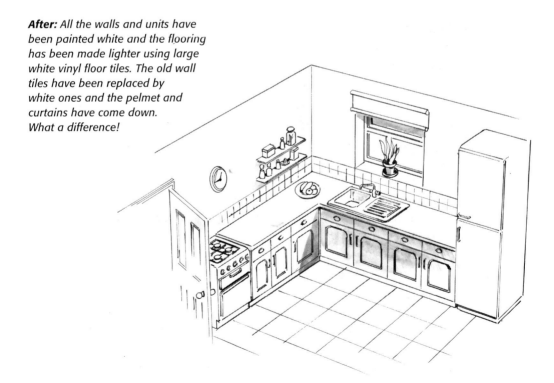

After scrubbing the bathroom free of grime you will only need to do a few things:

- Paint the walls white vinyl silk.

- Replace the tiles with white or creamy tiles.

- Install a huge, frameless mirror.

- Replace shower curtain or scrub shower glass.

- Replace carpet (if you have it) with vinyl flooring covering in the palest cream.

- Install a wooden loo seat if you haven't already got one.

- Use brighter light bulbs.

- Buy some new white towels. (You can take these with you.)

- Get rid of fluffy bath mats and pedestal mats! (You don't have those do you? Buy plain white cotton mats instead.)

- If the tiles are already white, re-grout where it has gone brown.

- Re-seal around the bath.

- Toilet should be sparkling clean, smell nice and have loo seat down.

- If the whole family use this bathroom, keep the children's toys out of sight. It has to look like a grown-ups' bathroom.

Some more quick sale tips:

- If you want a quick sale make sure that you have your deeds ready or that you know where they are. They are either with the lender or maybe your solicitor. If you can't find them you will have to apply to the Land Registry for a replacement, which takes time and money.

- Make sure your solicitor knows all about your service charge – if you have one – and whether there are any impending works. This will save time.

- If you are a female, get your boyfriend/Dad/handyman/neighbour to help you fix all those annoying things that didn't get fixed. When viewing a property the purchaser will always notice the things that *haven't* been fixed rather than the things that *have*.

- Another quick fix is that old lifestyle trick. When selling a house, a girlfriend of mine hangs her Gucci dresses on the back of the door and has her Prada bags all over the bed. Then she strategically places her empty champagne bottles by the bin. It works every time.

- Finally, keep it simple. The buyer wants to be able to envisage himself living there. If you **de-personalise** your home this will be much easier.

A Warning – Pets and Children

The two things that will hinder your viewings are pets and children. I know this seems harsh but if you've managed to de-personalise and de-clutter your home so magnificently, why would you want your children and pets cluttering it up for you?

In order to see your home clearly, the viewer needs as few distractions as possible. Tripping over dogs – especially if the viewer is not a dog-lover – will only make him rush around the premises and want to leave.

Unfortunately, dogs and cats only get in the way and, believe me, I'm an animal lover with a veritable menagerie at home. So, if possible, keep the dogs outside during the viewing. Cats are less hassle as they just seem to lie there all day but do make sure the chairs aren't covered in animal hairs, as so many people seem to be allergic to cats these days.

Smell

If you have animals, you may be blissfully unaware of the smell they generate. Get an honest friend to tell you if he thinks Fido needs a bath. Your home must smell wonderfully fresh before a viewing, not smell of wet dogs. I visited one house years ago and was greeted by a Vietnamese pot-bellied pig! Honestly. The estate agent threw her eyes to the heavens and just shrugged.

If your cat refuses to use the facilities outside and insists on a litter tray, pleeeeease remember to remove it before a viewing. And all those little dishes with food in them.

Children

What can I say? I've got two children and I couldn't put them in a cupboard every time we had a viewing, so we used to go to the local pizza restaurant and wait there. Unfortunately, it only takes ten minutes to eat a pizza so we explained our predicament to the manager and he was very sympathetic.

On other occasions we would hide next door and wait for the all clear. Most estate agents will agree that a viewing will go more smoothly if there are no children present – especially if there is a baby in the house. However, if you want to be present during the viewings, perhaps you could make arrangements for someone to look after the little darlings for a while.

What's in a Name?

According to one estate agent I spoke to, the name that you give your property can affect first impressions. He said that he would have no qualms about advising a vendor to change the name of their property if he thought it inappropriate or gave the wrong impression. 'For example, if it is called Foxglove Cottage when in fact it is a five-bedroom, three-reception room house, we advise them to change it to Foxglove House. The right name is very important.'

Apparently, in the countryside anything called The Old Rectory or Vicarage sells very quickly as does anything with Manor in the name. A friend of mine spent ages deciding between Farmhouse Manor, Old Manor Farm, The Old Manor House and Old Farm Manor.

Of course, pretension tends to creep into house names. I was filming once in a brand-new house on an estate that was called Nôtre Chateau! The awful thing was, the owners were very serious about it. No sense of irony at all.

One assumes there is irony and humour behind naming your house Costa Packit or Owl's Hoot or even Pheasant Plucker's Cottage. My favourite, though, is a house belonging to two doctors called Bedside Manor.

Whether your property has a name or a humble number, make sure it is easily seen from the street. There is nothing more irritating for the viewer who is looking for 78 Acacia Avenue, if the number is on the gate, which is hidden by a bush. *Especially* if he can't see 76 or 80. Large numbers on the door are ideal, whereas numbers on the gate are not. When the gate is open, which it should be, it will only be visible from one direction.

Also, remember if you have a Victorian house where the number is etched into the glass above the front door, you will need to have a light on, either inside or out, to make it highly visible.

If you live in a flat, make sure your name or flat number is quite clear beside the bell. Those labels that you shove behind plastic tend to fade very quickly.

chapter eight

Moving house painlessly

Choosing Your Removal Company

In an ideal world you would just go to sleep and wake up in your new home with everything unpacked and ship-shape. Wouldn't that be marvellous? Everyone knows that moving house is one of life's most stressful experiences and yet it needn't be. You need to be prepared and organised and retain a sense of humour for everything to be plain sailing. Not all of us, however, are prepared and organised, which is why it all becomes so stressful.

As a little girl I moved home dozens of time as an Army brat with a father in the Services. My mother became an accomplished house-mover and would have our new home looking straight within three days, with pictures on the walls and everything put away. So I suppose I had a useful training in how to move home painlessly.

Remember, no two house moves are the same, so the removal company will send out an estimator to assess the quantity of possessions you have, the amount of packing, the distance the van or vans will have to travel, the number of men involved, which floor you live on if it is a flat, and any other requirements and will base his quote on that information. You should get three quotes to make sure you get the best value (sometimes the famous names are the most reasonable), and make sure you show them the contents of the attic, garage and garden shed. These are often forgotten and will affect the quote.

When choosing your removal company make sure they are a member of the

BAR. The British Association of Removers is a regulatory body that imposes certain regulations on its members to do with insurance, training and code of conduct. If your company is not with the BAR make sure they have the necessary insurance to cover any damages.

Most removal companies will offer a range of services and it is important that you make clear what you require.

- **A standard move** – this is basically DIY where the removal company supply all the boxes, paper, bubble wrap etc. but you do all the packing. The company will then load, travel and unload.

    STRESS FACTOR: 7

- **Fragile packing** – the removers pack all the breakables only but you do the rest. They then load the van, travel and unload.

    STRESS FACTOR: 5

- **Full packing service** – they will literally do everything, including your clothes. They pack, load, travel, unload and unpack.

    STRESS FACTOR: 2

- **Combination service** – this is what I usually have and it depends on the individual household. They will do a complete packing service, load, travel, unload the boxes and leave them packed. Or unpack some. It depends what state your new house is in! It may not be ready to unpack everything. They will distribute the furniture and boxes into rooms as directed and then leave.

    STRESS FACTOR: 3

- **Storage** – you can have everything loaded into a container and stored for you while you are looking for something to buy. Alternatively you could do part move/part storage. During the estimate make sure he knows which pieces are going where – coloured stickers help – because this will affect the quote.

    STRESS FACTOR: 5

> **I**f you are selling some furniture prior to moving, make sure you tell the assessor because it could make all the difference between one container and two.

Removers will also provide special services for antiques and pianos, if they are needed. The really good removal companies have chaps who know exactly what to do with a Venetian mirror or a Beidermeier desk and will call in expert carpenters to take apart antique wardrobes or dressers. These are then reassembled at the other end. They have sophisticated pulley systems to get furniture out of top floor windows and experts who deal with unwiring and packing chandeliers. No problem is insurmountable. Whatever your needs, however humble or grand, they've seen it all before and are there to help you.

Once you have received your three quotes it is up to you to decide who will do the job. I usually go for the middle quote. When you have accepted their quote make sure you get it all confirmed in writing. You will need to tell them your moving date but if your house is still going through legal negotiations and you have not agreed a completion date, you could always give them a provisional booking. Do this as far in advance as possible. In fact, I usually get the removal people in before the house is even on the market.

Keep in close contact with them so that you can confirm the moving date as soon as possible (i.e. as soon as contracts have been exchanged).

The Cost of Moving

The cost of your move will depend on a variety of factors and not just how much stuff you have got. The assessor has to take these factors into account:

- The cubic capacity required to pack all your belongings. This will affect the number of vans you will need.

- Which service you require. If they are doing a full pack it can take three men five days to pack, depending on the size of the property.

- Access. If your home is on the fourth floor without a lift or the van can't park near your house it will affect the price.

- The timing. Fridays and weekends are always more expensive than weekdays.

- The amount of packaging.

- The distance the van has to travel and how long to unload/unpack. This sometimes means an overnight stay for the lads.

- Storage. The cubic capacity will affect the weekly rental.

TIP ···

If you are moving from Croydon to Leeds, for example, it may be worth getting a quote from a Leeds-based removal company. You don't necessarily have to use a firm that is based near your present home. They could be from your destination area. It might work out cheaper.

CHECK LIST ···

Check list for choosing your removal company

- Get three quotes.
- Show them everything including the attic, garden shed and garage.
- Show them all garden pots, statues and furniture that are going.
- Make sure they are with the BAR (or well insured if not).
- Check the small print in the quote to make sure that VAT, insurance, and packing materials are included. There should be no hidden extras.
- Discuss the range of services and tell them what you need. Each move is different, so go ahead and ask questions.
- Tell them about any furniture that is *not* going on the van.
- Once you have accepted a quote, get it in writing.
- Book your moving date. (Try to avoid weekends.)
- If things go wrong or you are behind on the packing let them know. The dates can change but you *must* keep in touch.
- Use coloured stickers if some of your possessions are going into storage.
- Agree a time when they can start packing. Sometimes this is days before the move.

Preparation – To Pack or Not to Pack?

Not to pack

I am strongly in favour of letting the removal men do *everything*. I mean every-thing. This is the least stressful solution. It might cost more – it will cost more – but if you have a job and a family, there aren't enough hours in the day to start packing bits of china. What price sanity? They are all very good at their job so let them do it. One removal chap I spoke to said that he actually prefers it if the customer leaves it all to them. 'You don't have to move a thing. Leave the pictures on the walls and the china in the cupboards so that the boxes can be labelled accordingly.'

They will pack all your clothes and hanging garments will be transported in mobile wardrobe boxes. It couldn't be easier. Your biggest contribution will be in the preparation and you can never start soon enough. Clear out all the junk that has been accumulating over the years. You don't want to start life in your new house surrounded by clutter.

It would be very helpful if you could draw a little plan of your new home, giving each room a name or number. If you give this to the removal company they will make sure all the boxes go into the right rooms. If you can be there on the day, so much the better. I'm usually standing at the back of the truck waving my arms like a windmill, shouting 'kitchen – bedroom 1 – sitting room.'

I usually pack all my personal bits and pieces like jewellery and office files and make-up etc. Pack a bag with anything that you might need in a hurry like:

- the contents of your desk;

- washing things;

- sheets, duvets and towels;

- change of clothes;

- tea, milk and sugar;

- loo roll;

- emergency rations like snack food;

- children's things (toys, nappies, food);

- bottle of champagne;

- plastic cups.

This way, when you get to your destination you won't be waiting for stuff to come off the van. While they are unloading and unpacking make them lots of cups of tea (they will need lots of tea during packing as well), so you might need to get some extra milk and sugar. (These boys are thirsty!)

Keep calm. Most removal men have a lovely sense of humour so the banter will help to keep you relaxed. If they are doing it all, just sit back and have a drink. They will assemble everything and put furniture wherever you want it. They will even carry heavy garden pots across the garden and place them where you want them.

> **O**ne removal man told me about a house he packed up into containers to be shipped to Montreal. Just as the containers arrived at the docks, he received a frantic phone call from the lady of the house saying, 'I hate Canada. Can't stand it. We're going to New York.' The shipment was rerouted to New York, was unloaded and delivered. However, before it was unpacked she rang again and said, 'I don't like New York very much either. We're going back to England.' Eventually her house contents were delivered back to Cobham, where she began, and unpacked.

CHECK LIST

Check list for not to pack:

- Have a massive clear out. Charity shops will be grateful for your clothes and some charities such as the Salvation Army will even collect furniture.
- Tidy up and sort out stuff.
- Make a plan of the new home with rooms numbered.
- Make sure you know where everything is to go.
- Children and pets should be elsewhere during the move (see page 135).
- Pack a bag of emergency rations and things you will need the other end.
- Have plenty of milk and biscuits. Be prepared to make lots of tea.
- Retain your sense of humour.
- Open the bubbly.

Here is a check list provided by the BAR:

- Confirm dates with the mover.
- Sign and return contract together with payment.
- Book insurance at declared value.
- Arrange a contact number.

How to **Make Money** from **Your Property**

- Dispose of anything you don't want.
- Start running down freezer contents.
- Contact carpet fitters if needed.
- Book mains services for disconnection.
- Cancel all rental agreements.
- Cancel standing orders in respect of mortgage, utilities and council tax.
- Notify doctor, dentist, optician, vet.
- Tell your bank and savings/share accounts.
- Inform telephone company.
- Ask Post Office to re-route mail.
- Tell TV licence, car registration, passport offices.
- Notify HP and credit firms.
- Make local map to new house for friends and moving company.
- Clear the loft.
- Organise parking at new home (for the van).
- Plan where things go in new home.
- Cancel the milk/newspapers.
- Clean out the freezer.
- Arrange minders for children/pets.
- Find and label keys.
- Address cards to friends and relatives.
- Separate trinkets, jewellery and small items.
- Sort out linen and clothes.
- Put garage/garden tools together.
- Take down curtains/blinds.
- Collect children's toys.
- Put together basic catering for family at new house.

> **I** once did a three-way move which really did my head in. Some furniture was going to the marital home, some was going to a rental flat and loads was going into storage. Thank goodness for coloured sticky labels.

To pack everything yourself

Well, you're very brave. This is quite the most stressful way of doing it but of course it is the cheapest. Also, if you are very minimalist and don't have much stuff then it makes sense to do it yourself.

If you don't need a professional removal company you could always hire a van, pack the boxes, get a friend to help you load up and drive it yourself. Ring around for quotes on the van hire and make sure it includes insurance and breakdown cover.

(STRESS FACTOR: 10!)

If you *are* using a removal firm but are doing all the packing yourself, here is a list of things to help you prepare:

CHECK LIST ··

- Book removal firm early.
- Plan ahead. Make lists of things to do. This helps prevent sleepless nights.
- Clear out all the unwanted items.
- Get packing materials delivered early. (You can never start too soon.)
- Start packing. All china and glass should be packed singly. Don't overload boxes. Put heavy items at the bottom and light at the top.
- Put books in small boxes, otherwise you won't be able to lift them.
- Label each box clearly, stating the contents. You could also put which room they are intended for.
- Pack pictures back to back and face to face in large boxes. Pad out any gaps.
- Use wardrobe boxes for hanging garments.
- Clothing in drawers can stay where they are.
- You will need plenty of sticky tape and several large felt pens.
- Get an electrician to dismantle wall lights (if you are taking them).
- Remember to let everyone know your change of address, especially gas, electricity and telephone companies.
- Remember to pack a bag with overnight things and a bottle of bubbly.
- Leave the vacuum cleaner out till last because you will want to have a quick flash about before you leave. (You'll be shocked by what's left under your bed.)
- See the BAR checklist above for all other reminders.

The life of a removal man is never dull. One chap told me the weirdest thing he ever came across was a preserved dog in a glass coffin. And apparently, some people forgot to remove things of a sensitive nature in the bedroom. Ahem!

Seven Ages of Moving

Most people move home during their adult lives approximately seven times. Rather like the seven ages of man, there seem to be seven key ages for property buying. The first age is between 23 and 28 after you've been renting for a while and the first property is sometimes bought with siblings or a partner.

The second age is when you get married, or not, as the case may be, and move to a bigger place. The third age is usually between 30 and 40 when the second child is on the way and suddenly you need a family home and a garden.

The fourth age is when families with growing children decide there isn't enough room in the urban environment and move further afield to find more space. This is exactly where we are at the moment. It's all about fishing, ponies, organic veg and a better, well, different, quality of life. Are there fairies at the bottom of my garden? There could be.

The fifth stage comes between 55 and 65 when the children have flown the nest – gulp – and you decide to downsize or move back to the city. At this stage I'll probably decide to go back into the theatre and will be just the right age to play Juliet's nurse!

The sixth age is from 75 onwards when you either move into a retirement home with a bit of extra security or into the granny annex to terrorise the children.

The final move is, well final, if you get my drift, and as I've just met a man who has only ever lived in one house for his entire life, I think this could be a load of bunkum. Never mind. Nice theory.

Tips on Staying Sane

One of my biggest tips for staying sane during the move (and sometimes the build-up to the move) is to have children and pets taken care of for the day. Ask family or friends to look after them for you because you need to be hands-free on the day. Children are unsettled by a move and can become demanding when you least need them to be. Younger children tend to cope better with a move and readily adapt to a new environment. Older children, however, can find it far more daunting so it is important that a really positive attitude is maintained towards the move. Whatever the reasons behind the move, don't dwell on any negatives.

Involve them in their new home as much as possible by allowing them to decorate their own rooms. Get them to pack and unpack their own belongings and have a bit of a sorting out session with them. Their bedrooms should be the first rooms that are finished and settled so that they feel secure and happy.

We took our two children to their new school a couple of times before the new term began and made contact with a couple of other mums so that we could get our children together. This helped a lot. It eased the anxiety of their first day at school. We also got to know the area quickly so that they could see all the fun things that there were to do. When you are unpacking and trying to sort out your new home, make time for the children because if they're happy, your life will be much easier.

Pets will also be guaranteed to get in the way. If you have four burly blokes shifting furniture, as I did, they don't like tripping over the cat! I asked my local vet for advice on transporting our cat and apart from getting the right equipment to put him in, she suggested keeping him indoors for about 10 days in order to convince him that this move was permanent. As it turned out we only kept him in for 2 days and then showed him around the garden. After he'd left his mark he seemed perfectly happy and never wanders off.

Dogs are different. They travel very well but are bound to be difficult to keep in, if you have a garden. If they tend to wander off, keep them on the lead when outside until they realise this is home.

TIPS

And here are some other tips:

- Make lots of lists prior to the move because if you try to remember everything it will cause sleepless nights. Your brain will be working overtime, so I've found that last thing at night I would make a list of 'things to do tomorrow'. This allows the brain to rest. Also, use the BAR check list and tick them off as you go along.

- Be ruthless with your possessions. I found that getting rid of a lot of our 'stuff'

– particularly the stuff that we didn't need – was immensely liberating and cathartic. If you find it hard to decide whether you need it or not try this little test. Is it useful? Does it have a function? Is it aesthetically pleasing? If it is a toasted sandwich maker that doesn't work but you said you'd fix it two years ago, then chuck it out. If it is a china ornament that you feel ambivalent about, chuck it out! (Ornaments have no function. You just have to dust them.) If it is a 4-year-old collection of *My Car* magazine, it will be heavy to transport, so chuck it out. You get the picture.

- Never look back. Leaving a home is bound to be an emotional experience, particularly if you have very fond memories of it. But you should be looking to the future and not dwelling on the past. Be optimistic at all times.

- If you are packing up yourself, get some friends round with some bottles of wine and make a party of it. It can be great fun.

- Ask a friend or neighbour to make supper for you and the family the night before the move. You won't be able to find any saucepans. (A good neighbour usually offers.) Or get a take-away.

- Take some cleaning materials with you in the car. Once the van has departed you will set off to your destination and probably arrive first. The last time you saw the kitchen it probably looked fine, but now that it's empty – oh dear. But don't get stressed. A quick wipe over with some Cif will work wonders. Alternatively, book a cleaning company well in advance of completion. Get the agents to hand the keys to the cleaners. After 4 hours you can move into a spotless home.

- Avoid the whole experience and escape. One family I know went to Florida while the removal company did the move. They left drawings, diagrams and lists of where everything was to go and refused to return until every teaspoon had been put away. The removal company even hung the chandeliers and pictures for them. (Well, we can dream.)

- If something is broken during the move, don't get angry or stressed. You are covered by their insurance and most things can be fixed anyway. If it can't be fixed, well, so what? I'm of the opinion that we attach too much importance to possessions.

- Register with the local doctor as soon as possible. Especially if you have children.

How to **Make Money** from **Your Property**

- Sticky labels. I should have been a Blue Peter presenter because I love sticky labels. Coloured sticky labels. You will find these immensely helpful.

- Be nice to the removal men and they will do *anything* for you. Especially if you're a girl.

- Don't be afraid to ask questions, whether it be to the removal company, the estate agent, your solicitor, the previous owner, the vet. They are all there to help you and understand how stressful the move can be.

- Don't put off until tomorrow what you can do today. I'm afraid it's so true prior to a move. The days will fly by and watching television won't get anything done. I found that the more I did, the more energy I had.

What to Do at the Other End

You've made it! You're in your new home. On the first night I'd try not to get too ambitious because you'll only end up knackered. Once the beds are *in situ* make them up and then sit down and have a drink.

I remember leaping around with joy when we made our big move to the country. It had taken four strong men – sometimes five – 5 days to pack 260 boxes plus furniture, on to three enormous trucks and two days to unload. They even had to remove a sash window to get something out of the top floor. By the Friday night they were all completely exhausted but I was exhilarated and excited by the whole experience.

It was the summer of 1999, in a heatwave, and I recall thinking how fit those guys must be. You never see an overweight removal man! They were drinking an awful lot of water. We had decided to send the children to stay with family for 4 days because of the tremendous upheaval so I made the final journey from Surrey to Gloucestershire with only our cat meowing loudly on the back seat of the car.

Once he was installed, I dashed around getting ready for the vans. At this point I should tell you we were moving into a building site, as our builders had been in the house for 2 months already. So there was no need for rubber gloves and Cif in my case because I had no kitchen to clean!

Despite this, certain rooms *were* ready for us to move into because I was determined to settle the children in quickly. So their rooms were finished, as was our office and the den/playroom. The rest of it was like camping I'm afraid.

When the vans arrived they unloaded all the garden stuff first. We had some pots and urns which were duly put into position. I had done a little layout of the garden and terrace so I knew where everything was to go. This is very useful because it stops you doing a double-shuffle (moving everything twice).

Because we were moving into a house that was in the process of being restored, there was no point in asking for an unpacking service as there was nowhere to put anything. So, apart from the children's stuff and office things most of it went into a store room to be unpacked at a later date. In our case it was the dining room.

TIP ·

If you do this, store everything in room-by-room sections, so that you can find the right box quickly. Put all the kitchen boxes together etc. Also, write the contents on the *side* of the box (the men usually write contents on the top), so that when they are stacked you can easily see what is inside.

After the second day of unloading I was beginning to feel like a windmill. My husband was busy re-wiring lamps and changing locks while I hurriedly got the children's rooms ready. At tea-time the children returned to find their new home in utter chaos but at least their bedrooms looked nice and seemed to get the thumbs up. The fun part for them was unpacking all their toys and deciding where everything should go. (As usual, hours of fun could be had with the cardboard boxes!) If you do the basic infrastructure for them, they can do the rest.

> **I** think you should tip the removal men quite generously but tipping is a highly personal thing.

The removal men left an hour later, after five extremely hard days and I was quite sad to see them go. The first thing to do was to unpack the necessary items like saucepans and cutlery. I suppose the kitchen should be a priority, but in our case it was all a bit haphazard.

Loud music and champagne are a great stress reliever. You might as well accept that it is going to be a bit chaotic for a while and this will help to keep you calm. Delegating little jobs is vital because you can't do it all yourself. We unpacked a few boxes and then went to bed tired and happy.

The next day you can really get cracking. Try to set yourself targets and this will motivate you. For example, 'Today I'm going to finish the sitting room!' I decided to do our bedroom even though it was not going to be our bedroom in the end. It is very important to get one room straight, as a haven that you can retreat to, to get away from the mess.

Slowly but surely you will see the boxes disappearing. Try to unpack as much as you can every day because the sooner your home is straight the better. This helps your peace of mind and enables you to channel your energy elsewhere. A chaotic home often means a chaotic mind. Clutter and mess are not conducive to harmony and stability.

Unless you are having building work done like we were, there is no reason why your home shouldn't be finished within two weeks. That includes pictures on the walls and everything! Honestly, you will feel so much better if you keep going until it is all done rather than putting it off for another day.

If you need shelves to put all your books on, get a handyman or carpenter in right away. Ask around. There is bound to be someone who can help you. It might be useful to locate a plumber as well, in case of emergency.

We had our builders living with us for another six months and slowly the house came together room by room. I would leap into the dining room to attack another batch of boxes because camping was beginning to lose its glamour. The children, of course, thought it was great fun to be living on microwaved food for two weeks in a kitchen that consisted of a windowsill!

If, after two years, you still have boxes that remain unpacked, get rid of them. You obviously haven't missed the contents.

CHECK LIST

- Make up the beds first.
- Settle the children's rooms.
- Unpack a little and often.
- Store boxes room by room.
- Delegate.

- Set yourself targets.
- Organise your bedroom quickly as a retreat.
- Get a handyman to help with shelves etc.
- Keep going until it is finished.

part two

Investing in the Private Rental Sector

chapter nine

How to buy the perfect rental investment

Should You Bother?

Being a landlord is definitely quite stressful at times but if you have decided to invest in the private rental sector there are various ways to ensure that you get it right, make a profit and even have fun. If you wanted an easy life you'd just stick your capital in the building society and watch it grow. But that's boring. That's no fun at all. You obviously want to do something more exciting with your money and, like me, you quite enjoy a challenge.

Don't get me wrong. Even with a chapter entitled 'How to Buy the Perfect Rental Investment' it is very easy to get it hopelessly wrong. I have and I've learned the hard way. Hopefully, you can learn from my mistakes.

To be a landlord you need to be strong, organised, practical, patient, good with builders and slightly mad. Unfortunately, I am only one of these and I'm not saying which one. You could always pass the management of the property on to an agent and let them deal with any problems, but you pay an extra 5 per cent of the rental for that and every hiccup afterwards costs an arm and a leg. As it stands, I pay 10 per cent to the agent for finding a good, paying tenant and everything else is down to me. (See Chapter 10, Choosing the Right Lettings Agent.)

Generally, after a 6-week period of teething troubles while the tenant gets used to his or her new abode, things quieten down and you stop dreading it every time the phone rings. I have found that it pays in the end if you appear to want to pamper your tenant and are keen to sort out any problem as swiftly as possible.

After a few calls they start to feel guilty about calling you out and sort the problem out themselves. If you appear diffident or slow to react to a request they will ring more regularly and at unsociable times too.

The secret to staying sane as a landlord is to have a good back-up team and an organised filing system. It helps if you have a tame plumber or carpenter whom you can call out in an emergency and someone strong to help with humping all the furniture around. The filing system is necessary because you need to keep tabs on when your gas safety certificate is up for renewal or your inventory needs updating.

Basically, there are more people renting than ever before. The average age of the first-time buyer is now 29 so there is huge demand for rentable properties both in the cities and in less affluent areas. The lettings industry is set to rise by 13 per cent over the next 5 years and this is probably due to employee mobility, more people in higher education, divorce rate, possible increases in interest rates, shortage of affordable housing and the availability of personal finance for investment in Buy to Let.

The Buy to Let scheme has revolutionised the rental market. In the old days, lenders would penalise the borrower if the property was a second home or was to be let, with the result that only very expensive apartments for company directors or cheap bedsits were available. There was little in between.

Now, however, the middle market has been opened up, with professional investors, like me, being able to secure special, low-cost mortgages in order to become the new breed of landlord. (See Doing the Sums overleaf.) Some of us buy property instead of taking out a pension whereas others are looking to boost their monthly income, but it's worth bearing in mind that the main profit lies in the capital growth of your property rather than the income received in rent.

But Buying to Let isn't going to make you rich overnight. Very few people realise how complex investing in property can be and, as I said before, it is easy to get it wrong. The wrong property in the wrong place at the wrong price could spell disaster. But you're not going to do that are you? If you remember to take good advice from lettings agents about the type of property you should buy and who your tenant is likely to be, you won't go far wrong. They have no hidden agenda, unlike the estate agent who is trying to sell it to you.

There is a new style of tenant with a higher disposable income and a stylish lifestyle that needs to be reflected in their home environment and the good thing about Buy to Let is that it has shaken out the long-standing landlords with the old-style properties and brought in the younger investor. To succeed as a landlord, your property has to have a fashionable edge and flexibility is most important. You have to be prepared to live with the fluctuations in the rental market, the void periods, the highs and lows. If you have money to invest in a second property and are prepared to take the heat, then go for it.

CASE STUDY ···

Michael and Elizabeth had a two-bedroom flat in London. Michael's company wanted to relocate him to their Carlisle office. Rather than sell the London flat, they were able to persuade their mortgage lenders to give them a second mortgage (Let to Buy) for a house in Carlisle and rent out the flat in London using an agency. 'It was only possible because house prices in the north of England are so much cheaper than London, and rental income in London is so high. In fact the rent for the flat actually covered both mortgages!'

Doing the Sums

Arithmetic not your strong subject? Never mind. It's not mine either. Basically, this is how it works. Once you have found the property you want to buy to let – more on that later – you can raise a loan against it – a special Buy to Let mortgage at normal rates which is available through most banks and building societies – and the rent you receive should cover the monthly repayments and other expenses, leaving you with a profit. If Granny has left you a nice chunk of cash in her will, even better. You have no repayments, just rent and capital growth.

Yields — CALCULATE YIELD. 6.9% if £720 mnth.

The yield is the way you judge your investment performance. It is the annual rent as a proportion of the market value of the property. For example, if you buy a property for £90,000 and the annual rental income is £9,000, the yield is 10 per cent. This is always gross. Once you have deducted fees, repayments and overheads, the net return is much lower. I always aim for 10 per cent yield but some landlords are getting much more.

Please don't think that only really expensive properties are good for letting because the rental yields are usually higher on the cheaper properties. Smaller, cheaper homes will garner a higher yield because the biggest area of the market is for single, young professionals who want the smaller units. Therefore demand is high for one and two-bedroom flats.

For example, if I bought a one-bedroom flat in Leeds for £90,000 and let it for £800 per calendar month (p.c.m.) that would be an annual rental income of £9,600, so the yield is 10.6 per cent.

Whereas if I bought a really smart three-bedroom flat in an exclusive part of Leeds for £250,000 and let it for £1,600 p.c.m., the annual rental income would be £19,2000 which is a yield of 7.7 per cent. So it doesn't necessarily follow that bigger is better. However, if you can get £25,000 for it then you're up to 10 per cent yield. It will depend on location etc. and these variables will occur in most towns and cities.

The most obvious way to make a bigger annual profit is to buy a flat that is in terrible condition, do it up yourself and then let it to a higher end sort of tenant. This is what I usually do. The turnaround has to be quick though because every week it is empty is a 'void' week where you have no paying tenant. I try to have my flats ready for rental within 4 weeks. The void periods in any lettings play havoc with your sums, so I always base my projected rental income on 46 weeks of the year, which gives you 6 void weeks for turnaround between tenants. Some years, of course, this may not happen if you have a tenant on a long let.

There are many expenses and hidden costs to take into account when doing your sums, for example:

- mortgage repayments;
- agency percentage;
- service charges (if any);
- stamp duty;
- Land Registry;
- council tax when the property is empty;

- cleaning between tenants;
- Gas Safety Certificate;
- redecorating;
- inventory clerk;
- updating furniture;
- advertising.

ASK
DANI.

> **A** Gas Safety Certificate is a government requirement and your agency will need to hold a copy in their office. These are quite expensive but prove that the boiler and all appliances are sound and in good working order. They need to be renewed every year, not just at the start of a tenancy. Some agents insist on an electricity certificate too.

Do you need an inventory?

As all my flats are let furnished I have an inventory clerk who draws up a comprehensive list of all the contents in the flat. She will usually be provided by your agents, but you the landlord are responsible for the fee depending on the length of the inventory. Do not try to do it yourself. Leave it to the professionals. She also notes the condition of every piece and the general state of the decor. These inventories are very detailed to protect both the tenant and the landlord. For example, if it states 'mark on left side of mattress' or 'scuff marks around kitchen skirting' when the tenant checks *in*, you cannot deduct that from their deposit when they check *out*. That would be unfair. (See page 148, Furnished or Unfurnished?)

If, however, the inventory clerk notes some breakages or dilapidations during the check-out report, this can be deducted. A deposit of 6 weeks rent – in my case – is usually secured from the tenant, and this is held by the agents, not the landlord. This makes the tenant feel happier about getting it returned. Usual wear and tear is taken into consideration because you can hardly expect someone to live in your flat for 2 years without leaving a single scratch. However, some landlords are quite unreasonable about this and give the rest of us a bad name. I *only* deduct for items that have gone missing, breakages and damage.

If you are going it alone without a lettings agent – good luck! (See Chapter 10, Choosing the Right Lettings Agent.) Obviously there are risks involved, but the deposits and rent can vary from landlord to landlord. Some ask for 4 weeks' security deposit, and a month's rent. Some ask for 6 weeks plus first and last month.

If your flat is unfurnished, you won't necessarily need an inventory clerk but it helps to note the state of the property in detail to prevent an argument at the end of the tenancy. This report should be signed by both tenant and landlord.

security
Deposit

Questions you should ask yourself before Buying to Let

- Will this property let easily? (See Identifying your Tenant, page 153.)
- What will my capital growth be?
- What are the overall running costs? (See list page 145.)
- Am I going to have void periods? Is there plenty of demand in this area?
- What should I spend on doing it up? Depends on the condition of property.
- What is the likely annual rental? Ask the local lettings agent.
- Set against the purchase price, what is my yield? (See Doing the Sums, page 144.)
- Am I overlooking any hidden costs? Such as void periods.

Hopefully this will help you do your sums. If you can make a tidy profit, terrific. But don't forget the tax inspector. He just loves unearned income! However, you *can* set your mortgage repayments off against your rental income and only pay tax on the profit after costs. But remember, if you are borrowing money, the main profit lies in the capital growth. Never borrow too much, otherwise the voids really eat into your profit.

CASE STUDY

One chap I know had no desire to be a landlord at all but fell into the business by chance. He inherited a flat on the south coast which was unsaleable and unusable so he spent a bit of money doing it up and turned it into a really fabulous looking one-bedroom flat. He rang the local lettings agents and they let it immediately for a fantastic return.

Surprised by its success he started to look for other grotty flats in a good location in the same area but they had to be empty. He would secure a loan and, between exchange and completion, the decorators would move in and he would advertise the property. On completion it would be ready for the tenant to move into, therefore covering all his outgoings immediately.

He lets all his flats unfurnished and only to professional people on long lets of one year minimum. He sticks to one-bedroom flats in prime locations near the shops and transport links because he wants his flats to be the most desirable. He now has over 20! In his particular case he is looking for maximum rental return rather than capital growth as he isn't interested in the resale value. His yields are in the region of 18 per cent. This is extraordinary but he has a lot of energy and tenacity, and he proves that the lower end of the market is where the higher yields are.

Furnished or Unfurnished?

Some time ago almost all flats and houses coming to the rental market were offered fully furnished, as a result of prohibitive legislation that made it very difficult for a landlord to gain repossession of a property if it were let unfurnished.

I've always preferred to let mine furnished simply because the property always looks better when it is fully dressed, i.e. beds made, towels in bathroom, pictures on walls, kitchen utensils visible etc. Some people have no imagination whatsoever.

However, when the legislation changed in the mid-1970s and the new Fire and Furnishings Regulations were brought in, the market saw a turnaround with more landlords preferring to let their properties unfurnished, because of all the hassle with changing curtains and sofas and mattresses. (Be careful when buying at auction, as I do, because some things just don't comply with the Regulations.)

The demand for furnished flats has now diminished, and we are getting more in line with our European counterparts. In fact, 50 per cent of the market is for unfurnished property. This is quite a dramatic change. Problems still tend to arise when dealing with Americans though, who often have larger pieces of furniture that do not fit easily into smaller English homes. So they may decide to take the flat furnished and put everything of their own in storage. The landlord needs to be very flexible and even though the demand is for unfurnished you should always show the property fully furnished. This gives the tenant a proper feel for the ambience of the house and, believe it or not, a furnished room will look bigger than an unfurnished one.

Most large family houses will be rented unfurnished, with everything being shipped over from abroad. However, you still need to furnish it, just in case. This can be a real pain, I know, as storage is expensive but of course your rent will reflect that. However, by showing it furnished the tenant may decide to keep several pieces, including beds, and you won't have to get rid of much.

Also, there is much demand for homes for those who are between selling and buying. Again 50 per cent will want to let it furnished because it is far less hassle just to stick everything into storage, and 50 per cent will want it unfurnished because they are not sure how long they are going to be there. Storage is pricey and they want their home comforts. So, flexibility is the key. And the possession of a large truck would be handy!

CHECK LIST ···

To furnish or not to furnish?

- Lower end will probably want it unfurnished.
- However, student lets will need to be furnished.
- Middle market could be either: 50 per cent require unfurnished but you must show it furnished.
- Upper end. If it's in the city, probably furnished, but could go either way.
- Upper end – family home. Usually unfurnished.
- Be flexible.
- Get a van.

> **U**nless you comply with the Furnishings (Fire and Safety) Regulations 1988 you could be fined up to £5,000. All upholstery, curtains, mattresses and sofas have to pass certain flammability tests and must be thus labelled.

If you do furnish your property, you will need to ensure all furniture and fittings look immaculate every time the property is let to a new tenant. Keep everything simple and easy to renew. If anything becomes too dirty or cannot be fixed it should be thrown out and replaced. Keep the property in good decorative order. You may need to touch up paintwork at the end of every tenancy, so keep a note of the make and colour of paints.

Finally, leave a smart folder of instructions, guarantees and advice for operating anything such as the cooker, washing machine, shower, central heating, and giving the whereabouts of meters (gas and electricity) and stop-cocks for the water supply. Include information on quirky aspects such as temperamental boilers and make sure tenants know what to do with rubbish.

What and Where to Buy

CASE STUDY ··

In the summer of 1989 I found myself between properties, having sold my flat in Knightsbridge and wanting time to find a real gem. So I decided for the first and only time in my life, so far, to be a paying tenant.

On the hottest day of the year, I moved into an exquisite flat, arranged over two floors in Belgrave Place, just off Belgrave Square in Central London. Posh isn't the word. Delusions of grandeur is more like it. It had duck egg blue silk curtains and fine antiques everywhere. On the first morning after moving in, I wandered bleary-eyed into the main communal hallway to pick up my newspaper, only to hear my front door slam shut behind me. (Beware of fire doors, that's my advice. They close without warning.) As I was only wearing my pyjama top and fluffy slippers I was in a bit of a predicament. No money, no keys, what to do? After a little sob, I plucked up courage and walked briskly across Belgravia to a friendly hairdresser, who I sort of knew, to phone the agents who came to my rescue with a spare set of keys.

As a landlord now myself I think it's quite a good idea to have done time as a tenant. You learn a lot about what and what not to provide. For example, my dear old landlord had probably had this flat for quite some time, as the washing machine had only just seen off the mangle and the ancient mattress on the antique bed was made of horsehair and extremely lumpy.

Therefore, I deduced that mattresses and washing machines needed to be replaced frequently and of the very best quality.

What to buy

With so many single young professionals and first-time buyers leaving it until they are 29 to buy, according to statistics, the biggest area of the market is in one-bedroom flats. Even the more affluent 30-somethings want to rent because it gives them flexibility and mobility.

I have one-, two- and three-bedroom flats and the one-bedder is always the easiest to let. Admittedly, these are all in central London, but research shows that it is the same up and down the country in city areas. Further away from the cities, but still within easy commuting distance, the larger family houses are very much in demand. This is due to relocation of families visiting from abroad on two- or three-year secondments.

Every pocket of Great Britain has its rental market but obviously it differs greatly from area to area. It is always best to seek advice from a lettings agent if you are thinking of investing. She (and I say she because it is nearly always ladies in lettings) will know what the requirement is for in your area. Here are some examples:

- In a university town she may suggest you buy a small terraced house and let to four students. (See Letting to Students, page 156.)

- In Swindon, she may suggest a house on a brand-new estate for an executive in one of the nearby car plants.

- In the heart of Surrey she may suggest a family home near the American school.

The only areas I would stay away from are the very rural countryside areas and obvious tourist traps such as Stratford-on-Avon. These are great for holiday homes but that is a very different section of the rental market. (See Chapter 11, Buying a Holiday Home.)

Whether you buy a house or a flat very much depends on the demand. I would say start small and see how it goes. If you have been left a property in someone's will – lucky you. I would spend some money bringing it right up to date because tenants are getting fussier these days and, with so much choice, your property will need to have an edge. With the arrival of Buy to Let mortgages came an influx of new landlords all keen to invest in the private rental sector. This increased supply so much that the tenant was suddenly offered a remarkable choice. He no longer found brown lino acceptable. He wanted laminate flooring. He demanded power showers and an eye-level cooker! This flushed out the older generation of landlords with a 'that'll do' philosophy and means that now, if you want to attract the upper end young professional, your property must be highly attractive. A well-presented property will let more quickly than a run-of-the-mill one.

Studio flats

A studio flat is definitely a risky proposition because given the choice a tenant would much rather have a separate bedroom. I know this from experience having bought a studio flat in London, spent oodles doing it up and was then unable to let it. They have limited appeal at the upper end of the market and being an old clever clogs it was extremely hard to admit that I'd made a mistake.

'Obviously they are popular with students' said one agent I spoke to, 'because it is usually all they can afford. But 400sq ft can be difficult to sell. They are land hungry too so developers are choosing not to include them in projects any more.'

A studio flat tends to have a ceiling price so it is a mistake to throw loads of money at it if the property simply isn't worth it. Even with a smart address I

How to **Make Money** from **Your Property**

found mine difficult to let and even harder to sell. However, having said that, in the right location (i.e. close to a university) it could be just the thing for a student.

Where to buy

Location, as ever, is crucial when buying to let. Tenants need easy access to transport links whether they be in a city or a 40-mile commuter journey. Even students don't like to cycle too far to the campus and you will find that there are areas of the university towns where they like to live.

Most tenants, whether they be corporate or otherwise, like to be fairly close to the local amenities, such as cinemas, parks and restaurants. If you are buying out of town you will need to consider whether it has a parking space, how far the railway station is and where the nearest school is (if it's a family home).

CHECK LIST

- One-bedroom flats are the easiest to let.
- Stay away from very rural areas.
- Avoid studio flats unless you're aiming at the student market.
- Victorian houses in university towns offer good yields to the investor.
- Buy close to road and rail links with a fast route into the nearest city.
- Buy close to local amenities like restaurants and cinemas.
- Target a specific sort of tenant.
- Don't buy a flat in a shabby block where the hallways and stairs are in need of attention.
- Don't buy in a known 'dodgy' street.
- Security is important.
- A flat with a terrace or nice view will always let well.
- A family house with a garden in easy commuting distance of the nearest city will command a premium.

In an area with a high demand for fairly reasonable rental accommodation, such as Oxford, why not buy a house and convert it into flats. Of course you will have to get planning permission and building regulation approval first which usually takes at least eight weeks. Check with the planning department of the local authority and find out what their attitude is to such an application – they are usually very helpful. This could make sound investment sense for letting. Take good advice before buying anything though because the local agent might tell you that there is nil demand for flats in her area and to stick with the house. Some areas or streets are clearly designated as 'house' streets or 'flat' streets.

Identifying Your Tenant and What They Want

It is very important before you start to invest in rental property that you clearly identify your target area of the market. In other words, who is your tenant likely to be? Obviously, there is a very wide spectrum and the price, location, style and decor of the property will all come into play once you have decided which end of the market to target. I mean, if you buy a student let you don't want it to be in the most expensive part of town where they loathe bicycles, and you wouldn't put antique furniture in there.

Simlarly, if you are going for the corporate let, they will need more space for entertaining and will expect very high quality furnishings.

It is a fact that the properties that are the most up to date, recently redecorated, well presented and well equipped will let fastest. These young professionals, with their disposable income, demand apartments within high specification new developments in desirable locations. They like high-tech designer living. It is an extension of their designer-led, label-conscious lifestyle.

Middle market

So, let's look at the middle market. You've found a nice one-bedroom flat in a great location close to all the amenities. This is what, ideally, it should look like.

The look:

- Stripped wooden floors, in the hall, kitchen and sitting room. Carpet only in bedroom.

- *En suite* bathroom in white with chrome accessories.

- Power shower in the bathroom.

- Tiles, laminate or vinyl flooring in the bathroom.

- Neutral decor throughout flat. I use soft creams or taupe on walls and off-white woodwork.

- Neutral, unfussy curtains.

- Good quality lighting. Spotlights, lamps, downlighters.

- Kitchen should be modern, bright, well lit and well equipped, with dish-washer, ceramic hob, microwave, washer-dryer etc.

- Fitted wardrobes in bedroom and lots of storage elsewhere if possible.

- Furniture must be sturdy and of good quality. Modern, light and bright.

- A dining table with four chairs should be in the main living area. If there is no dining room, maybe a fold-away table.

- Try to create a thoughtful, 'together' look without it being too designery.

I have found that the more neutral everything is, the more successful it will be. In one flat, I have everything in shades of cream, mushroom, taupe and grey – the curtains, sofa, linen, tablecloths, lampshades, everything – and it looks great and lets really quickly. The secret is to make it look carefully thought out without being too designer conscious. One or two really good pieces of furniture will lend the flat an air of class and large mirrors are a must. They are practical and will also help to open up the space.

LIGHTING is really important, especially if it is quite a small flat. I use down-lighters and wall lights quite a bit and spots in the kitchen.

THE KITCHEN should be all white with maybe coloured tiles. Cream tiles look great but green or blue could add a nice contrast. I equip mine fully with crockery and cutlery but you could take advice on this. A good oven with separate hob is advisable because old-fashioned kitchens are out. If there is no room for both a washer and a dryer then a washer-dryer will do. Make sure your tenant has all the instructions on how everything operates and make sure they are all serviced regularly.

THE BATHROOM should have a white suite with power shower. (You will need to install a separate pressure pump, if the water pressure isn't up to it.) Even though I love carpet in *my* bathroom at home it is a real no-no in a rental. Tiles, wood laminate, or vinyl at a push, will keep most people happy. On the walls I usually tile the whole room, which is expensive, but it saves redecorating every few years as steam plays havoc with paper or paint. You can buy fabulous large (12 x 8in) tiles that look like marble or plain white with a slight wave to them. Most people hate shower curtains so if you can install a glass shower screen, then great. If not, change the curtain after each tenancy as they soon look revolting. If you have room for a separate shower cubicle, that's even better.

The bath taps should have a cradle with a separate shower attachment. I always install these even if the shower is in the bath as it gives the tenant the option. All the taps and accessories should be in the very best chrome, but not too modern as they will date. Try a very classic design.

The toilet should be low-level with a wooden loo seat – don't ask me why, it just looks better – and bidets are a thing of the past. They are no longer a requirement and are an unnecessary expense. I always put a large mirror in the bathroom to double the space and for practical reasons too.

THE BEDROOM should have plenty of cupboards, and if you are furnishing it (see Furnished or Unfurnished, page 148) provide two bedside tables, a chest of drawers, mirror, a double bed with a *good* mattress and neutral carpet.

THE REST OF THE FLAT, hallway and sitting room, should be as neutral as possible but with very good furniture. I always put pictures on the walls but if tenants want to hang their own, that's fine by me. (The contract stipulates, though, that the flat must be reinstated as it was on hand-over.) I feel that the flat should be presented in such a way that the tenant feels immediately at home and wants to move in straight away.

TIP ···

If you are managing the flat yourself, it might be a good idea to 'dress' the property after the inventory clerk has been in to do her check-out report. If professional cleaners have been in, you will need to remove all those bits of silver foil they put under furniture feet, make the bed, change the light bulbs etc. One hour of titivating can make all the difference.

Lower end

If you've identified your potential tenant as requiring something at the lower end of the market, that's good. Nothing wrong with lower end because, as I said before, it often means higher yield. It also means you adjust your budget for any necessary rebuilding or redecorating.

If the tenant is on a tight budget he is not going to be so fussy or demanding about decor. If you decide not to furnish it (see Furnished or Unfurnished, page 148), this will help keep costs down and also provide less potential for damage. The property should be bright and freshly painted throughout in white. It is the cheapest colour to buy and easy to redo when necessary. Use a vinyl silk on the walls or even eggshell on the stairwell as it is easier to wash down than emulsion. I would put a hardwearing industrial carpet throughout the property in a flecked grey colour. This hides the dirt and stains but still looks good. Laying wood flooring here would be an unnecessary expense.

The bathroom and kitchen will still need to be presentable but not necessarily up to the minute. Take advice from the agent on this because obviously a dishwasher is a luxury that not many will expect.

If you have bought a property that will house four or five people – good luck! Any house in multiple occupation is bound to bring its own set of problems.

Letting to students

If all the students know each other then obviously it is an advantage but more often than not, you get a group of strangers living together and the health hazards are rife. Make sure you get a deposit from each of them and install a fire alarm. Most students have never done their own washing before so the plumbing needs to be rock solid. A dodgy waste-pipe will only lead to disaster.

However, students are taking more care of their property these days, according to several agents I spoke to, and require good quality fittings. This is where it is false economy to buy cheaper white goods because they get such heavy use. A good washing machine, dryer, microwave, fridge and dishwasher even, will last longer.

Students need furnished accommodation and the better class of student won't want brown 1950s furniture and a formica kitchen. Paint the whole place white and have pale, unfussy curtains. If the floors can be stripped wood with rugs that would be dead cool; if not, heavy duty carpet will do the job. Students like heavy, chunky furniture that is contemporary and it needs to be hard wearing. There are several mail order companies I use that make good quality furniture at a bargain price. Buy sofas with loose covers, in a dark colour, that are easy to wash. They will need a dining table and chairs as well, and most bedrooms should have double beds.

If you can install a separate shower as well as one in the main bathroom this will be a plus factor. They will need a separate loo too.

I'm afraid, as a landlord, I have always said that I would be nervous of letting to students. I know the poor dears have to live somewhere but I wouldn't trust them in my garden shed, let alone in one of my flats. (One student I knew managed to flood his digs within a week of going up.) However, if you are prepared for the hassle factor because of the high yield, it could be a very good investment indeed.

There will be constant squabbles about the rent, probably leading to one or two of them walking out on the lease. To make things simpler you could draw up a contract with one student whom you put in charge. Prepare a detailed inventory, ask for a deposit up front and arrange a direct debit for the rent. The perfect scenario is if one of your offspring is going to university. You buy the property, kit it out and put *them* in charge. Not only does your little darling have a nice pad to share with his mates, but he also gets to learn about responsibility, both domestic and financial.

CHECK LIST ···

Check list for student lets:

- Good plumbing is essential.
- Install a fire alarm.
- Buy good quality washing machine, separate dryer, fridge, microwave, dishwasher and vacuum cleaner.
- Paint the whole place white.
- Use heavy duty carpet and simple curtains.
- Buy sofas and chairs with loose covers in a dark colour.
- Buy good, sturdy furniture because it will get heavy wear.

- They will need a dining table and chairs.
- Install a separate shower.
- Bedrooms should have double beds.
- Kitchen must be fully equipped.
- Prepare an inventory.

Upper end

Anything at the upper end of the rental market can have limitless possibilities but the more expensive the property, the lower the yield tends to be. If it is in a fancy location, or exceptionally large, or exquisitely decorated with antiques, it will be deemed upper end. This sort of property appeals to the corporate tenant on a company let but the void periods may well be longer. In the big cities your tenant is likely to be a big cheese from a foreign company, or bank, over here with his wife and family.

I have let to embassy staff in London and they definitely require a parking space. Some of them like a cleaner provided or even accommodation for a live-in housekeeper.

If you are aiming at this market, take advice from your letting agent on what is required. The interior decoration needs to be of the very highest standard and can be quite luxurious. The colours don't have to be completely neutral but steer away from strong shades. Americans love big, spacious bathrooms with power showers and they love antiques. I use the auction rooms a lot to furnish the bigger flats and have tapestry wall-hangings and a mahogany dining table with eight chairs. They will normally require one or two reception rooms and at least two bathrooms.

If the tenant is young and wealthy he will want something very contemporary and hi-tech, whereas if the tenant is older – i.e. married – and wealthy, he will probably go for something more traditional and soft.

One of the best tips I was ever given by an agent was to remember that when couples are viewing it is usually, 90 per cent of the time, the lady who will make the final decision. So the decor, for example, can lean slightly towards the feminine. Only slightly. Women notice good quality curtains and soft furnishings, and are more impressed by the quality of kitchen and bathroom. Men are generally more influenced by factors that will make a statement about their standing – the price, the location – whereas women are influenced by factors that will make family life easier and more comfortable.

> **W**omen tend to procrastinate far less than men, which helps in the rental market. If you offer them the right look they'll say 'Great. When can I move in?' Whereas a chap will say 'I'll just see six more.'

When furnishing an upper end property the quality will have to follow right through to the linen, crockery and cutlery. For these rentals, the tenant expects crystal, not glass.

In London, the Americans love apartments in those old mansion blocks with panelled hallways and marble floors. They love the whole 'Englishness' of it all. They are also very security-conscious so any property that has secure parking, entryphones, gates, porterage and video cameras is a plus. Of course, the service charges are very high in apartments like that, so remember to take that into account when doing your sums.

CHECK LIST

Check list for upper end:

- Must be in the best location.
- Fixtures and fittings must be very high standard.
- Bathrooms should be spacious, with no carpet.
- Decor should be quietly elegant.
- Good fabrics essential.
- Must have parking.
- If furnished, go for quality and a few antiques.
- The women make the decisions, so pander to feminine requirements.
- Must have spaces for entertaining.
- Kitchen should be fabulous.
- Security essential. Porterage a plus.
- If it's a family home, out-of-town, must be near good rail links and schools.

My Top Ten Mistakes

Over the years I have made some prize-winning mistakes with my rental properties. When I started out it was all trial and error, but I was given some great advice along the way. Here then, in all their glory, are my Top Ten Mistakes, which hopefully will prevent you from being as daft as I have been, if you're thinking of investing in the rental market.

1. **Don't carpet the bathroom floor**. I have always, so far, carpeted the bathrooms with the same sandy-coloured carpet as the rest of the flat because that is what I like. This is a no-no as most tenants, especially Americans, prefer tiled or vinyl flooring. It is also more hygienic and easier to clean.

2. **Don't paint the walls in very strong colours**. I once painted a flat in terracotta, which looked amazing, but the more neutral a flat the quicker it will let. Try not to let your own taste take over. Soft creams and taupe are currently in.

3. **Don't use cheap door handles or knobs**. I bought handles from a mail order catalogue thinking they were great value (i.e. cheap), when in fact they were just 'orrible 'andles. They all broke. This is a false economy. Buy the best that are built to last.

4. **Don't buy a nice flat in a naff location**. This is so obvious but I did it and paid the price. It should be near a station, local amenities and in a nice street.

5. **Don't use cheap furniture**. If you're going to furnish, furnish well. Cheap stuff just breaks or chips and your deposit does not cover normal wear and tear. Chairs need sturdy legs and washing machines should be pretty sturdy too. (Tenants can be fairly tough on white goods.) Don't leave prized family antiques in a rental if they are heirlooms, as your deposit may not cover any damage.

6. **Don't buy furniture from auction rooms that doesn't comply with the 1988 Furnishings (Fire and Safety) Regulations**, otherwise you will have to

reupholster the whole lot. I thought I was being really clever buying sofas at auction, but ended up spending more on reupholstery than on a brand new one.

7. **Don't over-clutter the kitchen**. Most tenants like basic pots and pans – I always use good quality stainless steel – but don't need gizmos. I always used to put in too much stuff, only to be asked to remove most of it.

8. **Don't buy cheap curtain tracks**. The plastic track is OK for most domestic situations, but in a rental you need steel track that you get in hotels. My curtains in flat number two are currently stuck due to fitting the wrong tracks.

9. **Don't skimp on the plumbing**. Trying to save money on a plumber without a personal recommendation has caused me major aggro. Why spend money on getting the bathroom to look right if the plumber doesn't know his warwick fitting from his cannon valve? American tenants, in particular, expect the best from their bathrooms.

10. **Don't try to let it yourself**. I get so many letters from people dealing with the tenant from hell just because they are trying to save that 10 per cent. It just isn't worth it. An assured shorthold tenancy (see Chapter 10, section on Dealing with Rental Contracts) will give you peace of mind and protection. Find an agent who knows the area and let them have the hassle of checking references etc. Always listen to your instincts about a tenant.

One last word of advice: open everything that comes in a box *before* you leave the shop/warehouse/plumbers merchants. This will save you a return journey if they have given you the wrong thing, which they usually do.

How to **Make Money** from **Your Property**

The Terrors of Being a Landlord

The life of a landlord is never dull. Particularly if you are a 'hands-on' landlord managing the property, or properties, yourself. I like to manage my flats because:

(a) I save 5 per cent;
(b) I can see what's going on.

If there is a problem in one of the flats it is up to me to sort it out, so the tenant rings me at home and says 'Help!' Some tenants don't like to deal direct with the landlord, having had a bad experience in the past, and would much rather deal with an agent. This is fair enough, but my agents will always tell the tenant that I am a pussy cat to deal with and will sort out their problems with alacrity.

On the whole it hasn't been too bad but it can be very stressful sometimes. Here is an extract from my diary dated January 1998:

'It's all been a bit traumatic recently, what with a change-over of tenants in three of the flats all happening within six weeks of each other. Don't ask me how that happened, but I seriously hope they never coincide like that again. I'm completely cream-crackered. There are always the inevitable teething problems but then one tenant says "please remove a bed and a table", so poor Neil becomes Pickfords for the day. I then rush around like a lunatic replacing linen and calling plumbers because we have not one but two plumbing problems and one of my plumbers has gone AWOL. Something to do with a divorce.'

A tenant is likely to ring you within a few hours of moving in and say 'I can't get the oven to work'. I then say 'Have you switched it on at the main switch?' A few weeks later it will be 'The hall light isn't working'. 'Try changing the light bulb' is my usual response.' A sense of humour is essential.

One chap dragged me up to London because the spin drier wasn't working. As it was brand new I was rather alarmed, so I went to have a look. I discovered that the filter was full of lint, so the machine had shut down. After removing a handful of fluff, it was fine.

The most difficult part of being a landlord is facing up to the void periods when the market goes a bit quiet. This is the kind of situation that sorts the men from the boys. You need to be stoical and tenacious, and prepared to lower the rent quite dramatically. At least your property will be competitively priced. The way I see it, I'd rather have my flats let at a lower rent than have a void period of two months. It works out the same in the end. Most letting agents will agree.

Also, the more presentable the property, the quicker it will let. If things are a bit quiet, I'll start repainting skirting-boards, replacing saucepans and changing lamp shades, just to give it an edge. Sometimes a complete redecoration is necessary. You should do this every three or four years anyway. (Upholstery should never look grimy.) I always make the flat look dressed by scattering glossy magazines around and putting towels in the bathroom. A lot of other rental properties look a bit 'bald' and unwelcome without this.

You need to be persistent with your letting agent too. (See Chapter 10, Choosing the Right Lettings Agent.) If you're not happy, change agents.

If you are managing your rental property yourself, you will need to have a list of phone numbers close to hand, in case of emergency. Once you have found a good team, try to stick with them. You will need:

- a plumber – who is Corgi registered (so that he can issue the Gas Safety Certificate);
- an electrician;
- a handyman for fixing odd jobs;
- a decorator;
- a gardener – maybe;
- a window cleaner;
- a cleaner.

You will also need the number of the inventory clerk, your lettings agent, your tenant's work number or mobile number and, if it's a flat in a large block, the porter's number.

CASE STUDY •

Of course, we've all heard stories about the tenant from hell and you have to be prepared for that. As a landlord I am all too aware of the risks and pitfalls, which is why I always use an agent to draw up a proper assured shorthold tenancy contract.

I heard about a truly horrifying case from a Mr George Bowers, who told me about his mother's house in a town in the Midlands. She let it to an employed man and his family but when he lost his job and went on unemployment benefit the problems began. His wife and children left home and the council refused to continue paying his rent, so Mr Bowers's mother had to give him 2 months' notice. Two weeks before he was due to leave, the tenant called her and told her that he would not be moving out after all as, to quote Mr Bowers, 'The Council had advised him that if he did move out, even under the terms of his legally-binding tenancy, this would count as making himself voluntarily homeless, and they would not be obliged to house him. They advised him to sit tight and wait for my mother to evict him.'

She was already owed months and months of rent, and was forced to take him to court in order to regain possession. When she eventually got her house back it was in a dreadful state and everyone felt thoroughly demoralised, and exhausted. This is an astonishing tale but not an unusual one according to my solicitor. He told me that one is unable to take action against the council for proffering this advice as it is just a quirk of the law.

Pets

On a slightly lighter note, pets can become a bit of a problem for landlords. One of my tenants wanted to bring his cat up from the country and I had to explain to him that the managing agents of this particular block have stipulated in the lease that absolutely no animals are allowed. Unfortunately, it is not the landlord's decision to make.

On another occasion, my tenants moved out having had two rabbits in residence with them without my knowledge. The state of the carpet was, well, interesting.

However, in houses it is a different story. The landlord can make his own rules but if you are going to allow pets you need to think about cat-flaps and fencing etc.

Evicting the Tenant

Oh dear. This is a horrible situation for anyone to find themselves in, so I just hope you have a contract with your tenant.

Eviction is a tricky business and, as my solicitor was quick to point out, the theory is excellent but in practice it is another story. If the landlord has an assured shorthold tenancy agreement, which most of us have, it means he can serve 2 months' notice to quit and then gain possession. This is only if the tenant has been there for more than 6 months. If the tenant refuses to budge you get a court order served and have them formally evicted but this can take 3 months. If they have broken the terms of the lease the letting agents could start this process but then you have to prove that they have not kept the property and contents in good repair and condition or whatever. As soon as a tenant starts being tricky, you should seek legal advice.

This is why I tend to go for company lets or let to young professionals. They are less likely to cause you hassle and have a need for mobility and spontaneity.

chapter ten

Choosing the right lettings agent

Why You Need One

Q Why use an approved letting agent when it is going to cost you 10 per cent or more of your rental income?

A Because it is the only way to ensure that your let is hassle-free, financially sound and that all the proper references have been checked out.

I know some landlords who try to cut corners in order to save money but then you hear about the tenant from hell who won't pay and won't budge and the landlord ends up losing a lot more than his 10 per cent. He loses not only rent, he loses sleep and peace of mind. And legal action isn't cheap either.

So, my advice is **always use an agent**.

The best letting agents are usually part of one of the main professional bodies such as the Association of Residential Lettings Agents (ARLA) or the National Approved Letting Scheme (NALS), which has a government-based code of standards for letting agents. These organisations will offer protection to both the landlords and tenants from incompetent agents who often operate without even a minimum level of professional indemnity insurance.

Choose three agents in the area of the rental property and invite them to view. I have found in the past that the closer the agent is geographically to the property, the better. In lettings they don't like to travel too far, whereas in sales it doesn't seem to matter.

Unlike sales, however, you are not obliged to place your property exclusively with one agent. You can have as many letting agents as you like! If your instincts tell you that this agent is honest, reliable and trustworthy and will let your property to a good tenant, then you can instruct them to go ahead and they will reply in writing with the agreed rental fee as discussed.

It may be advisable to listen hard to the agent who is quoting the lowest rent they think they might achieve. If she says £600 p.c.m. (per calendar month) and another says £640 p.c.m. and the third one says £800 p.c.m., I would be inclined to say, 'Let's market it for £640 p.c.m., but that's negotiable. I'll accept £600 if the tenant won't go any higher.' **Note: If you instruct more than one agent to let your property they must all be quoting the same rental**.

Some agents quote rent per calendar month and some per week but this is usually only for the higher rents.

Rather like selling your home, you need to shop around for a good lettings agent that you like. Ask to see their lettings brochures and their Terms and Conditions of Business and ask lots of questions about their various services: you will soon be able to make that decision.

CHECK LIST

- Choose an agent who is part of ARLA or NALS.
- Get three agents to view and quote on possible rental.
- Ask to see their brochures and Terms and Conditions.
- Choose an agency close to the property.
- Instruct one or all three agents.
- Agree the rent.
- Rent is usually quoted p.c.m. (per calendar month), unless it is quite high when it will be quoted weekly.
- Agree terms. (See What they Cost, overleaf.)

What They Cost

Most letting agents provide a variety of services so it really depends on your particular needs and how much hassle you are prepared to take. For example, if you are going to be living abroad you will need a full management service in order to deal with the day-to-day running of the property, like finding a plumber if there is a crisis.

If you are living around the corner from the property you may only want the basic letting service.

> **R**emember, some corporate tenants from the big international companies will not consider renting a property unless it is professionally managed.

So here, then, is a list of letting services that *most* agencies will provide and **what they cost**. However, these percentages can vary slightly from agent to agent and are also negotiable. If it says 10 per cent, they may accept 9 per cent. No harm in asking!

- **Basic letting service**   **10%**
  This is of the total rent payable, payable in advance of the tenancy.

- **Letting and rent collection service:**   **12.5%**
  Although some agents include collecting the money by direct debit as part of their basic 10 per cent. If you are being charged 12.5 per cent this is usually payable at the same time as the rent is received (i.e. monthly).

- **Letting and management service:**   **15%**
  This varies, but usually you pay 10 per cent of the total rent in advance and 5 per cent at the same time as the rent is received.

- **The tenancy agreement:**   **£150**
  This is shared between the landlord and the tenant and is for drawing up the standard contract, which is called an assured shorthold tenancy agreement (see page 173). If the tenant renews his contract you will usually pay half that fee and split it with the tenant (£75 ÷ 2 = £37.50). This is as well as the commission.

- **The inventory**   **Variable**
  The cost for this, and it is essential you have an inventory if your property is furnished, will vary depending on the size of the property. It will include the check-in and check-out and note all dilapidations. You should discuss this fee with your agent and the Tenancy Agreement should provide for the check-in to be paid for by the landlord and the check-out by the tenant.

- **Advertising:**   **Nil**
  Hurrah! The good news is that the advertising, marketing and photographing of your rental property is all covered by the commission.

- VAT is added to all commissions, fees and charges.

- Insurance of the building and your contents is entirely the responsibility of the landlord. Your insurance company must be informed if the property is to be let. Some insurance companies get a bit twitchy about letting, so settle this first.

- The landlord pays for ground rent, service charges and general maintenance.

- Council tax is paid by the landlord when the property is empty.

- The tenant pays for gas, electricity, telephone, water rates and council tax during the tenancy.

- You must inform your mortgage company or anyone lending on the property that you intend to let the property. Some will require additional clauses protecting their interests in the tenancy agreements.

- Check your agent's 'empty property' policy. If the property is unoccupied for a while between tenancies, will the agent check it regularly and will they charge to do so?

- Tax – if you are abroad for more than six months of the year you will need to obtain tax exemption from the Inland Revenue, otherwise the agent will deduct 23 per cent of the rent.

- Find out how long after the rent is due it is likely to be in your account, so you can adjust your standing orders. A slow agent, combined with the banking system, can mean that you don't get your money for 2 weeks or more after the rent is paid.

What You Can Expect for Your Money

A good residential lettings agent should do all of the following:

- offer pre-letting advice on presentation;
- find you a suitable tenant;
- take up references;
- prepare the tenancy agreement;
- collect the rent;
- submit statements of account;
- inspect the property; inventory.
- deal with maintenance problems – if managing the property;
- close the tenancy.

Here is what you can expect for your money and why it is worth parting with that 10 per cent. You are offered peace of mind and the knowledge that if it *does* go horribly wrong, you *will* be able to get the tenant out.

For 10 per cent, your **basic letting service**, the agent will do the following:

- Agree the rent to be quoted.
- Market your property appropriately.
- Hopefully, find a tenant.

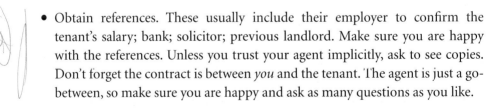

- Obtain references. These usually include their employer to confirm the tenant's salary; bank; solicitor; previous landlord. Make sure you are happy with the references. Unless you trust your agent implicitly, ask to see copies. Don't forget the contract is between *you* and the tenant. The agent is just a go-between, so make sure you are happy and ask as many questions as you like.

- Obtain your approval of the tenant. (I always listen hard and trust my instincts. On one occasion, I was told that the tenant and his family were unable to pay a deposit as their house had burnt down and they were still waiting for the insurance money to come through. They assured me the money was on its way. I'm afraid, call me heartless, that I said no. There are lots of sob stories out there. Beware of falling for them.)

- Prepare the Tenancy Agreement and obtain your signature and the tenant's signature.

- Arrange for an inventory and a check-in report to be prepared at the beginning of the tenancy.

- Collect and hold the deposit. This is usually 6 weeks' rent.

- Notify the services – gas, electricity, telephone, water – of the change of tenant at the beginning and end of the tenancy.

- Notify the local authority about the change of occupant for council tax purposes.

- For 10 per cent some agents will also make sure that the rent, whether it be monthly or quarterly, goes straight into your bank account. They will then submit statements of account. Others charge 12.5 per cent for this, payable when the rent is received.

For 15 per cent, the **letting and management service**, the agent will do a great deal more. Basically they are managing the property and dealing directly with the tenant over every little hiccup that may occur. Or big hiccups, depending on the problem. There have been times when I've thought 'If this tenant doesn't stop bugging me, I'm going to have to hand it over.' Similarly, I have thought 'I'm glad I'm not paying 15 per cent for this one. He's an angel. Never calls. No problems. Wonderful.'

So, as well as all the other stuff, they will do the following:

- Pay the ground rent, insurance premiums, service charges etc. from the rent received.

- Inspect the property three or four times a year.

- Deal with routine management matters such as 'How does the washing machine work?' to 'Please get rid of this table'.

- Deal with minor works or emergencies such as 'The heating doesn't work' to 'Oops, I've flooded the kitchen'.

- Deal with redecoration, renewal, repairs and replacements. This is the bit I really enjoy but if you are out of the country they will do it with your verbal authority.

- Lodge any insurance claim.

- Organise professional cleaning and repairs after the tenancy, that are noted in the check-out report. These are paid from the rent.

- Obtain estimates if a major redecoration is necessary.

> **The Landlord and Tenant Act 1987**
>
> Section 48 of this Act stipulates that the tenant should be provided with an address in England or Wales for the landlord, so that the tenant may serve Notices upon the landlord. Ouch! If you live outside the UK, you must provide an address in England or Wales. This can be your agent's address. (The Landlord and Tenant Act is only applicable to England and Wales because Scotland and Northern Ireland have totally different land-holding laws.)

Dealing with Rental Contracts

Legal safety requirements

First of all let's discuss the various regulations introduced by the government. Obviously, safety in the home is very important but even more so when your home is occupied by tenants.

- **Smoke detectors:** The Department of Environment introduced new regulations requiring any new building (built after June 1992) to have smoke detectors installed. If your property is older than this they recommend that battery-operated detectors be installed on each floor.

- **The Furniture and Furnishings (Fire Safety) Regulations 1988:** I have mentioned this before, but it is essential that all your upholstered furniture, soft furnishings (i.e. loose covers, headboards, cushions), beds, mattresses and pillows be fire resistant. Most items bought these days will comply and have little tags attached, which you should leave on. If you have antiques in your rental property, anything pre-1950 is exempt.

- **The Gas Safety (Installation and Use) Regulations 1994:** This is the gas safety certificate that you need to provide annually after all the appliances have been checked by a registered (CORGI) gas installer or British Gas. He will charge you handsomely for this service and costs may depend on the number of gas appliances.

- **The Electrical Equipment (Safety) Regulations 1994:** This stipulates that all your electrical goods must be safe and tested regularly, although it doesn't insist on annual checks. Any old appliances should be removed, because tenants want the latest looks. A dodgy toaster isn't worth the hassle.

The contract

Once you have chosen your letting agent, or agents, look carefully at their terms and conditions. They will all vary slightly. Not just the percentages but the way you pay. (See What they Cost, page 168.) Some want the whole 10 per cent of one year's rent *up front*; some will take it month by month.

Even though the tenant may say he wants the flat for a year, they will often ask for a break clause after 6 months. This is to protect him should he change his mind about the flat or his circumstances change and he needs to move. He will need to give you 2 months' notice to quit or face a penalty. This is to protect you *NOTICE* so that you have time to find another tenant.

The standard rental agreement is an Assured Shorthold Tenancy, which means that after 6 months you can give the tenant notice, if there is a problem. Two months' notice to quit, in writing, will be required. This has to be a special form, so get your solicitor or agent to do it. Remember if the tenant refuses to move out you cannot throw him out without obtaining a court order.

The rest of the lengthy contract basically stipulates that the tenant must keep the premises clean and in good condition; the tenant mustn't destroy anything; the tenant must clean the windows; the tenant must repair damage; the tenant must leave the premises exactly as he finds them; the tenant cannot use the premises for immoral purpose (ho-ho!); the tenant mustn't make a noise; cannot have pets; cannot lop down trees; cannot sub-let; must pay the rent on time etc., etc. It's all fairly straightforward, but if you want it thoroughly explained, your solicitor, or indeed your agent, will take you through it.

You will need to provide four sets of keys to the agent and I usually keep a set in case of emergency.

keys

Check the management set-up of the agent. Find out the name of the person who will be dealing with your property. If the roof is falling in and you are in Abu Dhabi you'll want to have one person to talk to. Sometimes smaller agents can be better in this regard. You don't want the buck passed around a large office!

Check day-to-day management procedure. You don't want to be bothered about a call-out for £35 to change a tap washer, but you do want the agent to inform you before they spend £500 of your money on a new washing machine.

Help the agent and tenant by providing as many instruction books and guarantees for appliances as you can.

Once the contract has been agreed and signed by both parties, and the date to commence tenancy has been fixed, the tenant can move into your property and you can call yourself a 'landlord', or a nutcase. Whichever you prefer!

There are other ways of letting your property – some of them not strictly legal – but if you choose to go it alone by advertising, interviewing, letting and rent collecting by yourself, then you're a braver person than I. The risks are obvious and you stand to get your fingers burnt. But good luck anyway. I'm only here to offer advice.

Security Deposits

I went to a very smart property do at the US Embassy the other night, wearing my landlord's hat of course. Everyone I met was really charming and rather curious as to why I was there. When I told them, they were amazed. I suppose they imagine all investors to be big and hairy. There was a lot of the 'Cor, I wish I had a landlord who looked like you' sort of ribaldry and the occasional stunned silence. 'But I thought you were a Bond girl,' said one. For that please read 'You're not supposed to be smart as well.' I just gave him an enigmatic smile and said 'Mmm. I still have a licence to thrill.'

The strangest encounter was with one of the bankers who came up to me and said very pompously, 'So why are you here then?' 'Because I invest in the property market,' I replied, sweetly. 'You mean you own your own home? Ha ha ha.' 'Er, yes,' I continued, 'but I have a small portfolio of properties that I buy to let. The rental market is proving rather rewarding at present.' I'm sure I saw a large leather shoe going into his mouth.

The danger, of course, is getting too smug about all this and the fact that I've never had a dodgy tenant. However, I had a heart-stopping moment recently and now face the reality that things can go wrong. One of my tenants announced that she was leaving her flat in 6 weeks' time and would not be paying any more rent as we were holding her *6-week deposit* and that could cover it.

I freaked because not only is this against her contractual agreement but if there was any damage to the flat, I wouldn't have her deposit to pay for it. Sadly, we landlords are to blame for this sort of behaviour, which is not unusual because according to the National Association of Citizens' Advice Bureaux (NACAB) recent research has found that landlords could be robbing tenants of millions of pounds a year in this way.

Some private landlords who deal directly with the tenant, rather than through an agent, are withholding deposits for the flimsiest of reasons, even if the tenant has cleaned the flat properly and there are no breakages. Normal wear and tear should be taken into account, so for example after 2 years, a landlord shouldn't really charge for minor scuff marks and dirty upholstery, but they do. Some landlords even charge if you don't put everything back in exactly the right spot.

In my case, my agents find the tenant and *they* always hold the deposit, not me. This is invariably returned in full unless, of course, my tenant has done a tango with a felt-tip pen all over the bedroom walls.

Your agent will usually hold the deposit (it is not always 6 weeks' rent but must be mutually agreed – 8 weeks is the legal maximum) in a designated client account with interest accruing to the tenant. However, not all agents pay out the interest to the tenant *or* the landlord. All damages, breakages and dilapidations will be paid out of it at the end of the tenancy. Some agents will mediate over how much deposit to return, while other agents will not get involved unless you have a full management service. In that case, it is up to you to negotiate directly with the tenant. This is where a fully detailed check-out report is invaluable. When carried out by a third party there can be no dispute over a stained rug or cracked hob. The only dispute will be over how much to charge.

My tip here is – *don't be greedy*. Don't think of a figure and double it. Be accurate. Be fair. You'll win the respect of your agents and feel better about it in the long run.

Long Lets Versus Short Lets

A mute tenant, on a 4-year let, who pays on time, is my idea of landlord heaven. Long lets have always been my preference because they are far less traumatic. Short lets or, worse, holiday lets (see Chapter 11) have such a rapid turnaround that I couldn't possibly manage them myself and I would need an army of cleaners and decorators.

However, the demand for short lets has been booming, due to employee mobility, and particularly in the summer months. Yields of 20 per cent are now achievable, due to the huge demand from corporate tenants and holidaymakers. Admittedly, this is mainly affecting London and the major cities but, apparently, the big companies want more flexible terms and are prepared to pay more for the shorter let.

For example, a good flat renting for £400 a week on a long-term basis could fetch as much as £650 a week on a short let. That would include gas and electricity, and you would be expected to provide a fax, TV, satellite and cable, maid and laundry service. They become serviced apartments really.

If you have a flat in a very good location, very central to all amenities and with a very high specification finish, it may be worth considering short lets. A short let can be anything from a week to 3 months.

The down-side of all this rampant profiteering is that the high turnover of tenants can cause greater maintenance costs and more damages. Your insurance will go up (be sure to inform your insurance company or else they may well refuse to pay a claim) and the agent's commission is higher:

- 10 per cent commission becomes 15 per cent for 3 months or less
- 12.5 per cent commission becomes 17.5 per cent for 3 months or less
- 15 per cent commission becomes 20 per cent or 21 per cent for 3 months or less

Your other costs will be incurred more frequently, like cleaning, tenancy agreements and inventories. So you need to do the sums carefully and see if it is really worth it. The void periods between short lets can be longer and the stress will be greater I'm sure. A good tenant ensconced for a nice long time will do me fine, thank you.

Short lets:	**Long lets:**
Higher yield *but*	Lower yield *but*
greater maintenance costs;	less maintenance;
higher insurance;	lower insurance;
higher commission;	lower commission;
longer voids.	shorter voids.

chapter eleven

Buying a second home or holiday home

Of course, it sounds rather grand to say that one has a second home. 'Do come to the country for the weekend darling. Scintillating company. Just bring a little *fois gras* and some Krug. Henry says we can all play croquet on Sunday, as long as Charlotte agrees not to cheat.'

In reality it is all very different – unless you're loaded and have an army of staff. The Friday afternoon drive is a nightmare because you have to wait for the children to finish school (if you are without kids then presumably you can beat the rush) and when you get there you spend the next 2 hours lighting fires, filling the fridge, getting the heating going etc. In the summer it is slightly more idyllic but only if the sun is shining and everyone likes barbecues. Then a gloom descends at about 5 p.m. on the Sunday when you start thinking about the ghastly return journey.

My advice to anyone thinking of buying a second home is: be a guest instead! Second homes are a very expensive luxury. Stay with friends, go to country house hotels, rent a cottage but think seriously about tying up all that capital in a house that is hardly going to be used and is not making you money. Even visiting one of the loveliest hotels in the *Relais et Chateau* guide every other weekend will cost you less money and cause you less grief than owning a second home in the country.

Where to Buy

If, however, you buy a second home *as an investment* then fine. Just make sure it is in the right location and will let easily. This is not as simple as it sounds and holiday homes have a different set of problems. You can't use it yourself as often as you would like because during the summer holidays when it is at peak rental, you have to go somewhere else. (See Making a Return on your Investment, page 181.)

The hot spots for holiday homes are the obvious counties like **Cornwall**, **Dorset**, **Suffolk** and **Gloucestershire**, with the **Cotswold villages** doing exceptionally well. A holiday home must be aimed at the tourist, whether home-grown or from abroad, so the obvious attractions will steer you towards a good location: **Stratford upon Avon**, **York**, **Chester**, **Edinburgh**, the **Cornish coast**, the **Yorkshire Moors**, the **Welsh mountains**, **Windsor Castle**.

As most holiday homes have a weekly turnover it is advisable to hand over the administration, marketing and financial aspect to one of the many companies who specialise in renting out country holiday homes. They are experts in their field and take all the hassle out of it. Some of them charge 21 per cent commission, while others go as high as 49 per cent for marketing your home. They deal with properties ranging from twee little thatched cottages to huge baronial castles.

The most successful holiday let is a two-bedroom cottage, which can sleep four or five, in an idyllic country location. If you are thinking of investing in this market, these companies will advise you on what and where to buy and send information packs on what is required, right down to the teaspoons. (See Furnishing a Holiday Home, page 179.) Their standards are very high, so no nylon bedspreads and shag-pile carpets!

Also, don't think that a holiday cottage will only be occupied during the summer months. Some properties are particularly popular over the Christmas period, especially the slightly larger houses (sleeping eight to ten) with real log fires. Two families will often get together for Christmas and fancy the typical rural retreat. All you have to do is lay on the snow!

CHECK LIST ···

Holiday Homes Check list:

- Two-bedroomed cottages let the easiest.
- Buy in idyllic rural location *or*
- Buy near tourist hot spot *or*
- Buy near the coast.
- Talk to holiday cottage rental companies, and get their brochure and information pack.
- Property must be fully furnished.

CASE STUDY ···

Mrs Wilson inherited her mother's house in Devon 2 years ago and on the advice of friends decided not to sell it but to turn it into a holiday home. She approached one of the well-known holiday companies and they sent her a package of information. She redecorated the entire cottage in off-white and duck egg blue and replaced all the curtains. Luckily all the floors are either stone or wood but she bought a few rugs for the bedrooms. Everything else was fine except for the mattresses, which were replaced, and she had to buy a few extras like a baby high-chair and a cot, but the investment was well worth it. She leaves all the organising to the holiday company and now receives cheques for £300 a week in high season. She has no loan on the house and is thoroughly delighted that she decided not to sell it.

Furnishing a Holiday Home

I have to confess to being very traditional when it comes to decor. I like a comfortable, practical environment that is easy on the eye. The difference between decorating a rental investment and a holiday home is that a rental property must be very neutral to suit all tastes, whereas a holiday home can feel a lot more like your own personal home and should have a very comfy, lived-in, child-friendly ambience.

According to the holiday rental companies, the very traditional, cosy cottages let the best. If you have an inglenook fireplace you will score very highly. A thatched roof also appeals, as does a country-style kitchen. Remember, these people want an escapist holiday for a maximum of 2 weeks. They're not investing a lifetime in your property.

> **A**merican tourists want the archetypal 'cute' English look that they see on television. Miss Marple has a lot to answer for.

I have stayed in several holiday homes across the British Isles and the one thing that struck me was the repeat business that the successful ones were doing. If you want to make money out of a holiday home you will need that repeat business. If a family are happy in your home they will return year after year and this is particularly prevalent in foreign investments. (The one absolute must abroad is a swimming pool.)

So here is a rough guide to furnishing your holiday home (the rental companies will send you lists of what you should provide. This will include a cot, a high-chair, a stair-gate, an extra foldaway bed etc., etc.):

- Keep chintziness to a minimum.

- Use warm colours in fabrics and upholstery.

- Choose hard-wearing fabrics.

- Choose a heavy-duty carpet.

- Leave pictures, vases and ornaments around to create a home from home.

- Buy good quality mattresses as they last longer and ensure repeat business. (If I can't sleep I won't go back.)

- Make sure the heating is efficient and plenty of hot water can be provided.

- Provide good, clean linen.

- Provide extra duvets, blankets and pillows.

- There should be plenty of comfy chairs and sofas.

- There must be a TV.

- The kitchen should be fully equipped with enough crockery for however many the house can sleep. (Everything will be on the list.) Good cutlery is a plus. I once stayed in a place where the knives cut into our palms.

- The whole place must exude a pleasant, comfortable air that makes people feel relaxed. That is the idea of a holiday, after all.

- Washing machine and dryer should have instructions nearby.

- One of the bedrooms should have twin beds.

- Bathrooms don't need to be up to the minute but a white suite is preferable and a shower is a plus.

Don't forget, all furnishings must meet fire protection standards and upholstery fabrics must be fire retardant.

Remember the house will need to meet the highest standards of cleanliness and repair. Your house will be graded by an inspector from one of the holiday companies (if you choose to go through them) and they are likely to offer advice on any changes they deem necessary. They want you to get the highest rent, so they get a higher commission! Obviously, the more your house has to offer in terms of style, comfort, location and facilities the higher the grading will be. A grand Georgian rectory with eight bedrooms is bound to be in a higher band than a two-bedroom cottage but it won't necessarily let as frequently. I'd stick with the cottage if I were you. If you have an inglenook fireplace, a thatched roof and a country kitchen, you're on to a winner.

Making a Return on Your Investment

The holiday lettings business has turned into a multi-million pound industry and there are some people who are going into it full time. They buy a house with lots of land, outbuildings and barns, which they turn into holiday lets (with permission of course). Some have as many as a dozen units that they let and will even build a swimming pool complex as well. If they are living in the main house it means they can manage and oversee the units themselves. Alternatively, you could purchase a property in need of renovation at a bargain price, do it up, let it out and have a solid asset that would increase in value.

This is big business and needs an army of staff and massive administration, but it is certainly a way of making a return on your investment. It's not for the faint-hearted, but if you are thinking of going into holiday homes in a big way, it will need 100 per cent commitment in order to make the business work. I don't think it is possible to run an operation like this as a side-line.

Insurance and Rates

It is advisable to include public liability cover in your insurance policy. This covers you if a member of the public suffers injury or damage as a result of you or anyone acting on your behalf failing to take reasonable care.

If you let your holiday home for more than 140 days a year, the rates change from ordinary domestic to the more expensive business rates. Keep this in mind when calculating the income from your investment.

However, running holiday homes is a notoriously fickle business on which it is extremely difficult to base any financial calculations. It certainly isn't based on 52 weeks of the year. With clever seasonal marketing you might be able to base it on 32 weeks of the year, but in France the figures are based on only 16 weeks. *Mon dieu!* That's high season only.

Remember, rents are disproportionately high on holiday lets, compared to long lets on an assured shorthold tenancy. So, for example, a nice cottage in the Cotswolds might rent for £1,000 per week at peak season. Assuming it is only let for 16 weeks that would be £16,000 minus your commission (which varies from company to company) of roughly £4,000, leaving £12,000 out of which you have to pay all maintenance, borrowings, cleaners, laundry, repairs and tax. This might not seem too bad if you can cover all costs and still make a profit.

The biggest return on your investment, however, will be the capital growth. Rather like the private rental sector, it is not the rental yield that will make you rich but the bricks and mortar itself. The basic rules apply. Buy a holiday home or second home in the right location, for a good price, make it look the business and in time you will be sitting on a gold mine.

Buying in France

Like many before me I was sorely tempted to buy a holiday home in France. Having rented houses in the Dordogne for the family hols and seeing what kind of return can be achieved, I started looking into it. However, after doing the sums and realising that we would never be able to use it at the height of the season (due to lost revenue) we decided against it and continue to rent other people's homes.

But buying a house in France is a great deal simpler than in the UK. Here is what happens.

Once you have made an offer that has been accepted, you have to sign a contract called the *Soussigne Signe* – or *Compromis de Vente* – which is a simple six-page document, and pay your 10 per cent deposit. You don't need a mortgage pre-arranged but the contract will contain the '*Clause Suspensive*', which has three reasons why the sale may not go ahead and that would enable you to get your deposit back. They are: if you can't get a mortgage; if the government decides it wants to purchase the property or land, to protect a neighbouring farm for example; if searches come up with something untoward. If none of these occur the sale must proceed.

All the legal work and negotiations are carried out by the local *Notaire* who works for both parties – the vendor and purchaser – and who is basically two things. He works for the government as an official tax collector and as a solicitor. He will do the conveyancing, the searches and generally do the best for you, but unlike an English solicitor, he doesn't advise. Now the bad news. There is a whopping 10 per cent purchase tax, but this includes all the Notaire's and estate agent's fees. The lucky vendor pays nothing unless it is his second home, and then there is a capital gains tax. Finally, the Acte de Vente is the completion after everything has been checked. The Notaire will set a date, sometimes 3 months away, but this is simply a final date by which time all paperwork must be completed. Often it is achieved within 6 weeks.

Property in France is still excellent value and in the south-west nowhere is too remote. Most people want to be near a village or small market town; they want good facilities and a pool. The pace is much slower than at home and, of course, the climate is wonderful. Life is very gentle and stress free. The perfect holiday if you like self-catering.

The down-side of buying a holiday home abroad is finding an honest management company to look after the running of it. They do exist, of course, but you need to do very thorough checks on their services. A friend of mine had a house in Portugal, which he let all through the year but it was beset with problems. His managing agents were always calling up and saying things like 'The pool's filtration system has broken down' or 'The downstairs loo is blocked', so they would call out engineers and charge the bill to him. 'The problem was, I had no way of knowing if these things were really happening,' he said, 'I just had to take their word for it. The maintenance costs were astronomical. Instead of making a profit, it was costing me £10,000 a year to run.'

TIPS ••

Buying Abroad Tips:

- Research the area – go on holiday there at least a couple of times to get a feel for the place.

- Check what rental incomes are like in the area.

- Recruit a specialist agent and lawyer to help with the legal documents.

- Check the deeds to the property and planning permission.

- Remember notaire and other fees will add about 15 per cent to the purchase price.

- Make sure you have sufficient funds – you can pay cash, release equity in your UK home or take out a mortgage to pay for your holiday home.

- Do not hand over 100 per cent of the money at any one time.

- Clarify rights of way and services such as water, sewerage and electricity.

- If the property needs any work, only use registered professionals, check their credentials and get written quotes and invoices.

How to Make Your Home Pay for Itself

Assuming you are comfortable with strangers in your home – and I wouldn't recommend any of the following options if you are a single girl or single mother, for obvious reasons – there are several ways to make money out of your home. By making your home 'go to work' so to speak, you will be able to afford that new roof, sun-room or extra bedroom. This is all about 'maximising the potential' so that when it is time to move on, your property has not only paid for itself but added enormously to its own value.

Bed and breakfast

I happen to love staying in British bed and breakfasts because they are so much more personal and charming than a hotel. If I'm working away from home, I feel less lonely in a B&B. They have a cosy, homely atmosphere that you rarely find in hotels.

If you have the sort of house that will lend itself to becoming B&B accommodation, it can be a wonderful way of making money. You need to be fairly fit and gregarious by nature and quite organised to prevent any double-booking but other than that, it is quite straightforward.

The English Tourist Board (ETB) has over 4,000 establishments, which are inspected by them, but there are another 9,500 who choose not to be with the ETB who can be found in publications such as *Bed and Breakfast Nationwide* or *Alistair Sawday's Special Places to Stay in Britain*.

My friend Wendy lives in a rather imposing Queen Anne house just outside Exeter and recently opened up her family home to paying guests. She isn't registered with the ETB or in any guidebooks, but still managed to have a hectic, thriving business during the summer months due to referrals from local hotels and businesses. 'It seems to work very well as the guests have their own front door, their own dining room and TVs in their *en-suite* bedrooms, so I don't find our privacy being shattered at all. Everyone is so nice. We get a lot of ramblers and twitchers who leave the house at dawn and come back for breakfast at 9 a.m. It's very civilised,' she said.

Wendy lets out only two bedrooms in her house, 'otherwise we have to install a fire-escape' and admits that the cash is very handy when it comes to redecorating or repairing the roof. She sought advice from the ETB who provide a detailed setting-up pack, but basically anyone can do it and there are no rules or regulations if you only let two rooms. If, however, you want to be listed with a crown rating in their little book, then there are certain guidelines that have to be adhered to.

If you install extra bathrooms or redecorate the bedrooms before opening for business, the setting-up costs are all tax-deductible, as are a percentage of all your running costs, like heating.

CHECK LIST ···

Check list for opening a B&B:

- If you only let out two rooms, you won't have to worry about fire regulations.
- Register with the Tourist Board for instant business.
- There are certain rules if you want a rating. (Like providing tea, coffee and kettle in the room.)
- *En-suite* bathrooms are a bonus and popular with customers. If you need to install them, it is tax deductible.

How to **Make Money** from **Your Property**

- Big breakfasts are usually expected.
- Apply for a 'setting-up pack' from the ETB.
- Provide good mattresses if you want repeat business.
- Decor should be warm and friendly.
- Get some cards printed and let local hotels and businesses know that you are now open.

Letting your home out for short lets

If the whole family are vacating your property for a 2- or 3-week holiday – if you live alone it is even simpler – you could consider letting your home on a short-term basis. Whether it is a flat in the middle of the city or a family house in a rural retreat, there are several companies nationwide who specialise in letting out homes. The money is considerable and the customer will pay because it is a *home* and not a rental investment.

Friends of mine in Wimbledon make a small fortune during the Wimbledon fortnight by moving out for 2 weeks! However, it is quite complicated and requires some effort and not a little upheaval. Here are some things you need to think about *before* you start emptying your wardrobes:

- Check that it is permitted under the terms of your lease, by the local authority or by your mortgage company.

- You will need to inform your insurance company and may need to take out extra cover.

- You will need to comply with the gas, electrical and fire safety regulations.

- All your furnishings and upholstered items will need to be fire-resistant and labelled in order to comply with fire safety regulations.

- Lock up valuables and store any rare and precious antiques.

- Clear away all personal bits and pieces and remove as much clutter as possible.

- The property should be clean and tidy.

- Empty wardrobes and drawers.

- Have an inventory taken.

How to **Make Money** from **Your Property**

If you use a short let company they will advise you on presentation and what to provide. This is your home, though, and not a holiday let so I strongly urge you to go through the proper channels and get the right contracts drawn up. Be prepared for upheaval when you return as a lot of things will have moved to different places. However, if it is successful and you do this often, you will find that it will change the way you live for ever.

The direct swap

This is slightly different in that there is no financial reward but your home will be paying for your holiday. The idea is to swap homes with a family abroad who want to come to the UK. All you pay for is the flights. There are companies on the internet who will put you in touch with a family in your desired location, from Atlanta to Zaire. Make sure you are getting what you want, including the car, otherwise it could be a bit of a raw deal.

So, if you don't mind strangers in your home, then the check list is the same – more or less – as above. Make sure your insurance company is informed.

Regarding swapping property, I heard about an actor, Chris, who fancied a holiday in Los Angeles and came up with a brilliant idea. He placed an ad in the *Hollywood Reporter*, which is the Los Angeles showbiz bible, suggesting a 2-week direct swap with his flat in Hampstead.

This proved immensely popular with producers tired of La La Land needing an injection of Cool Britannia, so Chris had the pick of the bunch and could dictate dates and terms. Everything was included, even the car, on the proviso that you looked after the place and watered the plants. Well, I know who got the best deal.

Chris arrived in LA with his family to find this enormous beach-front condo on Venice Beach. It had a huge bathroom with walk-in power showers, a refrigerator the size of the wardrobe, the sun was blisteringly hot and a Cadillac was parked out the back.

Meanwhile, Mr Producer arrived in rainy London to find Chris's Hampstead flat had only a bath with a hand-shower, a fridge the size of a gnat's armpit and a Vauxhall Cavalier out the back.

The movie location

Your home could be making money as a movie location or a location for pop videos, promos, photographic shoots and advertising layouts. Obviously, the more unusual, quirky or ancient your home is, the more likely it is to be used. But you don't have to live in a castle.

If you have an old bakery or stables; a ravishing garden or clock-tower; a really old kitchen or chapel; a modern glass penthouse or aviary, then contact one of the location finder companies, such as The Location Company (see Useful Addresses) and they will put you on their register.

Film companies pay quite well but can be a bit careless with the paintwork. There is so much equipment and so many people involved in these shoots that it is almost inevitable that some damage will be incurred. But it can be great fun too and you never know who you might meet!

I've worked in some fabulous locations over the years but the funniest was when I was filming in Belvoir Castle in Leicestershire. The grounds of the castle are quite breathtaking but they have dozens of peacocks roaming around, who are prone to screeching on a regular basis. Ever heard a peacock screech? This made filming extremely difficult because every time we got to the really poignant moment, a peacock would let rip and send us all into fits of giggles.

part three

Maximising
the Potential

chapter twelve

Making the most of your property

A Radical Transformation or a Cosmetic Touch-up?

This is the most crucial part of the book, I feel, because if you own a property, you have made an enormous financial commitment and presumably would like to see a healthy return on that investment, when you come to sell.

The value of your home will double every seven years. Approximately. This is a basic rule of thumb used by estate agents. So that's good news isn't it? Even better news is that you *could* double it even faster than that by clever investment in the property itself. You put a little more in (or add a little on) and get a whole lot back. A friend of mine does this for a living, buying up old wrecks, converting them into luxurious homes and selling them on. He doubles his initial investment every 18 months. Now, I'm not suggesting you become a mini developer, but your home should be regarded as a business investment whether you intend to live there for 5, 10 or 15 years. By maximising the potential of your home, you are increasing its worth.

Why is it that some people make a killing when they sell their homes while others barely cover their mortgage? If you were putting that money into the bank you would want the highest rate of interest wouldn't you? It's the same with property, only more so. If you get it right you'll have an even higher return.

Once in your home you need to decide how far to go to maximise the potential of your property. Is it a radical transformation, as in restoring a ruin, or merely a cosmetic touch-up requiring only a fresh coat of paint and a new bathroom? Most properties can be enhanced in some way both inside and out (see Transforming the Exterior, page 209), depending on your budget. Remember, a little goes a long way.

Extending Upwards and Outwards

If you love your house, the location is terrific, work is easy to get to, you adore the neighbours but are beginning to feel a trifle cramped, what do you do? It could be that the family is expanding – again – or that the sullen teenager is playing his music at 100 decibels. If you can't, or don't want to, move then the alternative is to either move up or sideways or both. A loft conversion or an extension?

You may think it an expensive decision but, let me assure you, it is a darn sight cheaper than stamp duty, estate agents' commission, solicitors' fees and removal bills. It is also an excellent way to maximise the potential of your home as it will definitely add value.

Converting the loft

In the dictionary, the definition of a loft is a 'room over the stable, especially for hay and straw', which is fine if you're Red Rum, but to most of us it's called the attic, or the place where all the junk goes. They are usually high up under the eaves, which means little standing-up room unless you're 2ft tall. They are not to be confused with the 'Manhattan Lofts', which are 2000sq ft and upwards of empty shell and hugely popular at the moment.

In the 1980s converting the attic space at the top of your house was all the rage and planning permission was fairly easy to obtain. Now, however, the local authorities are much stricter about consents and will insist that the roof line doesn't change and that only a rear mansard is permitted. Obviously, this depends on where you live but for those lucky enough to be granted a full front and back elevation it can prove to be a very shrewd investment.

Basically, a good loft conversion **can add twice as much as its cost to the value of your house**. This would be in a city or town where space is at a premium

Before: *Most attics, or lofts, are useful for storing all the household junk which could be hiding your best investment yet! Get a loan, get planning permission, get cracking.*

and would have to be a properly designed loft complying with the local authority regulations. This is most important as building regulations, and particularly fire legislation, are very thorough. For example, proper stairs are required if your loft is to be a living or sleeping area. One of those telescopic ladders will not do.

If you don't comply with buildings regulations, it will come back to haunt you when you sell. A surveyor will check to see if it has been approved by the council and if it hasn't the cost of rectifying the loft will be deducted from the selling price.

The cost

Loft conversions vary enormously in price depending on what you want, the size of the space, number of dormer windows and state of your joists, etc. Get several builders to quote for the job, or find a building company who specialises in loft conversions, of which there are many. Building societies are usually happy to loan you the money.

After: When you convert the loft make sure it complies with building regulations and has been well designed to maximise space. Here, a large bedroom with three sky-lights has been created.

The value

Depending on your location, the loft space should be worth twice what you paid for it. As I said before, this is in an urban situation where an extra bedroom makes all the difference. In the country, the situation is slightly different. An extension or conservatory is likely to add more value than a loft conversion, but it is still cheaper than moving home.

So, if you can't move home but need more space, converting the loft is one option.

> **N**ot all houses are suitable to convert. If you live in a terrace of fairly 'skinny' houses, with too few reception rooms, you could end up with something top heavy. Estate agents say there is no point having five bedrooms and nowhere to eat.

Check list for converting your loft:

- Use an architect who knows the local planning regulations.
- Get three building quotes.
- Build proper stairs.
- Remember smoke detectors.
- Install good ventilation and heating.
- A loft conversion will add value to your house, sometimes twice as much as it cost to build.
- It is cheaper than moving house.

Two of my builders were up in the roof the other day while I was fiddling about on the landing, when I overhead the following conversation:

'What's that Mike?'
'That's a bat, Pat.'
'A dead flat bat?'
'Yeah.'
'Nah. That's a fat flat rat.'
'No. The cat got the rat, Pat.'
'So that's a dead, black, flat bat?'
'Yup.'

Building an extension

Another way round the lack-of-space problem is to build an extension on to your home. This will add value *only* if it is done sympathetically, reflecting the style and age of your property. Unlike the loft, which is already an integral part of the house, an extension is a visible *addition*, which therefore must be aesthetically pleasing in order to increase value. It also needs to be in proportion to the rest of the building. It's no good building a giant sun-room on to a tiny cottage, or eating into precious garden space if it will leave you with little or no garden.

Remember, the value of your home will only increase if the property is in a desirable location to start with. You might not recoup your money if it is not. For example, adding an extra bedroom on to a bungalow on a really busy road, is probably not a good idea.

This sort of extension could add much needed space as an office or workroom and could be seen as multi-functional to any future purchaser. There is also the possibility of adding a further floor in due course. A real bonus.

With floor to ceiling windows, this extension lets the light flood in and it is a brilliant way of creating a larger kitchen and breakfast area.

This is a good example of a double-height extension with a sun-room, or extended sitting-room on the ground floor and a bedroom and bath-room above.

These are the sort of extensions that usually add value:

- an extra sitting room or den;
- a playroom;
- a downstairs loo and shower room;
- a larger kitchen;
- an extra bedroom and bathroom;
- a sun-room or conservatory;
- an *en-suite* bathroom;
- an office or workroom;
- a garage.

A friend of mine bought a wonderful stone cottage with an L-shaped kitchen that didn't seem to work at all. She eventually got permission to extend it, so that the L-shape became a huge square and now she can have a kitchen table in there where all meals are taken. It has become the hub of the house where just about everything happens and makes it enormously attractive to a future purchaser.

If you have the space, a double-height extension is a good idea and is usually not much more expensive than doing one floor. This way you can have a playroom, sitting room or whatever on the ground floor and an extra bedroom with *en-suite* bathroom on the first floor.

Of course, some people go mad and double the size of their homes with a massive reconstruction. This can look wonderful if you have used a good architect and good builders. If you have the space it can be a justified investment in your property but it *must* be in keeping with the rest of your house. (See Listed Buildings and Getting Planning Permission later in this chapter.)

Remember that under Planning Policy Guide 16 (PPG16) owners and developers have to bear the financial costs of discovering any archaeological findings. This can be hugely expensive if the dig drags on for weeks. It is not the sort of thing that a survey might warn you about (see Chapter 4, section on Building It Yourself for more on this).

For a large extension:

- obtain planning permission and Building Regulation Approval;

- use an architect;

- use good builders;

- construction should be of similar material and in same style so that it looks natural and not 'added on'.

> **Warning:** If you go ahead without getting planning permission it will affect your home in the future as you will be unable to sell it without the proper consents. This could result in a fine, imprisonment or having to take the extension down, so I suggest you go through the proper channels.

A small scale extension

Planning permission is usually not required for a small extension at the back of the house, as long as it doesn't increase the floor area by more than 23sq m or 10 per cent of the total floor area of the property. However, this does not apply if your property is in a conservation area. This includes conservatories and a garage but there are rules about the height and not reducing the space in your garden to less than 25sq m. If in any doubt, it is always wise to check with your local planning department.

In our old house, my husband built a long extension on to the back, which was in true Georgian style in keeping with the rest of our home. It added a couple of rooms and a downstairs shower room. After a few years it looked as if it had just 'evolved' rather than been added on and definitely added enormous value to the house. Of course, some planners don't mind utterly contemporary architecture being joined on to an historic building – look at the National Gallery in London for example – but I think one should tread warily when it comes to your home. Always think about what will appeal to the broadest market.

- **Do** tell your neighbours before applying for planning permission because the council will tell them anyway.

- **Do** use a reputable builder.

- **Don't** go for the cheapest quote.

- **Don't** try to save money by reducing the size of the extension.

Another 2ft all round could make all the difference long term and would be false economy otherwise.

Restoring a Ruin

If you insist on buying a wreck of a building – or, even worse, a listed wreck – you must be prepared for the bottomless pit syndrome. Our house was hardly a ruin when we bought it, but it is very, very old and the budget went out of the window extremely early on. If you are about to start work on an old property you must have a contingency plan and budget accordingly. The unforeseen and unexpected is bound to happen and not only costs you double but throws the schedule out as well. (Our builder was checking the joists under the floorboards when they all gave way under him. Chronic infestation apparently. That set us back a bit.)

Organise your finances. Estimate the value of the completed house first, then get three quotes for the cost of restoring it. The difference between these two figures is the amount you can offer for the property. Keep an emergency fund of at least 25 per cent of the building costs for anything unforeseen.

Your local council will be able to recommend an architect or you can contact the Royal Institute of British Architects. You will also need to find a surveyor – contact the Royal Institute of Chartered Surveyors.

Restoring a run-down house will only prove to be a good investment if it is the sort of property that someone else will want to buy in due course. The rules of location still apply, regardless. This is common sense one would think. But I know of one person who bought a water-tower near Birmingham for a very reasonable price. He then spent a fortune converting it into a home no one wanted to buy. Eventually he dropped the price so much that he only just broke even. This is something you will *not* be doing.

> **S**ome mortgage lenders are reluctant to lend you money if you are taking on a ruin, but there are now three or four building societies (such as Norwich and Peterborough and Ecology BS) who are keen to support people who would rather renovate than buy a new build. Ask around for the best rates. They usually monitor the upgrading and loan you money as you progress.

Restoration is all about bringing a building back to life, whether it be a church, a house or a railway station. If it is to be your home you must decide how far you want to go with it. For example, in our house we decided not to even out the bumps in the walls because I quite like that undulating unevenness. This is an old house after all. Similarly, we only replaced the stone mullions that had severe frost damage and left the others that just looked battered. Making your home safe, free of damp or wood infestation, watertight and warm is all that is required.

'You must understand your building before you undertake any restoration', said an English Heritage inspector I spoke to. 'Understand how it was built and how it came to be. If it is listed, why is it a cultural resource? If it's not broken don't mend it. It is important to keep old buildings looking old.' That is such an important tip. If you restore a house to within an inch of its life, you will take away its character. It doesn't need to look perfect, just loved.

VAT and Grants

Restoration and renovation is VAT exempt on some listed buildings when it is with buildings consent from the local authorities.

There are grants available for restoration but only if the building is considered to be 'at risk'. Grants are usually not available for standard home improvements – even to a listed building – unless there is no internal sanitation. Grants for disabled facilities etc. vary from council to council, so it is best to make applications to the relevant planning departments and seek advice. As soon as you ask for a grant you will have to comply with all English Heritage and Listed Buildings Regulations. (For more on this, see Listed Buildings, page 204.)

- Always replace like for like wherever possible as new materials won't work well.

- Avoid the temptation to rip out original features and later additions that are part of the history of your home.

- Use lime mortar instead of cement.

- Use old bricks instead of new ones.

- Find a reclamation centre near you for old roof tiles, old doors, old fireplaces, etc.

- Use reclaimed timber.

- Repair old windows and doors wherever possible rather than ripping them out and replacing with modern versions.

- Use old glass instead of new. It is far more interesting to look through.

- Use old-fashioned flat paint, such as the National Trust range.

- Never use brilliant white as it has too much blue pigment in it and is a modern invention.

- Use old-fashioned chalky whites.

- Eggshell paint on the woodwork – not gloss.

- Never paint stone mullions.

- On window exteriors use a colour that complements the period of the house. For example, Queen Anne would have white window frames, a period Cotswold stone cottage usually has stone-coloured window frames.

When restoring an old house you will probably want to put in new bathrooms and a new kitchen. It is important that they are in keeping with the rest of the house or you risk alienating any future purchaser. A techno-kitchen full of stainless steel would look incongruous, whereas a hand-made, traditional kitchen will add enormous value.

The bathrooms should have white suites and, once again, keep them looking traditional. People want fabulous bathrooms with all mod cons like power showers, heated towel-rails, down-lighters and even hidden speakers, but they don't want the expense of having to redo the decor.

If in any doubt about period detail or appropriate styles there are dozens of books available that will inform you about interior and exterior design. Getting the right doors or the right mouldings could make all the difference to your eventual sale price.

In a recent survey these were the areas that added the most value if you are restoring a house. In order of importance, you need to do the following:

- Install central heating.
- Good bathrooms.
- Kitchen suitably priced, appropriate style.
- A garage.
- A conservatory.

- Good insulation.
- An extension.
- Decorating. Should be fairly uncomplicated if you want to sell.

Obviously you will have to deal with fundamental basics such as the roof, walls, re-wiring, re-plumbing and flooring, etc.

Never underestimate the work involved! You will be on a roller-coaster adventure that is full of twists and turns, so be prepared for the journey.

> **I** cannot emphasise enough that it is imperative when taking on an old building that you get planning permission, or Listed Planning Consent; advice from the council; permission from English Heritage; comply with building regulations or whatever is applicable. Failure to do so could cost you dearly.

You can find out about your home in the local library, or you could involve an architectural historian if it is a very important property, but this could set you back a bit financially. If you are wondering about how much you can alter your home, the local authority conservation officer can pay a visit and will often give you free professional advice. However, if you are a bit nervous about an official visit there is a document called 'Planning policy guidance. Note 15', which you will find in the local library. Go to 'annexe C', which is the guide to alterations on listed buildings, and it will tell you everything from how to replace windows correctly, to which paint not to use and all about lime mortar. It is a true conservation bible.

Barn Conversions

I think old barns make wonderful family homes. A good conversion will give you all the mod cons and facilities of a modern home combined with character, charm and masses of space. They are cool in summer and warm in winter.

In the 1980s and early 1990s, barns were fairly cheap to buy because no one really wanted them but then some bright spark started making money out of the conversions and since 1996 the trend has seen a rapid rise in popularity, as they still represent good value for money.

Be wary when buying a barn if you are intending to do it up yourself, as some barns, such as old grain barns, don't make good homes, since they don't have any openings to convert into windows and planning permission is sometimes very tough to obtain.

> **B**e sure to talk to the local planning department before you buy a barn. They are very strict about installing windows, etc. and ideally you should employ an architect for maximum design impact.

A lot of barns are in the middle of nowhere so you may well have to start with the basic infrastructure, building roads for access and bringing in your own power supply, drains and water, etc. This will be expensive. However, if you find an old stone barn with a couple of acres and spend 50 per cent of the sale price doing it up, you will probably double your money within the year. Be prepared to use a good architect and the best local materials.

The fully timbered Sussex barns are my favourites but cattle barns, hay barns, and even piggeries will make terrific homes.

How to **Make Money** from **Your Property**

Before: Be wary of buying a barn that might not convert easily into a home. Talk to the planning department about installing such features as windows before you buy.

After: However with planning permission you can create a fantastic home. This barn has been converted into a charming, three-bedroom house with loads of space.

CASE STUDY ···

I met a chap who had converted an 18th-century piggery into a home. These have a much lower roof line so are usually on one level, like a bungalow. The exterior was exactly how it should have been with stone and exposed timbers, but inside it looked like a brand-new house on a housing estate. It was bland and characterless with a series of little rooms leading off a corridor. I was so disappointed. It was on the market when I saw it, for quite a high price because of the conversion, but it stuck there for 18 months and eventually he had to reduce the price radically. This is a good example of an investment in barns going wrong simply because the owner thought he could do a better job than an architect.

> **A** friend of mine bought a 250-year-old barn from Hurstmonceaux and asked a specialist to dismantle it, timber by timber. Each piece was numbered, transported and reassembled at her new home in Surrey. That's what I call style.

Listed Buildings

Living in a listed building definitely has its pros and cons. The main advantage is that your home is of special interest, both architecturally and historically, and there are usually wonderful stories associated with it. (Our house is listed and has a ghost called Lady Maude as well!)

> **B**efore moving here to Gloucestershire, we lived in another listed house in Surrey. For 300 years it was crown property and then Edward VII leased it to his dear friend and solicitor, Sir George Lewis. Lewis represented much of Edwardian bohemian society such as Burne-Jones, Oscar Wilde and James McNeil Whistler and would entertain them, along with Lily Langtry, to long weekend house parties. Now, the spooky thing is that before I married Neil, I used to live at 13 Tite Street in Chelsea, which was the house that James McNeil Whistler lived in, just up the road from his friend Oscar Wilde. So, a hundred years ago, Whistler lived in and visited the same two houses that I lived in!!

The disadvantage is that you can't do anything externally or internally without listed-building consent and even the smallest of home improvements may cost more than they would for a non-listed property. This is due to the special materials involved. For example, lime mortar will enable the building to breathe naturally, whereas modern plaster will not. But fear not. There is a huge market for 'interesting' houses, and assuming any work is carried out sympathetically and correctly, you should always be able to get your money back, and more.

There are about 530,000 listed buildings in the UK (460,000 in England, 25,000 in Wales and 45,000 in Scotland) and most of them were built before 1840. The listings are split into three categories:

- **Grade 1** These buildings are of paramount interest in a national context, and are mostly churches and public buildings.

- **Grade II*** (with a star) These are considered to be of outstanding interest but usually in a more local context.

- **Grade II** (without a star) These are of special interest and should be maintained and preserved. (More than 90 per cent of all listed buildings fall into this category.)

Don't be nervous of taking on a listed building as the results will be well worth it. However, to avoid getting into a wrangle with the local council, it is wise to ask for advice and permission before you do anything. Here are my tips for dealing with a listed building:

TIPS

- Remember, there is no such thing as a 'typical' listed building.

- Always seek advice on everything.

- There are various grants available – from English Heritage and the Heritage Lottery Fund – for owners of Grade I and Grade II* properties who wish to restore a building that is derelict or that has no indoor sanitation.

- The local council can provide you with names of builders who are experienced in conservation work.

How to **Make Money** from **Your Property**

- A listed home will not affect your mortgage application.

- All buildings pre-1700 and most from pre-1840 tend to be listed. Those of exceptional character post-1840 and selected buildings post-1914.

- Always get listed buildings consent for change of use and alterations. This is entirely separate from the need to get building regulation approval and planning permission.

- Read up on the history of your property.

- A listing applies to both the inside and outside of the property.

- Ask the relevant society for advice (such as the Georgian Group or the Victorian Society – see Useful Addresses).

- You shouldn't really change even the colour of your front door or the man from English Heritage will come round and smack your wrists.

Not all councils will be sympathetic to your needs and stick rigidly – too rigidly – to the rules. I heard about one chap whose cottage had a tin roof. He discovered it used to be thatched, until a fire in the 1800s, so he applied for permission to rethatch it as it was. He was turned down because the tin roof was now listed. So he appealed. He was turned down again. This seems such a shame because I'm sure the thatch would have looked prettier.

> **Y**ou know how some houses have a little blue plaque on the wall because someone famous used to live there? Well, it may be a wonderful talking point but it won't up the price and not everyone will be that impressed. When I was living in Chelsea, there was a magnificent house round the corner from me that used to belong to Bram Stoker, the author of *Dracula*. Someone spent a fortune doing it up but it remained on the market for ages and ages. I assumed that the blue plaque was a bit too spooky for some people.

Is a Conservatory Worth the Investment?

I absolutely adore conservatories. They let the light flood in and can be multi-purpose. From elegant dining room to children's play area they are the best kind of extension money can buy. The good news is, they *do* add value to your home and yes, they *are* worth the investment. An attractive, well-designed conservatory can potentially pay for itself many times over. Some estate agents estimate that you could double your investment if you install a really good one. Not only are you creating a distinctive feature in your home, which allows you to sit surrounded by your garden all year round, you are also creating an extra room.

However, it may be worth noting these points:

- Make sure the proportions are right. You'll only add value if the conservatory doesn't take over the garden.

- Don't destroy or hide attractive features of your house by creating a conservatory.

- Don't be tempted to buy something cheap. Poor quality softwood and single glazing is not the best investment.

- The average conservatory size is 3.5 x 3.5m.

- A larger (5m x 4m) bespoke Victorian style hardwood conservatory will cost much more but will be worth the investment. (Think re-sale value.)

- If money is no object, there are exquisite designs available, with underfloor heating, automatic roof vents and sun blinds.

- You may need planning permission, particularly in conservation areas or if your house is listed. Always ask the local council planning department.

- If the conservatory is at the back of the house with a glass or translucent roof and is not more than 70 cubic metres you shouldn't need planning permission.

- Conservatories should be built on proper foundations, solid enough to prevent damp and drainage problems.

- The National Conservatory Advisory Council (NCAC) has a register of vetted companies whose installations and accounts it has checked. Steer clear of the cowboys.

- The NCAC will give you independent advice on style, dimensions and whether you need planning permission or not.

A good conservatory is definitely worth the investment and could add twice what you paid for it to the value of your house. Whether it be very humble or very grand make sure the proportions are correct. A conservatory like this would be relatively inexpensive if it was bought from a DIY superstore and self-built.

An octagonal-style conservatory

However, a bespoke conservatory like this would be the top end of the market.

An orangery-style conservatory

The Georgians invented the orangery, the predecessor to the conservatory, which the Victorians built adjoining the house as a sort of morning room. An ex-boyfriend of mine lived in a beautiful Queen Anne house that was in dire need of some attention and restoration, but it had an exquisite orangery that he loved. He lived in only four rooms of his enormous mansion, which was freezing and threadbare, but every weekend I would dutifully traipse over there – mad fool that I was – and sit in his beloved orangery in two overcoats and two pairs of gloves. It had missing panes of glass and a leaky roof. It was all rather melancholy really.

Transforming the Exterior

Getting the outside of your house absolutely right is essential if you want to maximise your investment potential. In other words, if you are going to sell, look seriously at the exterior. Will it pull the punters in? Drive-bys are becoming ever more popular and if they do not like what they see, they will not – or might not – come inside. This is what is called kerb appeal. (See Chapter 7, the section on first impressions.) However, if you get the transformation right, it could add thousands to the asking price. After two decades of an architectural style-crisis during the 1960s and 1970s, builders, developers and architects have realised that a building that is aesthetically pleasing is going to be far more successful than one that is not. That goes for everything from supermarkets to semi-detacheds.

I received a letter from a couple who own an L-shaped brick-faced bungalow, which was built in 1972. It said, 'What would you suggest we do to enhance the exterior of our bungalow? It's present appearance is rather dull.' So I went to see them to have a look at the problem for myself.

In one year they have added enormous value to the house due to the various improvements they have already made to it. They put in a fabulous kitchen, new bathrooms and ripped out a ghastly brick fireplace. The garden is lovely and lots of serious planting has been taking place in order to cheer up the frontage. But the unfortunate thing about the look of the house is the way the garage door dominates and the front door is obscured by the corner of the L-shape. I think we could enhance it even further by creating an American-style, New England look.

Firstly, I would put ship-lapped horizontal timber cladding over the brick work and paint it off-white. In fact, one gable end was already timbered. Along that side wall, I suggested they knock down a little white wall and brick pillars to create a rustic timber pergola starting at the outside corner running right through to the garden. With wisteria or evergreen clematis climbing over it this would then become a covered walk-way. Four-inch diameter rustic poles should be used as uprights.

The window height of the only facing window seemed very high so I would lower it by about 5in and change the window to a traditional six-pane casement window. Now the front door. Well, the door could stay where it is, acting as an inner door if we created a porch. I would like to see a conventional, panelled door as the new front door, painted a very dark blue and with beautiful, brass door furniture. The garage door would then have to be painted off-white to bring it in line with the timber cladding and, because it too has horizontal lines, it should almost disappear.

However, when I suggested that we move the garage altogether, they jumped at the idea and we quickly found a new location for it to the side of the house, with access straight off the road. This would enable them to use the existing garage as a much needed dining room, as they love to entertain.

This was a much better idea because with that garage door out of the way they can create a really lovely L-shaped fascia to the house. With more timber cladding on the newly created wall and matching six-pane casement windows it would give it a perfect symmetry. I would be tempted to grow something up it like honeysuckle or yellow climbing roses, and have lots of pots full of colourful flowers. It could look really charming and for minimum outlay have maximum impact. In April 2000 I estimated it would cost them in the region of £2,400 to do this work, adding at least £12,000 to the overall value of the property.

A gravel drive is always more attractive than a tarmac one and ivy can always be used to great effect to hide a horrid wall. Pebble dash has a huge 'naff' factor so a rough sand and cement render can be used over it and then painted. If your house has a 1960s tile-hung top half, try painting it all white, including the tiles, and adding shutters to all the windows in a mid-blue. It will give it a New England look and set you apart from the others in the street.

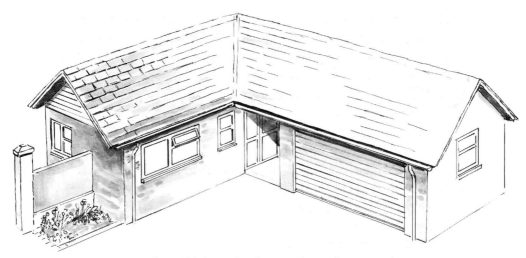

Before: *This bungalow has a rather ordinary exterior, where the garage door dominates, which does not enhance its saleability factor.*

After: *Timber cladding gives the bungalow a fresh 'New England' feel. The garage has been converted into a dining-room and the use of plants gives added interest. The new door and windows add charm.*

CHECK LIST ••

Check list for improving the exterior:

- Windows can be changed to improve appearance.
- Cover pebble dash with render.
- Rendered houses will improve with a new coat of paint.
- Shutters can radically change a look.
- Use ivy or wisteria to climb up any unattractive walls.
- Use pots and tubs to break up the front of your house and to add colour.
- Change the front door. A panelled door (in dark blue) will look better than a modern semi-glazed door.
- Cut down trees (with permission) that may be blocking out light.
- See Chapter 7, How to Sell Your House in One Week.

Getting Planning Permission

You will need planning permission if you are remodelling or developing your home and if you are considering building your own home from scratch. You would think that this goes without saying but you'd be amazed how many people assume that they are exempt. As we have seen, small extensions and conservatories are usually exempt if they are less than 23sq m and swimming pools are exempt as long as they are more than 5m from any listed building or party wall. (See page 222, Should I Have a Swimming Pool?)

So, in order to obtain planning permission you will need to:

- contact your local district council or town council planning department and ask them to send you a Planning Permission Application form;

- if your property is listed, you will need a Listed Building/ Conservation Area Consent Application form;

- you will need a full description of the proposed works;

- fill in the form(s) and submit them with the required documents (scale drawings, layout plans, etc.) and fee to the planning department;

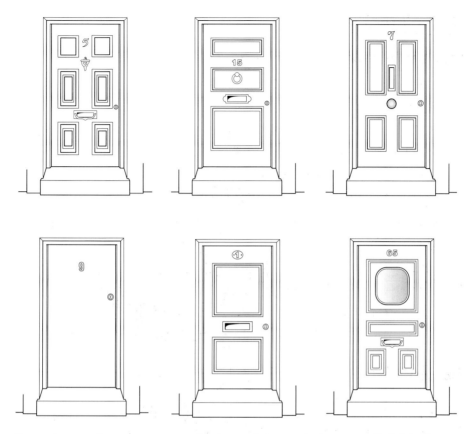

Remember your front door can completely transform your house. A panelled door (in dark blue) will look better than a modern door. Here are a few styles of door – top left is a lot more interesting than bottom left.

- if you are using an architect, he can handle the application process for you and meet the planning department first, to explain and pacify;

- don't forget you will also require Building Regulation Approval.

How long will it take?

How long is a piece of string? In other words, it depends on all sorts of things and each application will have its own set of problems. A new build can take up to 3 months for permission to be granted, whereas an alteration or extension can sometimes be passed in 3 to 6 weeks. However, this is a conservative estimate, as it has been known to take *much* longer. Be patient.

Dealing with Builders

Fact: One in ten people have suffered emotional stress as a result of problems caused by cowboy builders or tradespeople.

Good builders are hard to find, particularly if you are a female. The *Yellow Pages* has more cowboys in it than a John Wayne movie, so obviously a personal recommendation is preferable. Even then, one should always get at least three estimates for the work involved. They usually turn up after 6 p.m. straight from another job and should be clean, presentable, affable and professional. In my book, a scruffy first impression means shoddy workmanship. If they go 'Yeah, yeah, right' during your briefing and don't write anything down, it means they make the whole thing up when they get home, including your estimate. The builder should, ideally, make copious notes while you walk him through the job, ask intelligent questions and show an inordinate amount of interest in your property. (I once fell for a builder who said he'd never seen such beautiful cornicing in a Victorian house!)

Instinct often plays a huge part in choosing a builder. If you like him and he presents you with a professional looking quote and has a van with lots-of-writing-on-it, then he's your man. Don't go for the cheapest estimate or the chap who can start first. Sometimes the dearest quote is the most honest because he has taken everything into account, and if he can't start for 7 weeks, it's because he's in demand. Get him to write a detailed quote that you both agree on and sign. If you suddenly decide to move a doorway you'll know why you're being charged extra.

If he's running the job for you, he will employ plumbers, electricians, carpenters and plasterers and this should all be included in the price. If it is a big job agree to retain 5 per cent of the final cost for 'snaggings', which should be payable after 4 to 6 weeks. If you find anything wrong, it's amazing how quickly they come round to fix it!

However, you might want to bring in your own decorators at the end and, if you're installing a sophisticated kitchen, that definitely requires the experts. Don't be bludgeoned into believing that your builder can do everything, as I have been. They can't. A good decorator isn't a plumber and a good plasterer isn't an electrician. Check out references as you would for any employee and don't for heaven's sake pay by the hour, no matter how small the job. I once paid a bitter price for letting a carpenter charge me by the hour and when I realised how long it took him to unload his tools, unfold his chair and unscrew his thermos flask, I nearly unhinged his work-mate.

> **A**n 'estimate' is a rough assessment of the situation as to how much the job might cost. A 'quote' should detail exactly the work involved and give you a breakdown of labour, work to be undertaken and materials.

CHECK LIST

Check list for choosing a builder:

- Get a personal recommendation.
- Make sure he's good at what you want done (i.e. a great plasterer can't fit a bathroom).
- If you can't get someone recommended, use a well-known company rather than someone out of the *Yellow Pages*.
- He should be smart, have a van, ask questions and write everything down.
- Be specific about the work to be carried out. Clarity will avoid those grey areas.
- Set your budget.
- Get three quotes. (As detailed as possible.)
- Check their references.
- Don't go for the cheapest quote.
- Ask if he will be subcontracting. Get names and references if he is.
- A builder who is registered for VAT is more likely to be above board.
- Avoid paying cash because it means you have no comeback.
- Ask how long the job will take. (Ho, ho.)
- Do not pay cash up front.
- For large jobs you should have a contract and *always* get planning permission.
- Electricians should be certified by the Institute of Electrical Engineers – this should be obvious from the letterhead. Central heating plumbers should be registered with CORGI.

TIPS ··

Plan ahead

You will never find an excellent builder the week before you want work to commence, as the best ones are all booked up for months. The only way to get the good guys is to book them provisionally as soon as you have put in an offer on your property. When you have *exchanged* contracts you can then make a firm booking because you will know your *completion date*. By the way, most sellers don't mind you traipsing around their property with builders, after exchange of contracts, because they will have become emotionally detached from it by then.

One in five homeowners has been a victim of cowboy builders. I don't want you to be one of them. Always check their references.

When hiring a builder they should be a member of the Federation of Master Builders or on the National Register of Warranted Builders (NRWB). This organisation offers the client a 2-year insurance plan to cover defective work-manship and materials of all registered builders and ancillary tradesmen, i.e. plumbers and carpenters.

Customers pay a 1 per cent premium on the total cost of the job, i.e. £50 on a £5,000 contract, which strikes me as excellent value for peace of mind. This cover remains valid even if the builder goes bankrupt or if a sole proprietor has died.

Of course not all builders are on the NRWB. He *must* be insured, and you must get a detailed estimate from him to ensure he covers all aspects of your requirements including electrics, plumbing, heating, glazing etc. in his quota-tion. Once accepted, this should be signed and agreed by you both or a formal contract could be drawn up. On larger jobs this is called a JCT contract, which is a proper legal document. If you keep changing your mind about the job this will obviously affect the charges. However, if the builder has not made thorough investigations and discovers unforeseen problems along the way, which are going to cost you more, this is his error and you can break the contract. You can either call in an independent expert or surveyor to give you their advice and alternative estimate, or go ahead with the builder *in situ*.

The NRWB offers excellent protection but if your builder doesn't have insur-ance it can all go horribly wrong. The small claims court only deals with claims up to £3,000 but they are seldom worth pursuing as you still have to pay your solicitor's fees, which can be fairly hefty. So, basically, **get a contract and check they are insured**.

A friend of mine in Esher foolishly gave her builder 50 per cent of his money up front, so that he could buy materials. She needed new roof joists, so he came in, removed the roof, tacked down a bit of polythene and then disappeared, never to be seen again. Unfortunately that was the night before the big storm of 1987.

Here's how to tell the difference between the good guys and the bad guys.

Good guys

1. He'll try to work to the agreed specification and timings that you both set.

2. He's more than happy for you to go and look at the other work that he's completed and check references. In fact, he encourages you.

3. He talks to you in plain English, explaining complex building terms so you understand.

4. He knows when to recommend a specialist, rather than trying to do the work himself.

5. If the job requires more than one builder, he'll supply qualified tradespeople to work on the job.

6. He'll provide you with a detailed invoice, which includes VAT, because he knows it's illegal not to pay VAT.

7. He's more than happy to provide you with a signed written agreement.

8. He uses dust sheets, never smokes inside your property without your permission and will always try to leave it the way he found it.

9. He'll update you on the progress of the job and inform you of any problems and additional costs along the way.

10. He's always contactable and returns your calls promptly.

Bad guys

1. He'd rather work to a verbal agreement, which can be difficult to enforce.

2. He looks worried when you mention that you'd like to check on some previous work and isn't too forthcoming with the references.

3. He bombards you with technical jargon, in the hope that you'll have no idea what he's talking about.

4. He claims to be an expert at everything and his favourite line is 'Yep, we can do all of that. No worries.'

5. His idea of a qualified tradesman is the one who'll do the job for the least money.

6. He's more than happy to accept cash – in fact he might encourage it to help him avoid paying VAT.

7. He's terrified of paperwork.

8. He'll leave a mess when he's finished and won't think twice about lighting up a cigarette while painting your living room.

9. He'll surprise you with extra costs and problems at the end of the job but keeps quiet along the way.

10. He's difficult to get hold of and never returns your calls.

Some builders use a verbal shorthand to each other so it is wise to know what on earth they are talking about. Always ask if you are unsure about anything. Agreeing to an RSJ without knowing what it is could be an expensive surprise.

A Builder's Glossary (Understanding the jargon)	
RSJ	Rolled steel joist. A steel girder to support the ceiling.
DPC	Damp proof course.
MDF	Medium density fibreboard.
T&G	Tongue and groove timber.
B&B	Bead and butt timber.
PAR	Planed all round (timber).
Architrave	A door or window surround.
Screed	A sand and cement finish to concrete floors.
Skim	A thin layer of plaster as a finishing coat.
Retention	The money you hold back to deal with snaggings.

Snagging	Fixing all those little things at the end of the job.
Sub-contract	If your builder employs another builder to do part of the work.
Jammy Dodgers	Biscuits that you *must* supply with cups of tea to keep your builder happy. Hob Nobs are a good substitute!
Elbow	An L-shaped joint usually used in plumbing.
Hot work	Anything using a naked flame.
Stud partitioning	Timber-framed partition walls.
A Yorkshire	A pre-soldered joint to join two bits of copper piping.

Do You Need an Architect?

There is no law that says you must use an architect, and if the job is fairly small and straightforward, your builder can probably work from your own designs, measurements and diagrams. A good level of communication is essential though.

However, there are many instances when I recommend you use an architect, and they are:

- if you need a planning application for an extension;

- if your property is a listed building and you are planning major reconstruction;

- if you are finding it difficult to get planning consent;

- if you are building your own home.

An architect is fairly easy to find. The best way is by personal recommendation, or if you see something you like, you could ask who designed it. I walked into someone's garden once when I saw a fabulous stone garage being built. When I discovered the architect's name I asked him to design a small job for me.

Alternatively, you could call the Client Advisory Service of RIBA (Royal Institute of British Architects) and specify what sort of architect you need – is it a barn conversion, a Victorian extension or a glass tower you are after? – and they will put you in touch with the right local architect. Don't forget to mention your budget, as some of these guys are *very* expensive.

If you are restoring or extending a very old or listed building you could call the appropriate organisation for help. The Victorian Society, The Georgian Group, etc., etc. all have lists of architects who specialise in their field. (See Useful Addresses.)

CHECK LIST ···

Check list for appointing an architect:

- Try to interview more than one architect so that you can get a feel for who will be best able to design the sort of thing you want.
- Ask to see their portfolio of previous work.
- Ask about their fees and whether they can do the work within your budget.
- Ask for references and check them.
- Will he be project manager on the job, overseeing the project from start to finish, or will he be handing it over once construction begins?
- Ask for details of exactly what service he will be providing for his fee.

The architect's fees will vary from job to job but there is normally a fixed fee for a planning application. Other than that it is usually based on a sliding scale, that being a percentage of the contract sum (the entire budget to the builder). For example, on smaller jobs it may be 12 to 15 per cent and on larger jobs it could be less than 10 per cent. On a new build it could be as low as 6 to 8 per cent.

The architect will be happy to provide plans that your builder can work from and will normally charge a flat rate for that.

> **W**e didn't employ an architect or have a project manager when we restored our house in Gloucestershire as there was no major construction work involved. My husband basically ran the job and told everybody what to do. I must confess though, that answering questions and making decisions quickly (we lived on site) became immensely tiring and stressful as we often had nine chaps here needing instructions. There were stone-masons, joiners, a master carpenter, electricians, plumbers, decorators and a labourer. It is exhausting, so if you build your own home I would advise you to employ a project manager.

Do Tennis Courts Add Value?

According to most of the agents I spoke to, a tennis court *will* add value to a large family house with sufficient gardens for it to be discreet. It mustn't encroach on the garden or be visible from the house. If you have the land, it will usually be a big selling point.

There are so many different uses for a court nowadays. Our son uses ours for roller-blading, basketball, scooting and, of course, tennis. It was definitely a bonus when we moved here and we all love it now. Unlike a swimming pool (see overleaf) they are easy to maintain. We sweep it regularly and use a moss spray and weed killer twice a year to keep the moss at bay.

The cost

Prices will vary according to the size and finish that you want. It could be tarmac, artificial grass, clay or grey/green grit, which has a much looser surface. If you're very posh, you could have grass. Get three quotes, which include the fencing, the nets, posts and white lines. It takes approximately 3 weeks to prepare and level the land and install the court.

The size

The Lawn Tennis Association recommended specification is 114ft by 56ft but if that's a bit of a squeeze in your garden it can be reduced to 110ft by 50ft. Now, however, there is something called compact tennis that was developed in Australia, which is authentic tennis played on a smaller court with smaller racquets, different balls and a lower net. The rules are exactly the same – this is *not* short tennis – but the compact court only measures 56ft by 28ft. Sounds quite fun to me.

I fancy turning my rather boring grey tarmac court into an emerald one, which you can do with a porous spray paint. Have an expert do it for you. Whether it will inspire my junior champion has yet to be seen.

> **I** heard about a big house near Guildford that went on to the market after the owner had flattened a piece of land, mowed the grass to perfection, painted some sharp white lines and then just looked at it. Clever chap made a killing. So, will tennis courts add value? Definitely.

Should I Have a Swimming Pool?

If you have the space and wherewithal to install a swimming pool, terrific. But I'm afraid it is a fact that an outdoor pool in the UK, even a heated one, **will not add any value to your property** whatsoever. They are expensive to install and expensive to maintain, and you will never get that money back.

But if you have children and friends who love to swim, then I can't think of a nicer, more sociable reason to spend your money. Many sunny afternoons have been spent around our friend's pool here, with the children happily splashing away for hours on end. If the pool is heated, it *will* get used a great deal, believe me, even in a dodgy summer.

However, if you are investing in a seriously grand house and fancy putting in an indoor pool, with sauna and jacuzzi, then that would obviously make a difference to the overall value of the house. I saw a sympathetically restored Georgian house in Somerset that had a pool complex in the orangery, which was very special. It's all a question of scale and price. A multi-million pound house almost demands a pool whereas a suburban semi does not.

Think carefully before installing a pool. It is appropriate with your property? Can it be discreetly hidden from the house? Where will the pump house be located? Will it be used enough?

> **T**he same amount of money spent on a conservatory could add double to the value of your home.

TIPS

Some swimming pool tips:

- Fully tiled pools are more expensive than rubber-liner pools and are costly to maintain.
- Most swimming pool companies recommend a rubber liner for an outdoor pool.
- The rubber liner will need to be replaced every 10 to 15 years.
- Tiled pools are fine in warmer climates or indoors.
- The annual maintenance costs are high due to heating, chemicals, filters, parts, electricity, gas and water charges.
- A swimming pool should never be drained down.

Estate agents will tell you that a house with a pool will sometimes put the purchaser off. This is particularly so if the purchaser has very young children or animals. They also fear the running costs.

You will need planning permission for your pool if:

- it is an indoor pool;

- it lies within the curtilage of a listed building or an area of outstanding natural beauty (AONB);

- any part of it is in front of the house and closer than 20m to the nearest road;

- any part of it is within 5m of the house or a party wall;

- if your pool covers more than 50 per cent of your garden.

Four instances when a pool is a good idea:
1. If it can be indoors as an integral part of a large house.
2. If you are building a holiday home complex.
3. If you are developing a hotel.
4. If you are investing in a foreign holiday home.

In all other circumstances, in the long run, your money is better invested elsewhere in the property. Let someone else have the hassle! Join a club. Go to a hotel. Bribe a friend. Make friends with that nice family down the road. Go on holiday. All these options are cheaper than building a swimming pool yourself.

Don't Forget the Garden

Another way to maximise the potential of your property is to enhance the garden. One agent I spoke to said, 'There is no point having a wonderful house sitting in a shabby, unkempt garden. Most people attach enormous importance to how the garden has been maintained.'

I'm not suggesting that you get in the landscape designers and remodel your garden entirely, although that would probably look wonderful, but to think about how best to present your garden. It will certainly add to the appeal of your property

Before: *A neglected garden will seem like an overwhelming undertaking to a new buyer.*

if there is a nice aspect across the garden from your sitting room. If it is all neat and tidy it will make it much more sellable. (See Chapter 7, the section on kerb appeal.)

If you have children and the garden has become one enormous playground covered in bald patches, *please* don't leave it like that if you are thinking of selling. A small investment in some new turf, a few shrubs, a repaired fence and a tidy up could add thousands to the price.

If you are a keen gardener and have lovingly tended your garden for years, the estate agent should draw attention to it in the details as a major selling point. I know of one lady who bought a property based on the beauty of the garden alone, without even stepping inside the house!

CHECK LIST ●

Garden check list:

- If you live in a city, a garden is not an expectation but a bonus. If you have a 25ft garden you are considered lucky. Make the most of it.

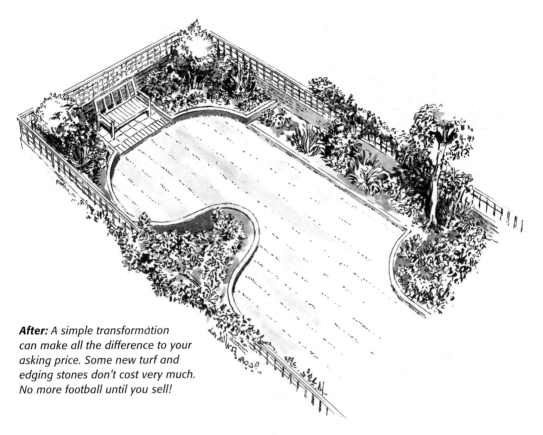

After: A simple transformation can make all the difference to your asking price. Some new turf and edging stones don't cost very much. No more football until you sell!

- If you are buying a flat, then a garden will obviously add value to the property. Garden flats are immensely popular, particularly if you have spent an extra bit on security. Use the garden as an added room to add value to the property. For example, in summer it becomes the dining room.

- If your garden is on the roof, then make it as lavish and well stocked as possible. You will add value only by making it look like an oasis of calm and not like an old roof with a couple of manky Christmas trees on it!

- If you buy a brand new home, planting out mature trees and hedging will instantly add value to your house as it will set it apart from the rest. But remember, first-time buyers like gardens that are easy to maintain.

- A garden with a wonderful view will definitely add to the value.

- The way we view the landscape is an integral part of buying a home.

Two friends of mine live in a tiny terraced house in South London with a really long, skinny garden. They have created a water feature, sitting areas, secret rooms and a canopied area with twinkling lights in their 'enchanted garden'. Without doubt they have added enormously to the value of their, otherwise quite ordinary, house.

Whether you have an enormous garden or a teeny-weeny patio, it is not to be ignored.

Dos and Don'ts of gardens

- **Do** maintain it.

- **Do** repair fences or stones walls.

- **Do** tidy up.

- **Do** employ someone for a few hours prior to selling, if you can't do it.

- **Do** invest in a few tubs and pots with bright flowers because you can take them with you when you move.

- **Do** think of it as an extra room.

- **Don't** neglect it.

- **Don't** leave things for the new owner to fix up.

- **Don't** leave it looking a mess.

- **Don't** think it doesn't matter.

- **Don't** leave the paths covered in weeds and cracks.

chapter thirteen

Transforming your kitchen

Should You Bother?

Ah, the kitchen. Of course you should bother! This is the most important room in the house and can make or break a sale. Even if you're not thinking of moving for a while, it is imperative to get the kitchen right because of the expense involved.

The kitchen has changed and evolved over the years from a place of drudgery to a multi-functional room used by all the family, and is very much the focal point of a house. If you have the space, a kitchen should have a wonderful ambience of cosiness where all is right with the world. Nowadays it is the room where most entertaining takes place, with the death knell being sounded for the dining room. So it has become a social environment and not just a practical place for cooking and washing up.

Therefore, as much thought needs to go into designing and decorating your kitchen as you would for the sitting room or main bedroom, if you want to maximise its potential. For example, what happens in *your* kitchen? Make a list of all the things you and the family tend to do in the kitchen. Do they (and you):

- do homework;
- play games;
- watch TV;
- read;
- use the phone;

- chat and gossip;
- do the laundry;
- cook;
- entertain friends;
- brush the dog;

- paint;
- do the washing up;
- do the ironing;
- use the computer;
- listen to music, etc., etc.

We do most of these things in our kitchen and it's utter chaos most of the time! But the list will help to focus your priorities. Are you part of a busy working family or a bachelor who eats out all the time?

Planning the Layout

Having made your list will help clarify the multiple uses of your kitchen. If you need somewhere comfy to sit, where are you going to put an easy chair? Is there room for the computer without taking away valuable work surface? Does the ironing *have* to be done in the kitchen or could you do it somewhere else? Ask yourself all these questions and the kitchen will begin to take shape.

If you are having a kitchen built for you by a specialist, show them your list and tell them about your various requirements. Be very specific because they will try to sell you extra units that you may not need when, in fact, you need the space for the dog's basket or whatever.

If you are doing it yourself, then terrific, because you will save yourself a fortune and, assuming you create something wonderful, will make an even bigger profit when it is time to sell.

Decide on your style of kitchen to create a theme. Will it be all gleaming stainless steel or country style? Will it be painted shabby-chic or immaculately smooth? Will it be natural wood or painted wood? Will it be fitted or free-standing? Will it be American chic or Arts and Crafts? Will it be Simple Farmhouse or Gothic Castle?

Obviously the choice is enormous these days but it would be wise to choose a kitchen in keeping with the age and style of your property. By that I don't mean a 1950s house should have a 1950s kitchen! Heaven forbid. Just that a modern glass and steel kitchen would look odd in a fully timbered house and a farmhouse kitchen would look odd in an urban penthouse. If you're unsure, go for simplicity. Whatever the size of the kitchen, here are some things to remember when planning the layout:

- Make a list of all the things you hate about your present kitchen.

- A kitchen should be based on a work triangle that links the cooker, the sink and the fridge. This is most important as it will increase efficiency. Don't have them too far apart. A couple of strides is ideal.

- The route between the cooker and the sink is the busiest so it needs to be free of traffic. If your kitchen is a thoroughfare put them on the same side.

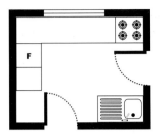

Bad layout: *The cooker is in the corner behind the door, the fridge/freezer (F) is in the middle of the work surfaces and is too far away. The sink is on the other side of the kitchen in a thoroughfare between the doors.*

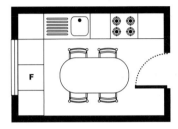

Good layout *for a small kitchen.*

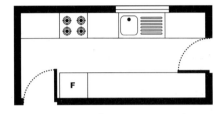

Good layout *for a galley kitchen.*

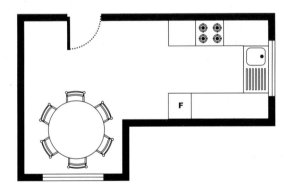

Good layout *for a large kitchen.*

- A tall appliance such as a fridge-freezer should be at the end of a run of work-top, not in the middle.

- A breakfast bar and kitchen table can double as a worktop.

- If you are having a dishwasher, put it close to the crockery cupboard to save travelling.

How to **Make Money** from **Your Property**

- Don't squeeze your cooker/hob into a corner as you will need space on either side.

- Try to have all your food stuffs and perishables in one area rather than in lots of cupboards. (If you have space for a larder this will make life much easier.)

- If you are very tall you don't have to have units at a standard height. A comfortable height for worktops is 5 cm lower than your flexed elbows!

- A comfortable height for the bottom of the sink is 25 cm lower.

- Leave space for open shelving or plate racks so that utensils or accessories can be seen and easily reached. Not everything has to be behind doors.

- Storage ideas come in many forms with endless possibilities. If space is at a premium ask about corner carousels, hanging racks, wall grids and wall-mounted TVs.

- If you have a central island it could be on wheels to change location when required.

The Budget and the Value

Whatever the size of the kitchen – and believe me even a tiny one shouldn't be overlooked – if there is room for improvement it will be money well invested. It will most definitely add value to your property in direct proportion to what you spend on it and the size of the property. If you live in a small flat and spend an astronomical amount on the kitchen, then the chances are that you might not see it reflected in the sale price.

But you'd be amazed what you can do on a budget (see Transforming your Kitchen for Less than £300, page 233) with just a lick of paint and a little ingenuity. There are plenty of DIY stores and kitchen warehouses selling ends-of-lines, and off-cuts of vinyl flooring are available at most carpet stores.

Kitchens can cost anything from a few hundred pounds to £60,000, if you are buying the whole concept. I would suggest that at the lower end of the scale you could more than double what you spend in the overall value of the property, whereas at the higher end of the scale you will just about get your money back.

For example:

You spend £500 on kitchen   £1,500 return
You spend £10,000 on kitchen   £20,000 return
You spend £40,000 on kitchen   £40,000 return

Now obviously, you wouldn't get very far on £500 if you were doing a vast country kitchen, that sort of budget is more for a flat, but it's all about scale and proportion. It depends what you want. You may not need to gut it completely. Instead, try some minor alterations.

> **R**emember, there is a big difference between an old kitchen and a kitchen that is out of date or simply old-fashioned.

Choosing the Décor

There is an enormous trend for traditional looking kitchens these days. They may be 'modern' in the sense that they are new and have all the latest conveniences, such as smoothly gliding drawers, but they are not modern in the contemporary sense.

When purchasing a house most people want to see a kitchen that is clean, bright, modern and practical. If your kitchen is out of date but the layout is OK, you could try changing the worktops, changing the door fronts from one of the many companies that supply just kitchen unit fronts and applying a fresh, bright colour to the walls.

In one of the kitchens I redid for a rental investment I simply:

- changed the worktop from brown to snowy white, which I got from a DIY superstore;

- installed a gas hob and separate oven instead of the old-fashioned cooker;

- changed the sink and taps;

- put up bottle-green tiles for a splashback;

- painted the walls white;

How to **Make Money** from **Your Property**

- changed the flooring from brown lino to cream vinyl;

- put up spotlights instead of the single bulb.

Luckily the cupboard fronts were fine so we just gave them a scrub. But the flooring and the white worktop made a huge difference and, with the green tiles, it looked quite glamorous! It seemed very light and spacious too, which is the key to a good kitchen.

Lighting is very important in a kitchen to lighten all the corners and under eye-level units. (See Chapter 15, the section on lighting.) Try to avoid strip-lights as they give off such a harsh, blue light.

The ambience is very important in the kitchen, especially if you are eating in there. Put spots or downlighters on a dimmer switch for cosy tête-à-têtes and use lamps. They don't need to be excluded from the kitchen! (We use candles at night.)

Don't be shy of **colour** in the kitchen. Obviously don't go too mad otherwise you'll be limiting the appeal – the idea is to be attractive to the broadest market – but clotted creams, sunflower yellows, Shaker blues, mint greens and pale lilacs can all look wonderful.

The right **flooring** can make a huge difference too. (See Chapter 15, section on flooring.) Pale wood laminate is all the rage but terracotta tiles may look more appropriate in your home. Unfussy, uncluttered flooring is important.

Here is a choice of materials that could be used in your kitchen:

- moulded resins give a smooth, linear effect with no joins;

- tiles, granites, limestone, marble;

- a variety of woods and MDF;

- mosaics;

- glass and mirror;

- stainless steel, copper, brass, chrome;

- wrought iron, aluminium, zinc;

- wicker;

- terracotta, York stone, reconstituted stone;

- coir and seagrass;

- vinyl or wood laminate.

If the layout is completely wrong, the only solution is to start again. The units could be saved and reused but the chances are that the floor will have to come up anyway if you are changing the shape of the kitchen. Plumbing may have to be moved if you are moving the sink and dishwasher, etc., and don't forget to have lots of plug sockets at worktop height.

Small is Beautiful

If your kitchen is tinier than a rabbit's hutch, it doesn't matter! It should look just as carefully thought out and can be very charming. There are under-size fridges available, baby freezers, tiny cookers and small dishwashers (though this is a luxury in a tiny kitchen). Put everything on open shelving such as stainless steel racks rather than having units with doors. If it is in a cupboard, use fold-back double doors so that you are not hidden from view if you have company and get the urge to stir your risotto!

In a tiny kitchen you can afford to put in black granite worktops for an extra wow factor. Black and cream look gorgeous together and will make the tiniest space seem stylish. Put an enormous clock on the facing wall for an added twist.

> **D**ark units were very 1970s, but they are still being sold. Please resist! Buy white or cream or wooden units that you can paint. Keep the room as light as possible. Simplicity is the key. Use quirky handles to cheer up plain cupboards.

Transforming your Kitchen for Less Than £300

I did a make-over on television last year that proved you don't have to spend very much in order to achieve the maximum effect. My brief was this: you have £300 to transform a rather dreary kitchen in a nice flat in South London, that is going on the market.

I love a challenge and I could see immediately where the problem lay. The units were old fashioned and needed a lift; the vinyl flooring was too dark; the window had a dark hessian blind keeping out the light; the splashback was a strange plastic cladding made to look like brick.

There was a place to seat four at a pine table and the basic layout was fine, so with a bit of help from my decorator this is what we did in two days:

- The units had a dark wood trim, so we undercoated the whole thing and then applied a soft apple green to the unit fronts and off-white to the trim.

- All the shelves, doors and woodwork were painted off-white.

- The flooring was replaced with a pale, creamy, marble-effect vinyl.

- The hessian blind and pelmet were taken down and the window was painted off-white. The glass was cleaned.

- The plastic cladding was removed and instead of tiles I used tongue-and-groove timber panelling as a splash-back. This was painted off-white.

- The walls then had two coats of pale lilac emulsion.

- The pine table was heavily varnished and a bit dated so I found a pale green checked tablecloth to put over it.

Total cost: £247.00

So I was well under my budget (this was April 2000), and the lilac and pale green looked fresh and contemporary. We had banished the wood trim, the cladding and the flooring for a lighter, more modern look. All the materials can be found in your local DIY store and some carpet warehouses have vinyl off-cuts available at discount prices. (Always test paint colours together to make sure they work well.)

The estate agent returned to see the flat and agreed that the newly transformed kitchen would not only appeal to a wider market but would add about £3,000 to the asking price. We all felt very smug!

Making It Work for You

It is essential that the kitchen layout is designed to make life easy for you. Not just the magic triangle but where you put everything is important as well. Prioritise your utensils and keep the busiest ones close to hand. A girlfriend of mine has one drawer for everything from cutlery to serving spoons and from cheese grater to sieves. As a result she can never find anything and spends 5 minutes rummaging around looking for a teaspoon. So, here are some tips:

TIPS ....

- Keep cutlery separate and use a drawer divider.

- Hang up the utensils and kitchen knives you use the most frequently.

- Put other utensils within each reach. Wooden spoons could go in a jar.

- Hang up colander, sieve, etc. for easy access.

- Use storage jars for things in packets like pasta, muesli, dried pulses. They are easier to use and attractive, too.

- Don't put the kettle in the corner where it is difficult to reach.

- Put up hooks for tea towels, oven gloves, etc. to save clutter.

- Categorise items and store together, e.g. all saucepans in one area, Tupperware together, casserole dishes together, baking tins together.

- Keep all crockery together to save travelling.

- Get drawers that glide smoothly.

- Chuck out things you don't use.

- Keep coffee, tea, sugar and kettle close to each other.

- Put all your 'foodie' bits in one area.

These are just a few tips to make your kitchen more efficient and to save you time in the long run. We all spend an enormous amount of time in the kitchen, so it might as well work properly. Another friend of mind has her fridge in the utility room, which is madness and makes her walk miles every day. Every time she wants the milk she has to go out of the kitchen, across a corridor and into the utility room, which must add unnecessary time to everything she does.

Home improvements are all very well but I'm afraid DIY can turn out to be a disaster. An estate agent told me that 'Sometimes we take on a property where clearly the owner has tried to change things with disastrous results. It would be wiser to employ someone to do it properly if you want to increase the value of your property.'

Anything to do with plumbing, electricity or gas should be handled by a qualified professional. If you enjoy carpentry or tiling, that's fine, but ask yourself how difficult the job is. Most people can apply paint to a wall but anything more difficult will involve reading, researching, learning and practising in order to get it right. Don't forget, if you are hiring any machinery (such as sanding equipment) to include the cost in your calculations.

If you are updating your kitchen with a view to selling, it would be a very wise decision indeed. The purchaser doesn't want to walk in and immediately start totting up the expense of changing everything. So make it easy for them. Do it *now* and you will reap the benefits. A few hundred pounds could add thousands to your asking price.

chapter fourteen

Bathrooms – getting it right

Do They Add Value?

The first time I realised that a bathroom could look anything other that utilitarian, I was 14 years old and on a yacht belonging to that late, great movie mogul, Sam Spiegal. I had just completed a movie for him when he invited the entire cast to join him on his magnificent boat, which was moored in the Med.

His bathroom had about an acre of black marble, gleaming etched glass and eight Toulouse Lautrec drawings on the walls! It was truly magnificent. A bit like something out of a Cary Grant movie.

From that moment on bathrooms were never the same again and I have always tried to recreate that glamorous movie look. Our bathroom at home is the closest I have got to achieving it, but without the Toulouse Lautrecs! (Sadly.)

Like kitchens, bathrooms are an incredibly important feature in any property. Whether buying or renting, they can be the deciding factor that clinches the deal. Women spend an inordinate amount of time in the bathroom – approximately 25,550 hours during a lifetime – so it might as well be a nice one. And, as you know, when a couple are buying it's usually the woman who makes the final decision.

So it makes sense to add value to your property by investing in a good bathroom that will appeal to the widest section of the market. Bathrooms are not cheap and can set you back a couple of thousand pounds, including labour, so it is important to get it right. Avocado suites are a thing of the past, I'm afraid.

Don't buy from expensive bathroom showrooms or DIY superstores. Try to find a little plumbers' merchants who can order for you direct from the wholesaler. You will get far better quality. Always negotiate on the price if you are ordering lots of stuff, but don't buy your tiles there. They will be cheaper elsewhere and offer more choice.

Any Colour as Long as It's White

As a landlord, I know that good tenants require good bathrooms. The same could be said for a seller hoping to achieve the asking price. If your bathroom has the edge, it will sell easily.

White ceramic has made a big comeback and coloured suites are now a throwback to the 1970s rebellion. If you think about it, bathrooms always used to be white in the old days. The Savoy, famed for its bathrooms, had white enamel and ceramics, as did the HMS *Queen Mary*. So *white* it is.

TIPS ·

Tips for bathrooms with an edge:

- I always install a fairly classic white suite with no frilly bits or funny shapes. Avoid the very modern styles or seashell scalloped edges as they will date quickly.

- Rearrange the layout of the bathroom if the first thing you see is the loo. Discuss with your plumber the various possibilities of swapping the loo and basin or moving the bath. A lot of it will depend on where the waste-pipe will go, especially in old houses.

- Power showers are all the rage and a definite plus. Put it over the bath if you don't have room for a separate shower cubicle, which would be preferable. It will probably require its own pressure pump as the water pressure in most buildings is so appalling.

- Shower curtains can look extremely naff, so a glass screen would be better. If this isn't possible, make sure the curtain is replaced before putting your home on the market.

- Chrome fittings are advisable as some people detest gold taps or brass fittings. Gold taps are all very well but remember that the towel rails, soap dish, loo-roll holder

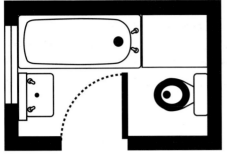

In a small bathroom try to avoid having the loo as the first thing you see when you open the door. This layout gets the most out of a small space. Keep it simple, but glamorous.

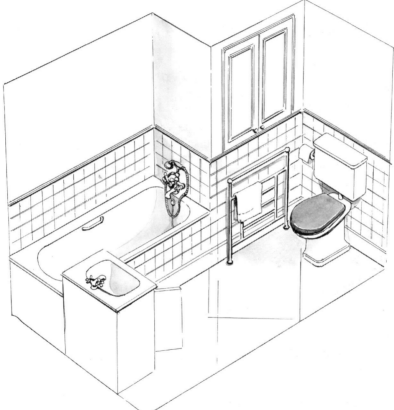

and hooks should all be in the same finish, so keep it simple. (I think white and chrome looks fabulous.)

- Always use mixer taps and have a handset on the bath *even* if there is a shower there.

- The taps should be the old-fashioned, knobbly type and not the modern round style that you can't turn off if you're all soapy.

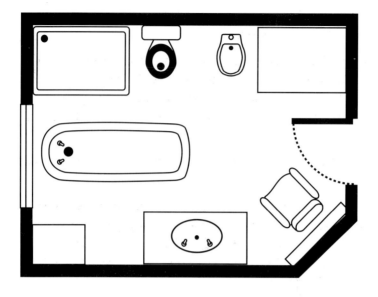

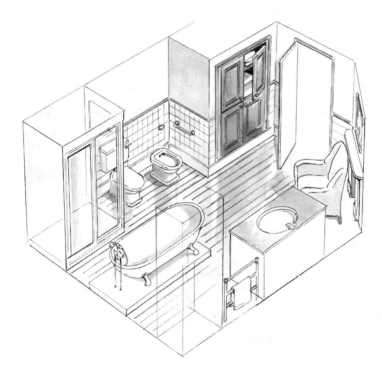

In a large bathroom you can have any number of layouts. A separate shower cubicle, free-standing bath and bidet are a great luxury if you have the space. The suite must be white!

- Gloss paint is quite funky in a bathroom, so give your bathroom two undercoats and two coats of gloss to make it fairly waterproof.

- Baths come in a variety of lengths and styles so if you haven't got the room, install a shorter one (500mm x 700mm). I always use pressed steel. Enamel baths are fabulous in old houses and if you buy one from a reclamation yard, you can get it re-enamelled. Try to avoid plastic and fibreglass baths, as steel is much better quality and not much more expensive.

- Bidets are no longer fashionable and certainly not a necessity in a bathroom, unless you have oodles of space.

- If the bathroom is tiny, I always recommend tiling the whole area up to the ceiling. This gives the illusion of space and height, and saves redecorating due to steam damage. I use bumpy white tiles with a high lustre and break it up with a rope border-tile, two-thirds up the wall that could be the same colour as your towels (e.g., navy towels and navy border looks great).

- Use colour as an accent to break up a white bathroom.

- Mirror one wall to make it seem larger.

- Put down-lighters into a bathroom rather than one central light.

- If there are no windows, good ventilation is a must to avoid condensation.

- If your bathroom is fairly spacious, treat it as a proper room. The tiled area can be contained and the rest could be sumptuously wallpapered. Have an armchair, a piece of furniture, lots of pictures.

- Storage is important, so get a carpenter to build a unit beneath the basin to house all those bits and pieces. Open shelves above the loo could hold all the towels.

- If there isn't much room for a radiator, install a vertical, ladder-style radiator, which will double as a warm towel-rail as well.

- Bathroom wall-lights have to be enclosed, but those movie-star bulbs on a strip look great for glamour.

- Women need light *in front* of their face to apply make-up, not overhead.

- Keep tiles simple. Patterns are too limiting.

- Buy large tiles instead of traditional 6in x 6in.

- When selling your home, the bathroom must be immaculate. Remove all limescale and polish up chrome.

Flooring

Bathroom flooring is a very personal choice and I happen to love carpet. There is nothing nicer than warm, soft carpet under my toes when I step out of the bath. However, some people, particularly Americans, will scream 'Yuk! Not carpet in the bathroom. How unhygienic. How gross.' Yes, I know. But as I said, it's personal.

If you like carpet too, that's fine. It should be the same colour as the bedroom if it is *en-suite*. Just make sure it's not too mouldy when you are trying to sell. Not attractive at all.

I have learnt the hard way that most tenants in rental accommodation prefer hard flooring in their bathrooms. It could be vinyl, ceramic tiles, marble, linoleum, even cork. So if you are doing up a property to let (see Chapter 9, How to Buy the Perfect Rental Investment), don't stint on the expense of good flooring because it is worth the investment.

In your own home, the choice is yours.

TIPS

- I have used ceramic floor tiles and they are easy to keep clean, but *so cold* under foot.

- Likewise marble. Of course you could go to the expense of underfloor heating, which would be very chic. It's quite easy to install if you are relaying the floor.

- Vinyl flooring should be laid by an expert but vinyl floor tiles are easy to use.

- In a small bathroom, sealed-rubber floor tiles are great for splashy kids.

- Frosted glass floor tiles look fantastic and are easy to clean.

- We have a shower-room at home where I have kept the natural flagstones and had them sealed. The shower is not enclosed, so all the water cascades on to the stones. It looks so organic and feels great. If you have stone floors it is perfectly possible to use them in a bathroom.

Showers Versus Baths

It depends whether you like standing up or lying down, I suppose! Even though we are slowly becoming a nation of showerers, I would advise you to put a bath in at least *one* bathroom (particularly the family bathroom if you have more than one) with a view to its selling potential. A flat or house without a bath at all will definitely be halving its market.

Most quality hotels have a bath and a separate shower, which is a great luxury, and all of the top developers I spoke to acknowledged the importance of having showers in their bathrooms. 'They are so much easier to use, for people in a hurry. In all our two-bathroom houses, one will be a shower and bath and the other will be just a shower-room,' said one. So there you go.

How Many Loos?

I read a very funny article the other day that suggested the number of loos one had indicated your social standing in society! Now, whether or not having three toilets will make you posh, I have no idea, but I *do* know that the number of toilets in a property can affect the price.

One estate agent told me that if a flat has an *en-suite* bathroom but no separate loo, it could be more difficult to sell than if it had a separate bathroom. 'You don't really want people traipsing through your bedroom to get to the loo,' he said. If it had a second loo it would obviously cost more to buy.

> The downstairs loo is now the epitome of inverted snobbery. If you have been pictured shaking hands with the Queen or have received a Christmas card from Tony Blair, you wouldn't dream of displaying it in the sitting room for fear of being thought pretentious. Gosh no. You just pray that everyone needs to wash their hands.
>
> One lady I know has a large photo of herself in the loo, taken from *Country Life* and underneath it says 'Lady Cecilia Twinkletoes, daughter of the Earl and Countess of Somewhere-or-other', just in case we didn't know.

All new builds tend to have one *en-suite*, one family bathroom and a downstairs loo. This seems the most sensible configuration and keeps the loo count up to a comfortable three. So if you have room to build another loo, it is obviously a good idea in today's market and will add those crucial pounds to the sale of your house.

Dos and Don'ts for Bathrooms

- **Do** make sure bathroom lights are installed by a qualified electrician.

- **Do** use a large mirror to increase space in a small bathroom.

- **Do** keep fittings simple and classic.

- **Don't** have the loo directly opposite the door.

- **Don't** carpet a rental.

- **Don't** use a fibreglass bath if you can help it.

- **Don't** use a coloured suite. Stick to white.

chapter fifteen

Basic rules and principles for decorating

I suppose it all comes down to whether you are investing in this property as a project that you wish to develop and then sell on, or to live in as your home for many years to come.

If it is the former, the basic rule-of-thumb is to keep the decorating style as uncomplicated as possible in order to appeal to the widest market. If you go madly *art deco* there will be a small number of people who will love it but you will be reducing your sale possibilities by an enormous margin. So keep it simple. The style of decor and finish should ideally reflect the period of your property and not fight against it (i.e. the architraves, windows, skirtings, door furniture, etc.), but don't spend a fortune on wallcoverings.

If, however, this is your home, you will want to inject a lot of your own personality and that of your family. There's nothing wrong with colour – I love colour – and if your teenage son insists on a purple bedroom, that's fine. Until it's time to sell. That's when you paint it cream, I'm afraid.

Here are a few tips I have picked up over the years from various experts and from sheer trial and error. Some of them are just common sense and some are brilliant, but none of them are written in stone.

Lighting

Lighting is the most important element for creating atmosphere. A single, central light can be very harsh.

TIPS ··

- Remember to sink wiring for wall lights, up-lighters and picture lights into the plaster before you start decorating.

- Down-lighters are fine in a kitchen or bathroom, but not advisable elsewhere as they can be too unflattering! Most designers I know ban overhead lighting in the living rooms.

- Spotlights are terrific for throwing light on to a feature such as bookcases, pictures or curtains.

- Spotlights and down-lighters should always be on a dimmer.

- Don't use spotlights over a basin as they create shadows on the face.

- Women like lights *in front* of the face to apply make-up, not overhead.

- Wall lights and lamps create a warmer atmosphere.

- All table lamps should be switched on from the door when entering a room. Put a low amp socket beside every 13-amp socket to do this. It saves you switching them all on individually.

- Picture lights can make an average picture look important.

- Big ceiling lanterns look great over the stairs.

- Up-lighters can be very effective behind a plant.

- Chandeliers should only be used with high ceilings.

- When dining avoid overhead lights – use lamps, wall-lights or candles.

- A mirror behind a light will double the effect.

- Bathroom lights needn't be boring – shop around.

- Use timers on some table lamps. They are good for security and welcoming when you return home on a winter's evening.

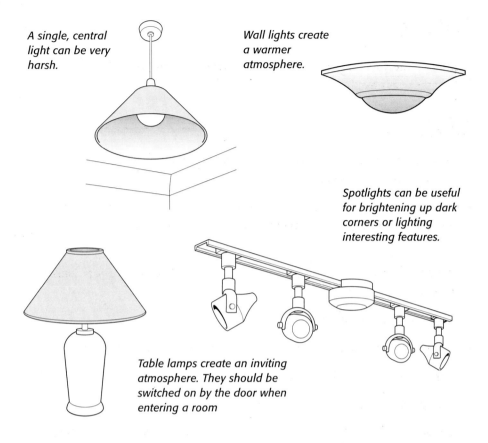

A single, central light can be very harsh.

Wall lights create a warmer atmosphere.

Spotlights can be useful for brightening up dark corners or lighting interesting features.

Table lamps create an inviting atmosphere. They should be switched on by the door when entering a room

Curtains

I really love curtains and feel that they can make or break a room. A good curtain-maker will help you decide on styles and widths, etc. I spend ages shopping for fabrics and always take little samples of wallpaper with me, to match up colours and shades. If you have painted walls, just paint a piece of paper, roughly 10in x 8in, with your wall colour and take that with you. Take snippets of fabric too if they dominate the room.

The shops will always give you a small sample to take away – take several to help you choose – but sometimes I pay for half a metre so that I can pin it up at home to help me decide. This is particularly useful if it has a large pattern. Choose your trimmings, your wallpapers and everything very carefully before you decide on your curtain fabric, because there's no going back once you've bought it. Don't make an expensive mistake.

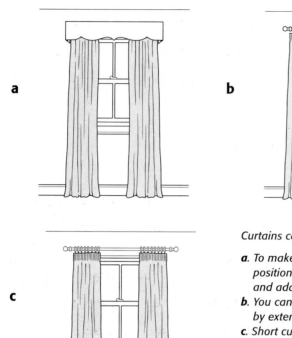

Curtains can create all sorts of illusions.

a. *To make a window seem larger position the track as high as possible and add a pelmet.*

b. *You can make a window seem wider by extending the poles.*

c. *Short curtains are informal and long curtains are more formal.*

If you live in the middle of nowhere, as I do, some fabric houses offer a postal service. You ring them up and say 'I'm looking for a coral leafy fabric with a cream background' or whatever you're after and they'll send you three or four samples. After you've decided which one you like – remember to check the pattern repeat – you can place an order and they will send it to you. Brilliant. In fact, buying fabric on the internet is becoming the way forward. You can access millions of samples from all over the world and even find discontinued lines.

TIPS

- Curtains don't have to be expensive. It is better to have generous, thickly interlined curtains of a cheaper fabric than skimpy curtains of a more expensive fabric.

- There are plenty of discount fabric shops selling ends of lines all over the UK.

- Linings improve drape and interlinings add insulation.

- To make a window look taller position the track as high as possible. Add a decorative pelmet to create the illusion of height.

- To make windows look wider, extend the track well beyond the frame on either side.

- Use a corded track for curtains that are tricky to pull.

- Trimmings go on the leading edge of curtains and fringing can look wonderful on pelmets or valances.

- 'Dress curtains' are only for show and don't actually pull. A blind will keep the light out. This is a much cheaper option for any room.

- Swags and tails look formal and only work on full-length curtains.

- Shorter or sill-length curtains are less formal and good for kitchens or cottages.

- Cheap fabrics like calico, muslin, hessian, plain cotton and lining material can make wonderful curtains.

- Thickly interlined, off-white cotton can look fabulous, particularly in a modern flat.

- Tie-backs and push-backs shouldn't be too high. Lower is more elegant.

- Net curtains are horrible. If you must have them, use voile instead.

- Live in the property for a while before splashing out on curtains.

- If your curtains are tired or dirty when you are selling your home, take them down. It is better to have no curtains at all than bad curtains.

- Make sure they don't cut out the light.

- Blinds can make a small room appear much larger.

Flooring

Flooring has become so much more sophisticated these days and we have a greater choice than ever. Walking into my local carpet showroom is a bit of an eye-opener now because he seems to sell everything *but* carpet. He has wood flooring in every shape and colour; 'Looks like the real thing Fiona. Who needs parquet?' He has glass floor tiles, fancy vinyl flooring that looks like marble, vinyl tiles, seagrass matting, wool tiles and, oh yes, out the back, some carpet.

Gone are the days, or so it seems, of wall-to-wall carpeting. Think carefully about what you want and, as ever, for the broadest appeal keep it simple and neutral. Swirly patterns are out.

Always get flooring professionally fitted if you want it to last. Vinyl flooring needs to be laid on hardboard or ideally plywood for a really smooth finish and good carpet should also be laid on hardboard before the underfelt (unless you have very even floorboards or concrete underneath.) However, vinyl tiles and carpet tiles are relatively easy to lay yourself.

If you have just moved into what will be your family home for years to come, I would advise spending a little extra on the carpet – especially the stair carpet – because cheap carpet will wear through very quickly and you'll end up spending even more money to replace it.

TIPS

- If you use wooden strip flooring, fit a layer of insulation to prevent sound transmission. Particularly if you live in a flat.

- Whether choosing wood, tiles or carpet, aim for continuity to get a seamless flow throughout the house or flat. This is easier on the eye than several different colours.

- Buy the best-quality carpet you can afford, if you intend to stay put for a while. It is false economy otherwise.

- Choose plain carpet *always* if you want to sell quickly.

- If you have good floorboards, just sand and varnish them.

- Painted floors and scattered rugs look good on a budget.

- Laminate flooring can look like the real thing. Most carpet showrooms sell it.

- Keep original stone or tiled floors, as they are an important feature.

- Bathrooms shouldn't have carpet. Particularly in a rental investment.

- Keep carpets fairly neutral.

- Choose wooden flooring whenever possible. If there are no decent floorboards, seagrass matting, or coir, looks great under rugs. Never use it in bathrooms or near the back door as it doesn't like getting wet.

Walls and Colour Schemes

Paint is my favourite product. You can do *so* much with just a coat of paint. You can transform a room, believe me. Our office at home was really dreary until I threw some terracotta paint at it and now it is a warm, friendly environment in which to work.

A lot of people put off painting a room because they think it's going to be such a hassle. Well, maybe taking down pictures and covering up furniture with sheets isn't your idea of a fun Saturday afternoon, but the results will be amazing. Get everyone involved. Once the paint is out, it will take only half a day (unless you're doing Blenheim Palace). Use those paint pads I mentioned before (available at all DIY and paint shops) for really good coverage. If you want to sell your home this is the most effective way of freshening it up. Even tired old wallpaper can be covered up.

In your own home you can be as adventurous as you like with colour. But when the time comes just don't try to sell it with navy blue walls and purple carpet!

TIPS ···

- Dark colours enclose a space but can create an atmosphere – especially in the dining room.

- Dark colours don't sell a property as quickly as pale colours.

- Use different colours to break up an open plan area.

- Less is more. Don't use too many busy wallpapers and borders.

- Use one pale colour throughout to open up a tiny space.

- *Trompe l'oeil* panels can add grandeur to a large, boring wall. (This is a specialist paint effect that will require an expert.)

- In old properties use flat, old-fashioned paint, such as the National Trust range, available from special paint suppliers.

- Use timber panelling, such as bead and butt, to give a room a more rustic feel.

- Room colours will affect your mood. Use subtle, soft colours for a serene environment. Muted shades of grey-green or grey-blue work well. Deep yellows like mustard and soft tobacco are good too.

How to **Make Money** from **Your Property**

- There are many neutral, stone colours on the market. These look good if you are nervous of colour. Use an off-white for woodwork.

- Brilliant white is too blue for old properties. Use an ivory or cameo white on wood-work.

- Use eggshell on old doors and windows, not gloss. Gloss is a modern invention.

- Ceilings should usually be white emulsion. If the ceilings are very high, a deeper colour will give the illusion of lowering it.

- White walls won't necessarily make a dark room seem lighter. Use lighting and mirrors.

- White on white can look very chic. Use different whites and cream furniture.

- Experiment with paint. It is the cheapest way to change a look.

Other Decorating Tips

Decorating is such a personal thing that an item thought of as highly stylish by one person could be deemed extremely naff by another! It is important that you are comfortable with your home and your living environment. Don't live with something just because some magazine tells you it's the height of fashion. Zebra-skin cushions will never grace *my* home but you might think they're fabulous!!

This book is not about interior design and I'm certainly not qualified to tell you how to design your home, but other books and magazines are a wonderful source of inspiration and information. Devour as many as you can for a variety of ideas. I think the key word is *simplicity*. Simplify your life and your home and you'll probably feel the difference.

If a home is loved it will be well maintained and that means redecorating every 5 or 6 years I'm afraid. This will serve you well in the long run when you want to sell your home because there will be less damage limitation. Windows, in particular, need constant attention due to inclement weather.

Anyway, here are a few tips I have picked up along the way. Once again, nothing is written in stone, but they might just help towards maximising the potential of your home.

TIPS

- Remember to do all the wiring, plumbing and cabling before you start decorating. Think of hi-fi wiring, security, lots of sockets, phone sockets, etc. Wires on the surface are ugly.

- If there isn't a focal point in the room, create one by installing a fireplace or bookcase.

- Decide on a theme or style for your home. Is it Georgian, classical, Mediterranean, funky modern, minimalist, bohemian, etc?

- Think of using glass to create space and light. Glass walls, glass stairs, glass tables?

- Let one object or piece of furniture dictate the colours for a room. You may have a beautiful blue lamp or a gold rug, for example.

- Use mirrors to bounce light into a room.

- Use mirror panels to double the size of a small room, like a bathroom.

- Use different textures to add interest.

- Overscaling looks a great deal better than underscaling. Big lamps look terrific, whereas teeny ones look cheap.

- Use patterns sparingly.

- Rooms always look smaller when empty.

- Buy cheap picture frames at auctions or car boot sales and spray them gold. Fill with pictures from catalogues or magazines.

- Hang lots of pictures close together for a more dramatic effect.

- Proportions are important. Don't have tiny furniture in a huge room.

- Be bold with cornicing.

- Auctions are wonderful places for finding good furniture at reasonable prices.

- If the budget is really tight, buy from junk shops or charity shops – the Salvation Army shops are brilliant – and transform pieces with paint and new handles or new fabric.

- Paint radiators the same colour as the walls.

- Use paint pads to apply emulsion to walls. It is easier and quicker than brushes.

- It is possible to paint old tiles or formica to transform a room. Ask in your local paint shop.

How to **Make Money** from **Your Property**

Conclusion

'Mid pleasures and palaces though we may roam,
Be it ever so humble, there's no place like home.'

J.H. PAYNE 1791–1852

It is so true when people say 'you only get out of life what you put into it'. It took me a long time to realise that in fact it is true about everything. Whether it be your job, your friendships, your relationship or your home. All of these will become more rewarding if you put a little extra effort into them.

Buying your home was an enormous financial outlay and I hope that, in some small way, I have helped to highlight various ways in which you can increase that capital. A little effort goes a long way – in property terms – to increasing the profit you should make from the sale of your home. Investing it wisely in the next property is essential if you are to continue making healthy profits.

Have fun with your property, especially if you are thinking of investing in the private rental sector and don't be afraid to make mistakes, as I have done. On second thoughts, now that you have read this book, you should absolutely *not* be making *any* mistakes! OK? Just go and make *loads* of money from your property and tell everyone how easy it is.

Useful addresses

Architects' Registration Council of the United Kingdom
73 Hallam Street, London W1N 5LQ.
Tel: 020 7580 5861. Fax: 020 7436 5269.

The Architecture and Surveying Institute (ASI)
St Mary House, 15A St Mary Street,
Chippenham, Wiltshire SN15 3WD.
Tel: 01249 444505. Fax: 01249 443602.
Email: mail@asi.org.uk.
Website: www.asi.org.uk

The Association of British Insurers
51–55 Gresham Street, London EC2V 7HQ.
Tel: 020 7600 3333. Fax: 020 7696 8999.
Email: info@abi.org.uk.
Website: www.abi.org.uk

The Association of Plumbing and Heating Contractors (APHC)
14 Ensign House, Ensign Business Centre,
Westwood Way, Coventry CV4 8JA.
Tel: 02476 470626. Fax: 02476 470942.
Email: aphuk@aol.com.
Website: www.licensedplumber.co.uk

Association of Residential Letting Agents
ARLA Administration, Maple House, 53–55
Woodside Road, Amersham, Bucks HP6 6AA.
Tel: 01494 431680.
Website: www.arla.co.uk

The British Association of Removers (BAR)
3 Churchill Court, 58 Station Road, North
Harrow, Middlesex HA2 7SA.
Tel: 020 8861 3331. Fax: 020 8861 3332.
Email: info@bar.co.uk.
Website: www.barmovers.com

Builders' Merchants Federation
15 Soho Square, London W1V 5FB.
Tel: 020 7439 1753

Building Employers' Confederation
66 Cardiff Road, Glan Y Llyn, Cardiff
CF15 7PQ. Tel: 029 2081 0681

The Building Societies Association (BSA)
3 Savile Row, London W1Z 1AF.
Tel: 020 7437 0655. Fax: 020 7734 6416.
Website: www.bsa.org.uk

Cadw (Welsh Heritage)
Cathays Park, Cardiff CF10 3NQ.
Tel: 029 2050 0200

Chartered Institute of Buildings Services Engineers
Delta House, 22 Balham High Road, London
SW12 9BS. Tel: 020 8675 5211

Consumers' Association
2 Marylebone Road, London NW1 4DF.
Tel: 020 7830 6000

Corgi (The Council for Registered Gas Installers)
4 Elmwood, Chineham Business Park,
Crockford Lane, Basingstoke, Hampshire
RG24 8WG. Tel: 01256 372200.
Website: www.corgi-gas.co.uk

The Council of Mortgage Lenders
3 Savile Row, London W1X 1AF.
Tel: 020 7440 2255. Fax: 020 7434 3791.
Website: www.cml.org.uk

Department of the Environment, Transport and the Regions
Eland House, Bressenden Place, London
SW1 5DU. Tel: 020 7890 3000.
Website: www.detr.gov.uk

The Electrical Contractors' Association
ESCA House, 34 Palace Court, Bayswater,
London W2 4HY. Tel: 020 7313 4800

The Electrical Contractors' Association of Scotland
Bush House, Bush Estate, Midlothian EH26
0SB. Tel: 0131 445 5577. Fax: 0131 445 5548.
Email: ecas@fol.co.uk.
Website: www.select.org.uk

English Heritage
23 Savile Row, London, W1S 2ET.
Tel: 020 7973 3000.
Website: www.english-heritage.org.uk

The Federation of Master Builders
Gordon Fisher House, 14–15 Great James
Street, London WC1N 3DP.
Tel: 020 7242 7583. Fax: 020 7242 0505.
Website: www.fmb.org.uk

The Federation of Overseas Property Developers, Agents and Consultants (FOPDAC)
3rd Floor, 95 Aldwych, London WC2B 4JF.
Tel: 020 8941 5588. Fax: 020 8941 0202.
Email: info@fopdac.com.
Website: www.fopdac.com

Fire Protection Association
Melrose Avenue, Boreham Wood, Herts
WD6 2BJ. Tel: 020 8236 9700

The Georgian Group
6 Fitzroy Square, London W1T 5DX.
Tel: 020 7387 1720

Glass and Glazing Federation
44–48 Borough High Street, London
SE1 1XB. Tel: 020 7403 7177.
Fax: 020 7357 7458

Guild of Master Craftsmen
Prest House, Exelby, Bedale, N. Yorks
DL8 2HB. Tel: 01677 427183

Historic Scotland
133 Longmore House, Salisbury Place,
Edinburgh EH9 1SH. Tel: 0131 668 8600

***Homes Overseas* Magazine**
Blendon Communications Ltd
207 Providence Square, Mill Street, London
SE1 2EW. Tel: 020 7939 9888

Institute of Electrical Engineers
Savoy Place, London WC2R 0BL.
Tel: 020 7240 1871

The Institute of Plumbing
64 Station Road, Hornchurch, Essex
RM12 6NB. Tel: 01708 472791

The Law Commission
Conquest House, 37–38 John Street,
Theobalds Road, London WC1N 2BQ.
Tel: 020 7453 1220. Fax: 020 7453 1297.
Email: secretary.lawcomm@gtnet.gov.uk.
Website: www.lawcom.gov.uk

Listed Buildings Information Service
Tel: 020 7208 8221

Listed Property Owners Club
Tel: 01795 844939

The Location Company
1 Charlotte Street, London W1T 1RB.
Tel: 020 7637 7766.
Website: www.thelocation.co.uk

National Approved Letting Scheme
PO Box 1843, Warwick CV34 4ZA.
Tel: 01926 496683.
Website: www.nalscheme.co.uk

National Association of Citizens Advice Bureaux
80–82 St John's Road, Tunbridge Wells, Kent TN4 9PH. Tel: 01892 539275

The National Association of Estate Agents
Arbon House, 21 Jury Street, Warwick CV34 4EH. Tel: 01926 496800.
Fax: 01926 400953.
Email: naea@dial.pipex.com.
Website: www.naea.co.uk

National Conservatory Advisory Council
NRWAS, PO Box 163, Bangor, County Down, N. Ireland BT20 5BX. Tel: 0500 522525.
Website: www.nrwas.com

National Federation of Roofing Contractors Limited
24 Weymouth Street, London W1N 4LX.
Tel: 020 7436 0387. Fax: 020 7637 5215

National Home Improvement Advisory Service
NHIAS, The Mount, 2 Woodstock Link, Belfast BT6 8DD. Tel: 0800 0851 246.
Website: www.nhias.org

The National House Building Council (NHBC)
NHBC, Buildmark House, Chiltern Avenue, Amersham, Bucks HP6 5AP.
Tel: 0845 845 6422. Website: www.nhbc.co.uk

National Register of Warranted Builders
Gordon Fisher House, 14–15 Great James Street, London WC1N 3DP.
Tel: 020 7404 4155

Northern Ireland Housing Executive
The Housing Centre, 2 Adelaide Street, Belfast BT2 8PB. Tel: 01232 317000.
Website: www.nihe.gov.uk

Office of Fair Trading
Field House, 15–25 Bream's Buildings, London EC4A 1PR. Tel: 020 7211 8000

Office of the Ombudsman for Estate Agents
Beckett House, 4 Bridge Street, Salisbury, Wiltshire SP1 2LX. Tel: 01722 333306.
Fax: 01722 332296. Email: post@oea.co.uk.
Website: www.oea.co.uk

Office for the Supervision of Solicitors
Victoria Court, 8 Dormer Place, Leamington Spa, Warwickshire CV32 5AE.
Tel: 01926 820082. Fax: 01926 431435.
Website: www.lawsociety.org.uk

The Royal Incorporation of Architects in Scotland
15 Rutland Square, Edinburgh EH1 2BE.
Tel: 0131 229 7205. Fax: 0131 228 2188.
Website: www.rias.org.uk

The Royal Institute of British Architects
66 Portland Place, London W1B 1AD.
Tel: 020 7580 5533.
Website: www.architecture.com

The Royal Institute of Chartered Surveyors
Database Resource Centre, Surveyor Court, Westwood Way, Coventry CV4 8JE.
Tel: 020 7222 7000. Email: info@rics.org.
Website: www.rics.org

The Royal Institute of Chartered Surveyors in Scotland
9 Manor Place, Edinburgh EH3 7DN.
Tel: 0131 225 7078. Fax: 0131 226 3599.
Website: www.rics-scotland.org.uk

The Royal Society of Architects in Wales
Bute Building, King Edward VII Avenue, Cathays Park, Cardiff CF10 3NB.
Tel: 029 2087 4753. Fax: 029 2087 4926.
Email: wrennm@cf.ac.uk

Royal Society of Ulster Architects
1 Mount Charles, Belfast BT7 1NZ.
Tel: 01232 323760

Salvo
Organisation of architectural salvage companies. Tel: 01890 820333.
Website: www.salvoweb.com

Save
www.savebritainsheritage.org
A conservation charity with a list of homes in
need of care and attention

Scottish and Northern Ireland Plumbing
Employers' Federation
2 Walker Street, Edinburgh EH3 7LB.
Tel: 0131 225 2255

The Society for Protection of Ancient
Buildings
37 Spital Square, London E1 6DY.
Tel: 020 7377 1644. Fax: 020 7247 5296.
Email: info@spab.org.uk.
Website: www.spab.org.uk

Timber and Brick Homes Information
Council
Gable House, 40 High Street,
Rickmansworth, Hertfordshire WD1 3ES.
Tel: 01923 778136. Fax: 01923 720724

Twentieth Century Society
Tel: 020 7250 3857

Victorian Society
1 Priory Gardens, Bedford Park, London
W4 1TT. Tel: 020 8994 1019.
Website: www.victorian-society.org.uk

What House?
Blendon Communications Ltd
207 Providence Square, Mill Street, London
SE1 2EW. Tel: 020 7939 9888

Property. Websites
www.assertahome.com
www.findaproperty.co.uk
www.fish4homes.co.uk
www.homepages.co.uk
www.homes-on-line.com
www.hometrack.co.uk
www.propertyfinder.co.uk
www.propertymarket.co.uk
www.propertyworld.co.uk
www.upmystreet.com

Financial websites
www.financelink.co.uk
www.ftyourmoney.com
www.moneyextra.com
www.moneynet.co.uk
www.moneyquest.co.uk
www.thomweb.co.uk
www.yourmortgage.co.uk

Index